AFRICAN ETHNOGRAPHIC STUDIES
OF THE 20TH CENTURY

Volume 77

COMMUNAL RITUALS OF
THE NYAKYUSA

COMMUNAL RITUALS OF THE NYAKYUSA

MONICA WILSON

R Routledge
Taylor & Francis Group

LONDON AND NEW YORK

First published in 1959 by Oxford University Press for the International African Institute.

This edition first published in 2018
by Routledge
2 Park Square, Milton Park, Abingdon, Oxon OX14 4RN

and by Routledge
711 Third Avenue, New York, NY 10017

Routledge is an imprint of the Taylor & Francis Group, an informa business

© 1959 International African Institute

British Library Cataloguing in Publication Data
A catalogue record for this book is available from the British Library

ISBN: 978-0-8153-8713-8 (Set)
ISBN: 978-0-429-48813-9 (Set) (ebk)
ISBN: 978-1-138-60033-1 (Volume 77) (hbk)
ISBN: 978-1-138-60034-8 (Volume 77) (pbk)
ISBN: 978-0-429-47100-1 (Volume 77) (ebk)

Publisher's Note
The publisher has gone to great lengths to ensure the quality of this reprint but points out that some imperfections in the original copies may be apparent.

Disclaimer
The publisher has made every effort to trace copyright holders and would welcome correspondence from those they have been unable to trace.

Due to modern production methods, it has not been possible to reproduce the fold-out maps within the book. Please visit www.routledge.com to view them.

THE KYUNGU, PETER

COMMUNAL RITUALS
OF
THE NYAKYUSA

MONICA WILSON

Published for the
INTERNATIONAL AFRICAN INSTITUTE
by the
OXFORD UNIVERSITY PRESS
LONDON   NEW YORK   TORONTO
1959

Oxford University Press, Amen House, London E.C.4

GLASGOW NEW YORK TORONTO MELBOURNE WELLINGTON
BOMBAY CALCUTTA MADRAS KARACHI KUALA LUMPUR
CAPE TOWN IBADAN NAIROBI ACCRA

PRINTED IN GREAT BRITAIN

To the BaNyakyusa

with affection and respect

CONTENTS

MAPS, PLANS, AND TABLES

LIST OF ILLUSTRATIONS

ACKNOWLEDGMENT

THE material presented here was collected by Godfrey and Monica Wilson under the auspices of the Rockefeller Foundation and the International African Institute between 1934 and 1938, and with the aid of a grant from the Carnegie Corporation of New York in 1955. Publication has been made possible by grants from the University of Cape Town and the International African Institute.

That the book could never have been written without the co-operation of very many friends will be obvious to readers. I wish, however, to thank particularly the chief Coloneli Makan'ata of Ilolo for generous hospitality and help, Mr. John Mwaikambo of Igalamu for friendship and able assistance over more than twenty years, the men and women of Lupata and Ilolo, the missionaries of Rungwe, and Mr. and Mrs. Peter Johnston of Tukuyu who received a stranger so charitably in their homes. Professor Dover Wilson has given himself unsparingly to make the reader's task less difficult and turn the barbarisms of an anthropologist into English.

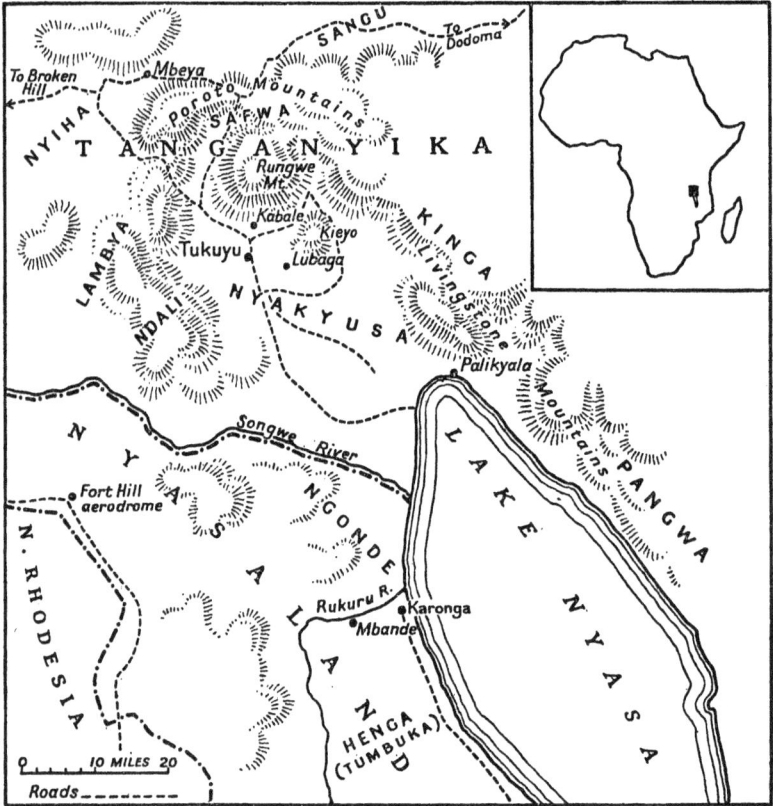

Map I. Country north of Lake Nyasa

CHAPTER I

INTRODUCTORY

THE peoples with whom this book is concerned, the Nyakyusa and the Ngonde, occupy an area shut in by mountains at the northern end of Lake Nyasa, and enjoy a culture which, though varying locally, clearly springs from a common basis and is traditionally attributed to similar origins. The most conspicuous features of their political organization are (i) the balance of power between chiefs and commoners; (ii) the 'coming out' ritual in which a generation of men which has governed for approximately thirty years retires and hands over the administration to its sons, retaining only ritual functions; and (iii) the system of age-villages.

All are agreed that chiefs and commoners belong to different stocks; the commoners being descended from the original occupants of the country while the chiefs trace their descent to a line of invaders who came down from the Livingstone mountains eight generations ago. According to the myth, they brought with them fire, and cattle, and iron tools, and they found a people who ate their food raw in a land 'without trees'.[1] Commoners are *abatitu*, black people, while Ngulube, an early ancestor of the chiefs, was 'pale'[2] and chiefs (*abanyafyale*) generally are said to have been lighter in colour and 'different in their bodies'. After generations of intermarriage between chiefs and commoners there is no consistent difference in physical type between them, but the range of physical type among the Nyakyusa as a whole is wide.[3]

Nyakyusa and Ngonde historians say that their chiefs are related to those of the Kinga, who live high above the Nyakyusa valley to the east in the Livingstone mountains, whence the chiefs came. The Kinga acknowledge the connexion and join with the Nyakyusa in sacrifice to their common heroes, but culturally the

[1] Possibly the lake-shore plain. The hills until cultivated are covered with either savannah or rain forest.

[2] Godfrey Wilson, *The Constitution of Ngonde*, Rhodes-Livingstone Papers No. 3, p. 10 (1930). According to the Ngonde version Ngulube was the *first* ancestor.

[3] cf. F. Fülleborn, *Beiträge zur physischen Anthropologie der Nord-Nyassander* (1902). *Das Deutsche Njassa- und Ruvuma-Gebiet Atlas* (1906).

two peoples are distinct. Their languages are not mutually intelligible and the Nyakyusa despise the Kinga as dirty in habit and
obsequious in manner. There were two main invasions from
BuKinga: (i) that of the 'sons of Lwembe' who settled south and
east of Tukuyu, and (ii) that of the 'sons of Ngomale' (or Kukwe),
who settled first at Kina below the northern crater of Rungwe
volcano, and then at Kabale in the foothills to the south-east.
Most of the present chiefs of the Nyakyusa belong to one or other
of these two lineages, and the chiefs of Ngonde are claimed by
both. The arrival of the chiefs of Lwembe's line may be fixed
between 1560 and 1650, i.e. before the settlement at the Cape, but
after the death of the first Christian martyr in what is now
Rhodesia[1] and the 'sons of Ngomale' followed them some generations later (vide infra, genealogies pp. 3, 27; p. 94). Two of the
invading heroes, Lwembe and Kyungu, became 'divine kings'
whose successors claimed spiritual authority over wide areas, and
the heirs of Kyungu gradually acquired temporal power also.

About the first inhabitants of the Nyakyusa valley, the abilema,
tradition is vague; however, it is clear that they were not one
people, but consisted of small, scattered, independent groups,
disparate in origin. Some were very early invaders from BuKinga,
others came from near Lake Rukwa and were kin to the Bungu
of the Rukwa plain. They occupied an almost empty country (as
their name indicates) but they found pygmy hunters[2] in the
Rungwe forests. The invaders themselves were primarily hunters
and honey-gatherers, though some, at least, of them began to
cultivate millet, beans, and pumpkins. One group of early
inhabitants, the Penja, which was pushed into the north-west
corner of the valley, has remained relatively discrete, though for
the most part they have fused with the conquerors.

It is clear that nowhere were the invaders allowed to establish
themselves as tyrants since, though their descendants rule over the
various chiefdoms, their authority is strictly limited by the headmen of the villages who are invariably of commoner stock. Moreover, while the most sacred persons in the country are, or before
the coming of the Europeans were, 'divine kings', descendants of
the original heroes, chosen by each generation to become their

[1] In 1561, cf. G. M. Theal, Records of South-East Africa, vol. ii, p. 126.
[2] The quality of relations with the Pygmies is summed up in the ironical name for
them 'Where did you see me?' (Umbwenekugu?) The tale is that they were very sensitive
about their size and the first question on meeting a Nyakyusa was always: 'Where did
you see me?' The only safe reply was: 'Far, far away!'

living representatives, to take their name, and to sacrifice at their groves, it was commoner priests who chose them and, as will be seen, put them to death when it was expedient for the good of the people. It is clear, too, from what source the commoners drew their power. The invaders were supposed to have brought into the country fire, cattle, crops, and iron; they were creators, the guarantors and preservers of fertility; and it was to foster and increase fertility that men worshipped and sacrificed at the groves of the mythical heroes. The aborigines, on the other hand, without fire, without iron, and feeding on raw meat as the myth depicts them, possessed one weapon of terrible potency, witchcraft, which no chief, not even a priest of the chief's lineage, could withstand or would dare to challenge. To the Nyakyusa the essential nature of the universe, established in history and in the institutions of their society, was reciprocity, a balance between chiefs and commoners, between cattle-owners and cultivators, between the creative power of the heroes and the black anger of the witches. The idea of a chief who was a dictator was as foreign as the idea of a single omnipotent creator. Moreover, there was a multiplicity of chiefs, no single central authority.

The heroic tradition, then, accounts for the differences between the chiefs and commoners and for the remarkable equilibrium that obtains between them. It accounts also, as we shall find, for the 'coming out' ritual, at least in part. It is strangely silent, however, about the origin of what is perhaps the most striking feature of Nyakyusa social life, the system of age-villages. The absence of any link between the myths of the heroes and the founding of age-villages is the more surprising in that the pattern of age-organization almost certainly came into the valley from the north-east. Only in East Africa was government based on age groups and the handing over of power from one generation to the next celebrated by whole communities. If the system of age-villages came in with the eastern invaders why is this contribution to civilized living (for the Nyakyusa regard village life as the essence of civilization) never mentioned? The only explanation we can offer is that the age structure is not necessarily linked with chieftainship, whereas the control of cattle and iron was the basis of power, and making fire was a symbol, not only of a new chieftainship, but of the vital creative force in the body of the chief. The heroic cycle justifies the relations between chiefs and commoners, but is not concerned with other institutions of the society.

The age system of the Nyakyusa has been described in detail in *Good Company*,[1] but, since it forms the basis of their social structure, a brief explanation must here be given for the benefit of readers unacquainted with that earlier volume. Within each chiefdom there are a number of villages composed not of kinsmen but of age-mates. Villages begin when small boys of eight or ten years build together at a little distance from their fathers. They are joined by younger brothers, as these reach the age when boys stop sleeping at home, until the eldest are in their middle teens, when the youngsters will be told to begin another village. The boys of a village have their own leader, a 'natural' leader, not specifically appointed, but they are subject to the headman of their fathers' village, and formerly fought as a group under his direction. But at the 'coming out' a headman for each village is selected from among its members by the fathers: if he dies, his heir—a younger brother or son—inherits his position, so that sometimes a young man becomes headman of an old men's village, taking the name and social position of his father. Only commoners are eligible as headmen: we knew one candidate who was rejected because his great-grandfather was a chief.

Two villages in each chiefdom are senior to the others and their headmen are responsible each for half of the country. During the 'coming out' ritual the chief marries two wives, 'mothers of the country', and one is established in each senior village or capital (*ikitangalala*). The eldest sons of these two wives are the heirs, and later divide the old chief's country between them. Most of the chief's junior wives are divided between the capitals but some may be settled in a colonizing village in unoccupied country. All the chief's sons build with commoners in villages appropriate to their age, and all save the two heirs are subject to the commoner headmen of their villages. They are entitled to some respect as 'sons of the chief', and those of strong personality gain a following and settle disputes between their fellows (as may any commoner), but only the two senior sons can claim political authority.

Before the 'coming out' the villages of young men and their fathers adjoin, for the boys have built on their fathers' land, on the fringes of their fathers' villages. But at the 'coming out' there is a new deal in land. The young men are established in the centre of the country and their fathers move to the periphery; it is not merely that fathers and sons exchange land, but all the boundaries

[1] Monica Wilson, *Good Company*, 1952.

are redrawn and only the fields in old craters (the most prized and fertile of all) are not re-allotted. Thus the villages of kinsmen of two generations adjoin, and often those of three generations.

On the old chief's death his village headmen become priests of the grove in which he is buried, and, in co-operation with his sons, the new chiefs, sacrifice there on behalf of the two countries into which his old chiefdom is divided. There is a nice balance of power between chief and village headmen in life, and when he dies his two heirs and the headmen (or their heirs) continue to share power, the power which belief in his spiritual force and their ability to guide it gives them. The success or failure of rituals is held largely to depend upon the personal relationships of the leading participants, chiefs and commoner priests.

Besides the ordinary commoner priests (the village headmen of a past generation or their heirs) there are priests of the chiefs' lineage, usually belonging to a junior line to which specific ritual functions, such as rain-making, have been entrusted, and whose office is hereditary in the same way as that of a chief. Kasitile (86),[1] the rain-maker, is such a priest: his grandfather was the brother of a ruling chief (43) and had been appointed as rain-maker (*umpelafula*) and priest (*unyago*), the two functions being separate but overlapping. As rain-maker Kasitile tended the rain stones, as priest he initiated the rituals in certain of the sacred groves, though he did not actually officiate himself. Kasitile was a key informant on ritual and a chapter is devoted to his history, since it epitomizes the relationships between chiefs and commoners.

As we have shown, most of the Nyakyusa and Ngonde chiefs claim some sort of kinship with one another. Those who are nearly related pray together at the groves of their common ancestors, and those more distantly connected join in sacrifice to their founding fathers, but in the communal rituals kinship is neither the dominant theme nor the exclusive principle of association, as it is in the rituals celebrated by private persons. In the communal rituals most of the priests are commoners unrelated to the dead who are honoured, and the sacrifices are held to benefit not only the descendants of the dead, but all those who live in the countries they once ruled. Nevertheless, the symbolism of the communal rituals constantly recalls that of the rituals of kinship; themes which pervade the death ritual recur again in the rituals of 'coming out' and 'cleansing the country'. This background is

[1] Numerals after a name refer to the genealogy of Nyakyusa chiefs facing p. 3.

accessible in an earlier book, *Rituals of Kinship among the Nyakyusa*,[1] and the details need not be recapitulated here.

Perhaps the reader has already noted a certain difficulty over tenses: 'is' tends to merge into 'was'. When we first visited BuNyakyusa in 1934 missionaries of various denominations had already been at work, and a foreign government in control, for forty years past. Between 1934 and my last visit in 1955 the changes have been great, but I use the present tense for things seen at first hand, whether earlier or later, and a separate chapter is devoted to the twenty years' change. It is well to recognize at the outset, however, that in 1934 the sanctity and power of the 'divine kings' was already questioned and their rituals were curtailed, and even the pagan cosmology of the Nyakyusa was beginning to exhibit traces of Christian influence. One striking example was the changing, or rather the fluid, connotation of the name *Kyala*.

Two new types of organization developed in BuNyakyusa with the arrival of the Europeans: churches which are based on a principle of association wholly new to the pagan tradition— common belief as opposed to kinship or contiguity; and a centralized system of government. To these have now been added trading concerns, of which the most important are co-operative societies exporting coffee and rice.

The subject of this book is (i) the traditional rituals celebrated on behalf of chiefdoms and groups of chiefdoms, and (ii) the changing ideas and values apparent as a section of the Nyakyusa turn from paganism to Christianity. In the concluding chapters an attempt is made to demonstrate the links between the changes in social structure and the changes in ritual.

[1] Monica Wilson, *Rituals of Kinship among the Nyakyusa*, 1957.

CHAPTER II

THE MYTHOLOGICAL CHARTER

In Nyakyusa mythology the heroes were creators of crops and animals and were driven out from BuKinga by a jealous father (or elder brother) who sought to kill them; but he found, when they had gone, that they had taken the fertility of the country with them, so he sent offerings after them, and still such offerings are brought to their graves in sacrifice. One of the heroes, Kyala (2), created crops alone, and of him it is said that each time his father or elder brother tried to kill him he rose again; another, Lwembe or Mbasi (3 or 15?), created both crops and animals, brought cattle, fire, and iron to the Nyakyusa valley, and left many descendants who spread over the valley as chiefs, ruling a people who had not known chiefs.

The names and events mentioned vary somewhat from one area to another; in some versions there were three brothers, though the eldest, Nkekete (1), being buried in Kisi country, does not concern the Nyakyusa; in another version the brothers had a sister who was the mother of Kyungu (16), the hero of Ngonde; but the general pattern of heroic ancestors who were creators and discoverers, and who brought to the old inhabitants of the valley such good gifts as crops and stock, fire and iron, and the institution of chieftainship, remains the same. They all had miraculous power and are vaguely connected with volcanic disturbance, such as continued in the area until recent times (*vide infra*, p. 16).

Here is an account by Kikungubeja, one of the priests of BuKinga, whence the heroes came:

Nkekete (1) and Kyala (2) were brothers, Mwemusi [the first Kinga chief] killed them. Mwemusi's men tried first to kill them by cutting their throats, then by throwing them into a little lake, then by heating a great stone and throwing it on top of them. Each time Nkekete and his younger brother Kyala rose again. Then they left the country, the two of them, and the earth rumbled as they walked. Nkekete (1) went to Mbela to build; Kyala (2), the younger, to PaliKyala. Then the men of Mwemusi followed Nkekete with a cow to entreat him because he had taken all the food with him. Mwemusi was angry with him and his younger brother Kyala, because they made food and they were

B

fierce warriors. They were first driven out, then later Lwembe (3) was driven out too. When Lwembe was a child, herding cattle with his fellows, he moulded cattle of clay and they became alive; so with lions and leopards, too; he also took up a handful of earth and it became beans or millet. His fellows told Mwemusi of this and he was astonished. Then Mwemusi sent men to watch; they went early in the morning and hid themselves and watched; they watched him making all these things. Then they wanted to kill him, but the forefather of Mwaka-lukwa [another Kinga chief] gave him two cows; he was a friend and said: 'Leave the country, they want to kill you, take these cows and eat them on the road.' Lwembe went away with Kissoule and Mwamaloba (Mwamalunguka) and two wives and all his animals.

These three, Nkekete (1), Kyala (2), and Lwembe (3), were driven out by Mwemusi, but Lwembe's younger brothers, the BaMwalukissa (4), were left. When Lwembe went away, Mwemusi's men followed him, wishing to kill him, but they feared his animals, and did not try.

Nkekete (1) set out to the Lake [Nyasa] and went into a stream; he is in the water now, in a stream with pools near the Lake, in Kisi country. Kyala (2) went and built among stones in a cave. When the Europeans came they took rifles and shot at Kyala in the place where he had built, so he moved to a different place. Of old he was in a cave washed by the waters of the Lake, but after the Europeans came he moved to his present cave at the boundary between Kisselelo's and Kisi country. Kyala had fowls there; some saw them in the old days and some did not. Nkekete is in a stream with pools in it; there (at Lumbila in Kisi country) men sacrifice a cow. Kyala's sheep are killed near his cave.

Neither Nkekete nor Kyala had any children, but Lwembe (3), who went off alive, begot many children. We speak with them. Nkekete and Kyala were killed, Lwembe was not. . . . All the Kinga chiefs when praying in the sacred groves say the names of their fathers who have died, and also the names of Nkekete, Kyala, and Lwembe, in that order . . . Lwembe was the youngest of the three brothers . . . Nkekete and Kyala only made crops—millet and beans. We ask for fertility of the soil (*imboto*), and sunshine, and rain from them, but not animals. From Lwembe we ask for milk, and fertility of men and cattle, and snakes, and goats, and sheep, and all crops. Lwembe has every-thing. We ask for sunshine and rain from Lwembe as well.

When Lwembe went down into Selya he found the hill people (*BaMwamba*) and the people of the plain (Mwakyembe's men)[1] already there. They feared him because he had all things, and they still fear him. He was greater than Nkekete. They cut Nkekete's throat, but they couldn't kill Lwembe. He made the small lakes—all of them. He

---

[1] In other versions Mwakyembe is a descendant of Lwembe.

went from Mwemusi's country down the path by Mwakalukwa's to Mwakaleli. He lived a year at Lumbila and found it too cold, and thence he went to Masoko, and thence to Lubaga. All men feared him and his animals.

In another version Lwembe's survival is linked with the possession of *ifingila*, the medicine on which still, today, the authority of chiefs is thought largely to depend.

Nkekete had much food and Mwemusi killed him because he had no *ifingila*. He killed him and he rose again. 'Why don't you die?' Mwemusi asked. Nkekete replied: 'I don't know, I have nothing, I am quite alone, I have no *ifingila*.' Mwemusi killed him again and he rose, many times. Then at last Nkekete said, 'I am tired.' And he showed Mwemusi and his men a razor (*ulwembe*) and said 'Kill me by cutting my throat with this', and they did and he stayed dead.

Mwemusi feared to kill Lwembe because he was very 'heavy'. He had *ifingila*, and when they tried to kill him they found his house full of animals, lions and others. . . . Once he turned himself into a stone when they tried to capture him. So Mwemusi told him to go far off, and he went with his two wives and two men, Kissoule and Kimonile. He went off riding on a lion like a donkey, with a lion behind his wives, and men were astonished when they saw him.

It is perhaps significant that Lwembe who survived is 'The Razor', by which Nkekete was killed, and the python from which *ifingila* medicine is made must be killed with razors and in no other way (*vide infra*, p. 60).

It is Lwembe's capacity to make things live and grow which is always emphasized:

Lwembe and another were given millet in their hands; Lwembe's sprouted, but not that of his fellow. He was told, 'You plant here and the other there.' The next day Lwembe's had sprouted, but not that of the other. He and his friend went to a hill in dry weather and wanted water. He just struck the earth and water came out. . . . He created leopards and kept them, and he moulded cattle of clay, he moulded them and they became cows, and his friends did the same and they remained clay.

When the heroes were driven out there was a fearful famine in BuKinga, for they had taken the fertility of the country with them, which is why, the priests say, sacrifices to them were begun by the Kinga. The priests of Lubaga were explicit on the point:

Mbasi (Lwembe 15?) came from BuKinga, he took the road to

Mwakaleli and came here and died. The Kinga went to BuSangu to buy food, for there was great hunger after Mbasi and Kyala were driven out, and wandering home they came here and met Mbasi. He said, 'Go home, there will be plenty of food, but I want my things.' He had left them at his father's place when he fled with his sister Kyungu. He asked for his leopard and otterskins, his drums, his bows for shooting birds,[1] his harp, mats, a stool, bamboo beer, and twenty hoes. . . . Then the Kinga went back and found their country full of food; and they brought all his things to Mbasi and even things like salt that he had not asked for. . . . This is how the ritual began. . . . Mbasi ruled because he had helped them in their hunger.

Kasitile (86), the rain-maker, speaking of the same incident, stressed only the hoes. Lwembe 'came to Lubaga and found a good place to settle, then he sent out messengers to Mwemusi (the Kinga chief) and said: "I want my hoes, especially my great, eyed hoe" (ilikumbulu ilya maso).' (The old ritual hoes had perforations—'eyes'—on the blades comparable to the perforations on other rain-making instruments.) Still today Kinga priests come to Lubaga to sacrifice to Lwembe (3), and they bring with them hoes.[2]

The hero of Ngonde, the Kyungu (16), was also associated with iron implements which he had brought with him—a spear, staff, stool, and a sieve used for making rain, which were royal insignia, and razors, spears, and knives of an unusual pattern, which long remained in the groves of the hero and his successors.

In the commonly-told Nyakyusa myth it was Lwembe who introduced fire to BuNyakyusa—'he found the original occupants eating their food raw'—and the fact that he conferred so great a benefit is the charter for the position of the chiefs, celebrated at every 'coming out'. The Kinga priests push the spread of fire back a little further.

Of old in this country [BuKinga] there was no fire, men ate food un-cooked; there were very few men in the country, most of it was forest. This was after Mwemusi came to Kinga country. Then one man, a hunter, went into the forest to hunt buck and otter, and he had dogs. And in the forest he made fire with a drill and cooked his food; and gave his friends cooked food to eat, and they were astonished.

---

[1] The bow and arrow are not now used among the Nyakyusa, but men in their thirties had used them when boys, for shooting birds.

[2] cf. Ludwig Weichert, *Mayibuye i Africa! Kehre wieder Afrika* (Berlin, 1927), p. 129, for a photograph of one.

Then the chiefs took it from him and spread it through the Kinga country . . . and to the Mahasi, the Ndali, the Nyakyusa. . . . It was taken to BuNyakyusa before Lwembe went, when he was a child, before the killing of Nkekete and Kyala.

In the version told by Mwandisi (107), the old blind chief of MuNgonde, the various events of the cycle are rather differently combined; there were three brothers in BuKinga, Lyambilo (12) or Ngutike, Kyala, and Mbasi, and a sister, Kyumba. Lyambilo discovered how to make fire with a fire drill. Kyala was clever at making food—maize and millet—and Mbasi was clever at making animals—cattle, lions, elephants.

Then Lyambilo, the eldest, was angry that his younger brothers should be so clever; he was jealous. First he made war on Kyala, he wounded him once, but he did not die; then he wounded him again, but still he didn't die; then the third time Lyambilo put a stone in the fire and made it hot and threw it at Kyala, and he died, and was thrown into the Lake. But as soon as he died there was a great famine, no rain fell and no food grew. So they had to pray to Kyala to give them rain, and they killed a cow to sacrifice to Kyala. And as soon as they had done this much food grew.

Still Lyambilo was jealous of Mbasi because he could make animals. But when he went to kill him he found so many animals with him, roaring lions, and elephants, that he was afraid and he ran away. And he brought some hoes to Mbasi to say he was sorry for having tried to kill him. Then Mbasi moved from BuKinga to the Nyakyusa hills (Mwamba). . . . Lyambilo stayed in BuKinga. . . . Mbasi came down to the plain on a visit and went back to the hills, but his sister Kyumba stayed down here and married a man and bore a son. Before she came there was no fire here, she brought fire, and so they called her son Kyungu in honour of his mother because she brought fire.

When Mbasi was at Masukulu (in the hills) he made one cow, but it soon died; then he moved to Mbambo and made another cow and this soon died; then he went to Lubaga (which is still called Mbasi) and there he made one cow again which bore many many calves, and he divided his cattle among his sons. . . . Mbasi was Lwembe.

In Ngonde tradition the first Kyungu (16) was a man, descendant of Ngulube the Kinga chief, and he travelled with three brothers and a sister westwards, passing south of Rungwe volcano, where he and his immediate successor were buried, one of them on Kieyo mountain. Their descendants went on to the 'country of the Bisa', then returned eastward to Mbande, the sacred hill which the Kyungu took from a Fipa hunter, Simbobwe. Like Lwembe, the Kyungu had a miraculous power of creating animals and it was by making elephants, buffaloes, and guinea-fowl for Simbobwe and his men to hunt, and climbing Mbande when it was deserted, that he captured it. Directly he reached the top he struck his drum and 'when Simbobwe heard the drums beaten on the hill he fled to his own country'. This Kyungu's successors on Mbande became 'divine kings' with miraculous power much like that of the Lwembe at Lubaga. One of his brothers became chief of the Namwanga; another of the Iwa; and a third became the rival of his sister's son for the chieftainship of the Lambya. Such is the Ngonde account. The Kukwe say that the Kyungus of Ngonde come from the same line as the chiefs of Kabale, while the men of Lwembe insist that he was descended from a daughter of their line (*vide supra*, p. 2). What connexion existed between the lineages of Lwembe and Ngomale is uncertain, but the assumption is that they, together with the chiefs of the Pangwa and Kisi, sprang from a common stock in BuKinga.

The commonest story of origin is that all the peoples of the area, save the Sangu, emerged from a 'dark house' (*nyumba nditu*) near the present Njombe, and came to Ilongo (KwiLongo) in the forest, in what is now Bena country. Nsamba, a Nyakyusa priest of the chief's lineage, with a reputation as a historian, spoke of a 'few men' coming from 'a rocky shore to the north-west' (Lake Tanganyika?) and travelling to the east shore of Nyasa, where they increased in numbers, and then spread northwards through BuKinga; Mwenifumbo, a noble of Ngonde, spoke of Ngulube the 'pale' having come to BuKinga 'from the north'.[1] But the Kinga priests knew nothing of the 'rocky shore' or northern origin; and if we take the direction in which the corpse faces when buried (the most certain criterion of the direction of origin) then the Nyakyusa and Ngonde people came from BuKinga, some travelling to the north of Rungwe volcano and some to the south, and the Kinga themselves came from the east.

Other evidence also indicates that the chiefs came from the east or north-east rather than the north-west. The cattle they brought were the short-horned Zebu type, like those of the Masai and other peoples of central and eastern Tanganyika and Kenya. They are quite different from the long-horned cattle of the Hima

[1] Godfrey Wilson, *The Constitution of Ngonde*, Rhodes-Livingstone Papers No. 3, p. 10 (1930). According to the Ngonde version, Ngulube was the *first* ancestor, but Nsamba began the genealogy four generations earlier (*vide* chart, facing p. 3).

and Tutsi who established conquest states to the north-west.[1]

Whatever the origin and adventures of the heroes they were important in Nyakyusa and Ngonde history because their graves became centres of religious ritual which linked together groups that were otherwise largely independent. The myths about them are the charter for chieftainship. They are depicted as benefactors who brought to uncivilized men not only the institution of chieftainship itself, but fire, cattle, iron, seed, and a creative power resident in their own bodies and those of their anointed heirs. But the myths also justify the power of commoners who first occupied the country and who have witchcraft in their bellies:

The commoners whom Lwembe found here were extraordinary. They were cultivators, but they had not yet got fire, they ate their food raw. It was we chiefs, it was Lwembe, who brought fire and cattle—he came and found the original occupants without cattle; hence the commoners say, 'We are the earth'. Commoners are different from us physically, they are black; they are awe-inspiring, they are witches. Before you Europeans came the chiefs like Mwaipopo (116) were not awe-inspiring, they feared the commoners very much; the commoners hammered the chief with their fists—yes, by daylight. And if the chief cut a man's bananas that man took the chief's. If the commoners were angry with Mwaipopo they fetched Mwangomo (124 whose chiefdom adjoins Mwaipopo's) at night by their witchcraft; he came in the night with his people and seized the cattle, both those of the chief, Mwaipopo, and those of the commoners. The next day the commoners said: 'It is we, we are angry. Why do you not look after us? Why do you not kill cattle for us?' Then Mwaipopo would kill two head of cattle and all the men in the country ate. . . . Mwaipopo and his equals were not awe-inspiring long ago, it is you Europeans who have created chieftainship and awe.

[1] cf. H. H. Curson and R. W. Thornton, 'A Contribution to the Study of African Native Cattle', *Onderstepoort Journal of Veterinary Science and Animal Industry*, vii, 2 October 1936 (Government Printer, Pretoria). An analysis of the distribution and migration of breeds in Africa.

H. B. Thompson and R. Scott, *Uganda* (1935), pp. 195 ff.

Fülleborn, *op. cit.*, pl. 68: 69.

M. Merker, *Die Masai*, pp. 157 ff., 1904, Berlin.

H. H. Johnston, *The Uganda Protectorate*, 1904, pp. 86, 105 (early photographs of Nyoro cattle).

The short-horn type predominates among the Nyakyusa, but some animals suggest an intermixture with Sanga cattle. The hump is regarded as a great delicacy and is exaggerated in the clay cattle which boys model. Cf. Fülleborn, *op. cit.*, pl. 72. The similarity between the ritual and symbolism of the Nyakyusa and those of the Ganda as described by Roscoe is marked. J. Roscoe, *The Baganda*, 1911.

The balance between chiefs and commoners is explicit. So also is their dependence on *both* cultivation and herding, and it should be noted that, though the Nyakyusa speak of themselves as stock men, they are not pastoralists to the same extent as the Masai or the Nuer. The number of cattle in Rungwe District today is less than half the human population, and men traditionally have done the heaviest share of cultivation.

In every version of the myth the tension between father and son, or older and younger brother, is stressed. In Nyakyusa society the father (or his eldest son who replaces him) controls the family property and exacts obedience from his juniors who continue to show their respect after his death by sacrifices. The tale of Kyala and Lwembe celebrates the triumph of the junior. Thus, at the heart of the very ritual which sanctifies seniority there is the assertion of the victory of the son and younger brother. The myth expresses the aspirations of subordinates—of commoners and junior kinsmen—as well as the power of chiefs and seniors.

As we have already noted, the heroic cycle makes no reference to the peculiar Nyakyusa institution of age-villages. Their charter is a quite separate myth[1] which tells of a chief who looked on his daughter-in-law and loved her and took her, and this so shocked men that in future fathers and sons built separately, so that a father-in-law should never see his daughter-in-law.

There are other hints of the eternal theme. Besides the saga of Lwembe there is another quite different tale of the origin of fire, which is less often related. In it a girl who had angered her father by breaking his drinking calabash fled from BuKinga to the Nyakyusa valley, where she found people who ate their food raw. She made fire and cooked for them and 'all women came to her to learn to cook'. The long-necked calabash, used as a drinking vessel and in prayer to the shades, is a man's most personal possession destroyed at his death, and it stands for a husband, while cooking is a symbol of the sexual activity of women, so the myth is perhaps a drama of incest, but we have no direct evidence of this.

This last is the only tale in which a woman appears as a benefactor. In general, the mythology is that of a strongly patrilineal society in which men are dominant. The wives of Lwembe who walked behind their lord, shepherded by a lion,

[1] cf. Monica Wilson, *Good Company*, p. 85.

I. CATTLE AT PASTURE

2. THE ROAD TO LWEMBE

are remembered, and the names of the two senior wives of a chief are often recited in genealogies because the heirs take their names from their mothers, but she-who-taught-cooking is the only heroine in her own right.

It is worth noting also that the rituals of kinship are linked neither with the heroic tradition nor with primeval incest. We could trace no myths regarding their beginning, save that concerning the origin of avoidance between father and daughter-in-law. The myth of the origin of death is a variation on the theme, so familiar in Bantu-speaking Africa, of the two messengers (a sheep and a dog in this version) sent to men by 'Kyala', one promising life, the other death. It provides no charter for the ritual.

And what of the relation between myth and history? The conquest of cultivators by cattle-keepers is the common theme of traditions in the lacustrine area, and it is quite possible that small groups of invaders, who brought with them iron tools and weapons and cattle, established themselves as chiefs over small unorganized groups of hunters and cultivators in an isolated valley three or four centuries ago.[1] The Nyakyusa valley and the plain of Ngonde have no iron ore, and the inhabitants were dependent, until the coming of the Europeans, on iron (*ikyela*) smelted in the hills to the east for weapons and tools.[2] The original inhabitants are said to have used wooden hoes exclusively—such hoes were still in common use in 1938[3]—so the myth of a Lwembe sending to BuKinga for iron hoes has a firm foundation in historical fact. But that the original inhabitants of the valley did not know the use of fire 300 or 400 years ago (when Lwembe arrived) is incredible. Here the record of one of the greatest events in history is fitted into the shallow time-scale of an isolated people. To them it is not *when* fire arrived that is really important, but *who* brought it; chiefs are chiefs to the Nyakyusa (as to other peoples in Africa) by virtue of this great benefit they brought to men.

[1] Namwanga tradition (recorded in the Mbeya District Book) tells of the introduction of iron fifteen generations ago. The Sangu tradition says that a tall, pale man from 'Somaliland' first brought iron spear-heads to BuSangu and his son established a hegemony by virtue of his superior weapons.

[2] cf. Monica Wilson, *Good Company*, p. 7. The iron deposits on the Livingstone mountains have recently been investigated by the Colonial Development Corporation. A 'titaniferous iron mountain' in the south of Njombe District was found to be 'smeltable'. *Tanganyika: Annual Reports of the Provincial Commissioners*, 1951, p. 51.

[3] Wilson, *op. cit.*, plate VII.

It is surprising to westerners, whose whole framework of reference is shaped by the conception of historical time, that the heroic myth is not more explicitly dated by the volcanic eruptions known to have taken place near Lubaga,[1] but to the Nyakyusa the sequence of events does not appear important except in so far as it determines seniority.

Nowadays, with the changing form of the society, there develops a new mythology. Kyala is described by younger men as a creator, apart and distinct from any hero or ancestor, and they reject any suggestion that he was once on a footing with Lwembe and Kyungu. The more conservative fit Christian names into the heroic myth. One version goes as follows:

Kyala had two sons, Kyala the elder who was Mbasi or Satano, and Kyala the younger who was Jesus. Kyala the younger made corn, and cattle, and fire, and cooked meat, and men ate; then Mbasi or Satano was furious because his younger brother was outdoing him, and killed him, and became the only one.

Here the traditional theme of the jealousy of the senior is dominant, but generally it is the power of the heroes over fertility, under the old dispensation, that is stressed.

Many people tell today of old prophecies concerning the coming of Europeans and of the triumph of a new religion. To the Christians these provide some bridge between the past and the present, for they interpret the words of pagan prophets as evidence of their foreknowledge of a truth they had not yet been taught.

[1] D. A. Harkin, 'The Sarabwe Lava Flow, Kiejo, Rungwe District', *Tanganyika Notes and Records*, September 1955, suggests that the most recent eruption in the district, that of Kiejo, took place about 1800, but this conclusion is based on the description of the eruption by *one* man, and the statement that his great grandfather witnessed it. That *some* ancestor of Andulile Kajigiri witnessed the eruption is likely, but had it taken place only three generations ago it might be expected that other families also would have had a tradition of the event. Kiejo is clearly visible from Mwaipopo's country and had the eruption taken place early in the nineteenth century either the chief Mwakagile (59) or his father Mwamukinga (43) must have observed it. Their descendants are emphatic that there is no tradition of their having done so, though it is commonly known that an eruption of Kiejo occurred in the distant past.

CHAPTER III

THE 'DIVINE KINGS'

(a) CHARACTERISTICS OF 'DIVINE KINGS'

THE heroic myths and genealogies proclaim the origin of chieftain-ship, and point to a distinction between ordinary chiefs and those we call 'divine kings'. Two remote ancestors who were pre-eminent are worshipped as heroes and creators, their graves are centres at which a large number of chiefdoms join in celebration, and living representatives are selected in every generation bearing their names. These are the 'divine kings', the Lwembe of Lubaga (in the centre of Nyakyusa country) and the Kyungu of Mbande near Karonga in Nyasaland. A third hero, Kyala, is associated with the cave, PaliKyala, near Ikombe at the north-east corner of the Lake, and he is worshipped in the same way as the other two, except that the priest of the cave is not his descendant and does not embody him. According to the myth, Kyala was the brother of Lwembe, but died without issue. However, the word for chiefs—*aba-nya-fyale*—is popularly believed to mean 'the sons of Kyala'.[1]

Kyala is one hero among others, but his name is *also* used in the sense of 'the lord': a chief is *kyala gwake* (his lord) to a commoner, a father is *kyala gwake* to his son or daughter 'because he created him' and a shade is *kyala* to his living kinsman (*unsyuka jo kyala*). Of one who performs a feat—something difficult—it is said 'he is Kyala'.[2] This usage is said to be very old, but there is yet another meaning of the word which is new. *Kyala* was used by the European missionaries (who first established themselves near PaliKyala) as their translation of 'God'. Today these three con-ceptions are inextricably mixed: Kyala the hero, Kyala 'the

---

[1] I am indebted to the Reverend Paul Fueter for drawing my attention to this point. It is doubtful whether *Kyala* and *fyale* in fact come from the same root. *Fyale* in Hehe means the daughter of a chief (A. G. O. Hodgson, 'Some Notes on the Wahehe of Mahenge District, *J.R.A.I.*, lvi (1926), p. 40). In Bena *nyakiyara* means 'my husband's father or mother' (A. T. and G. M. Culwick, *Ubena of the Rivers*, p. 196). In Ganda *mukyala* means 'lady', mistress of a household and garden (J. Roscoe, *The Baganda*, p. 44). cf. Nyika, *fiala* 'to beget, to bear' (J. L. Krapf and J. Rebmann, *A Nyika-English Dictionary*, edited by T. H. Sparshott, 1887).

[2] cf. F. R. Lehmann, 'Some field notes on the Nyakyusa', *Sociologus*, New Series, 1951, vol. 5, p. 66.

lord', and Kyala the Christian deity. In the sacrifices at Lubaga and the groves of various chiefs, the name Kyala was mentioned repeatedly, as will be shown. Some may interpret this as evidence of a traditional belief in an overriding deity. We think that in most cases it is used in the sense of Kyala the hero, or Kyala 'the lord', but after forty years[1] and more of missionary activity it is not possible to establish exactly what the traditional conception of Kyala was. Moreover, it will be obvious that many of the speakers quoted in later chapters now entertain religious notions which have been unconsciously, and sometimes profoundly, modified by Christian ideas, a phenomenon especially noteworthy in their references to Kyala.

All the Nyakyusa proper (that is those of Selya, the Lake plain, and Masoko) send cattle to sacrifice at Lubaga (the grove of Lwembe), and several of the Kinga chiefs send there too. The people of Ngonde send to the Kyungu at Mbande, but not to Lubaga, while the people living north of the Songwe did not ever send to Mbande. Some of the people of the Lake plain (Mu-Ngonde) and various Kinga chiefs send to PaliKyala as well as to Lubaga, but the hill people never send to PaliKyala, nor did the Kisi who lived around PaliKyala send to Lubaga. In other words, Lwembe and Kyala were 'brothers' and it was possible to sacrifice to both, though people living close to one centre did not send to the other. All those living south of the Songwe river looked to Mbande; those north of it to Lubaga or PaliKyala. Lwembe, Kyala, and Kyungu were ancestors, honoured primarily by their own descendants or by those of a brother, but they were also divine heroes who might be appealed to by unrelated people through their priests.

The distinction between a 'divine king' and an early ancestor who established a line of chiefs is not a sharp one, and we have indeed been uncertain whether or not to class Mwangomale (4K),[2] the founder (or at least a notable son) of the Kukwe line, with Lwembe and Kyungu. Sacrifices used to be made to Mwangomale at the grove of Kabale by a number of Kukwe chiefs, but we have no evidence either of the formal installation of a living representative in each generation or of sacrifices by unrelated people, and therefore do not include Mwangomale among the 'divine kings'. The early inhabitants of the Rungwe

[1] Field-work began in 1934.

[2] Numerals followed by K refer to the genealogy of Kukwe chiefs facing p. 27.

area, the Penja, have a grove, Lukata, where they worship their founding ancestor, and the Nyika living on the west bank of the Kiwira river have their grove, Lubaga, twenty miles or more from the Lubaga in Selya and unconnected with it. A third distinct group, the Saku, who were the first inhabitants of the south-eastern part of Rungwe District, have their own grove, Nkeso, where their progenitors Mwamakula and Mwalukinge were buried. None of these has anything like the prestige and sanctity of the Lwembe or the Kyungu, but they are probably the prototype from which the 'divine kings' developed.

What circumstances produced a 'divine king' at Lubaga and not (so far as our limited knowledge goes) at Kabale we do not know, but we can show how the 'divine kingship' at Mbande, near the Lake shore, developed rather differently from the originally similar institution at Lubaga which is forty miles from the Lake. The Kyungu gradually acquired political power in a way in which the Lwembe did not. Among the Nyakyusa the 'sons of Lwembe' spread through the country establishing themselves as independent chiefs. They acknowledged the mystical supremacy of the Lwembe, and sent cattle to him to sacrifice, but they were sovereigns in their own territories. Just what this mystical supremacy of Lwembe implied was and still is often a matter of dispute, as we shall see. On the death of a chief his country was normally divided into two independent sections, each ruled by one of his sons. One heir sometimes fought the other and reduced him to a subordinate position, but the number of independent chiefdoms appears to have increased fairly steadily, and their size did not diminish in proportion, for the Nyakyusa chiefs have been expanding their area of occupation over a long period, establishing themselves as rulers over scattered and unorganized peoples with less developed techniques than their own, or colonizing unoccupied forest country. Expansion into uncultivated forest is still going on (1955), and were it not for the vigilance of the British Administration it is almost certain that the Safwa people would have been conquered and absorbed like the Penja, Lugulu, and others before them.[1] In 1936 over 100 independent chiefdoms were recognized by the people themselves, and they varied in size from 100 to 3,000 adult men.

In Ngonde the development was different. In the early period all the sons of the Kyungu, save two, were killed, and the territorial

[1] cf. Monica Wilson, *Good Company*, p. 4.

rulers were not of the royal blood but 'nobles' (*amakambara*), descendants of the five leading men who had arrived with the Kyungu, of those he found already occupying the country, and of those who arrived after him. Later the slaughter of the Kyungu's sons ceased, and as they grew up they were established as subordinate chiefs through his territories, gradually taking over power from the commoners who had previously ruled, by a process familiar in other parts of Africa.[1] But the 'nobles' retained considerable power. At Lubaga the descendants of the two men who had arrived with the first Lwembe, and of some of those who were there before him, became priests, and priests only; in Ngonde those of similar origin developed secular, as well as ritual, functions.

The reasons why the office of Kyungu developed into a paramount chieftainship, and that of the Lwembe did not, have been examined in a previous publication,[2] and may therefore be dealt with very briefly here. The most important factor was that the Kyungu exported ivory and amassed wealth which was used to bind territorial rulers to him, while the Lwembe remained cut off from the outside world and did not trade at all. The geographical situation largely accounts for this. The ivory of Ngonde first went north, and later south-east, across the Lake, and Mbande was well situated for both routes. It lies eight miles from the Lake and close to a defile which leads from the lakeshore plain to an open table-land stretching north to Lake Tanganyika, the very route which engineers later selected for the Stevenson road. Lubaga, on the other hand, is forty miles from the Lake and the only routes northward lay over broken country and passes 8,000 feet high. Giraud remarks in his journal that the Nyakyusa were the only people he had come across among whom the chiefs did not claim at least one tusk of every elephant killed;[3] they did not claim it, for they had no use for the ivory; but the Kyungu's right to a tusk from every elephant killed was enforced.

The growth of a paramount chieftainship in Ngonde was slow. The early Kyungus lived within an enclosure on Mbande to which only their personal servants and the nobles of Ngonde had

[1] cf. M. Hunter, *Reaction to Conquest*, p. 380; H. Kuper, *An African Aristocracy*, pp. 13-14; I. Schapera, in *African Political Systems* (edited Fortes and Evans-Pritchard), pp. 60-1.

[2] Godfrey Wilson, *The Constitution of Ngonde*, Rhodes-Livingstone Papers No. 3 (1939).

[3] V. Giraud, *Les Lacs d'Afrique Equatoriale* (1890), p. 186.

access. It was the nobles who were the effective rulers of the country; the divine Kyungu was the centre, a source of mystical power, a numinous symbol of unity, but not a judge or an administrator. Gradually, however, the Kyungus emerged from seclusion; they descended from the hill of Mbande; later they ceased to live within a stockade; in the crises of the Ngoni invasion the Kyungu in office (a notable warrior before his accession to the stool) broke tradition by himself taking arms. 'When the Ngoni came their enmity was like that of the lions and their number like that of the ants, and so Kyungu Mwakasungula, seeing his people were terrified, took up arms in person, and said he would die fighting. And his people heard with awe and astonishment that he himself had come to fight and they determined to die with him.' The next stage was a development of the judicial functions of the Kyungu until, in the present generation, the transformation from god to magistrate was complete.[1]

We turn now to the detailed description of the rituals at each shrine.

(b) LUBAGA

Lubaga is a hill dominating the central part of the Nyakyusa valley and on its slopes are signs of old and intensive cultivation. There an early Lwembe (19) lived and was buried, there is the grove where he is worshipped, and there his descendant chosen as 'the living Lwembe' should build. According to tradition the 'sons of Lwembe' spread all over the Nyakyusa valley as chiefs, but two senior lineages, that of Mwampondele (27) and that of Mwakisisya (56), remained near Lubaga, and from them was chosen, alternately, the living embodiment of the 'divine king', the Lwembe. Men feared greatly to be chosen, for they feared to be 'killed by the grove', and indeed the Lwembe rarely lived long. He must not fall ill or all the people of the country would do so likewise; therefore if he ailed he was smothered by his priests who stuffed up his nostrils and other passages of his body. Towards the end of our stay in BuNyakyusa Kasitile made a formal statement on this point in the presence of another priest, Mwamakunda:

The Lwembes were not sick. They said: 'I am going, I have eaten food at home, at the place of the shade', and they died that day; they

[1] The change in the position of the Kyungu from the earliest period is discussed in detail by Godfrey Wilson in *The Constitution of Ngonde*.

were not ill, they were not troubled as we are. For later in the evening, while the Lwembe was still alive, the commoner priests removed his nails and hair; they came near and plucked them off. He shouted: 'Who is snatching at me?' They replied: 'No one', and then they smothered him with cloth in the nostrils and in the anus, and he went away [i.e. he died]. . . . They did it only when he had initiated it himself by saying: 'I have eaten food in the land of the shades'; they did not begin it themselves. . . . They collected the relics in a little bamboo flask, and a priest treated them so that Lwembe might not go away with the food to the land of the shades, that the fertility of the soil (ilifugo), this ifingila, might always remain above.

These relics, the hair and the nails, were held to be magically connected through their growth with the growth of crops.

While the Lwembe lived he was secluded—ordinary men did not see him—and he was subject to numerous taboos. For example, he might not tread in water lest the country should be flooded; he never bathed in a stream (as Nyakyusa men do daily) and was carried across any river when travelling; he must not sit on a green banana leaf lest the bananas in the country should fail, but was always provided with a skin to sit upon, and he ate only the middle portion of a banana throwing away the ends for 'if he finished the whole of a banana he would create hunger in the country'. No one might grasp his hand, or drink out of the same calabash as he, save the priests of his own age; if he drank from a calabash when travelling he took it with him, for 'if he left it behind he left hunger in that place'.

The selection of the Lwembe was in the hands of the hereditary priests of Lubaga and the hereditary Kinga priests, who come from BuKinga to sacrifice at Lubaga. The man they choose must be of good character—at the time we were in BuNyakyusa the only willing candidate was rejected because 'he is a bad man, a thief, they refuse to have a thief as priest'—he must exhibit in his own home the power of fertility. 'They don't catch just anyone, but one with children, and cattle, and fertility of the fields in his own homestead. If the man taken as chief is not fertile and rich there will be many sterile people in the homesteads, and much disease and hunger.'

When the priests had decided upon the man of their choice, they seized him and set him upon a sacred skin and a pad of leaves; and it was believed that once he had been set thereon he would die if he refused office; tales were told of a younger brother

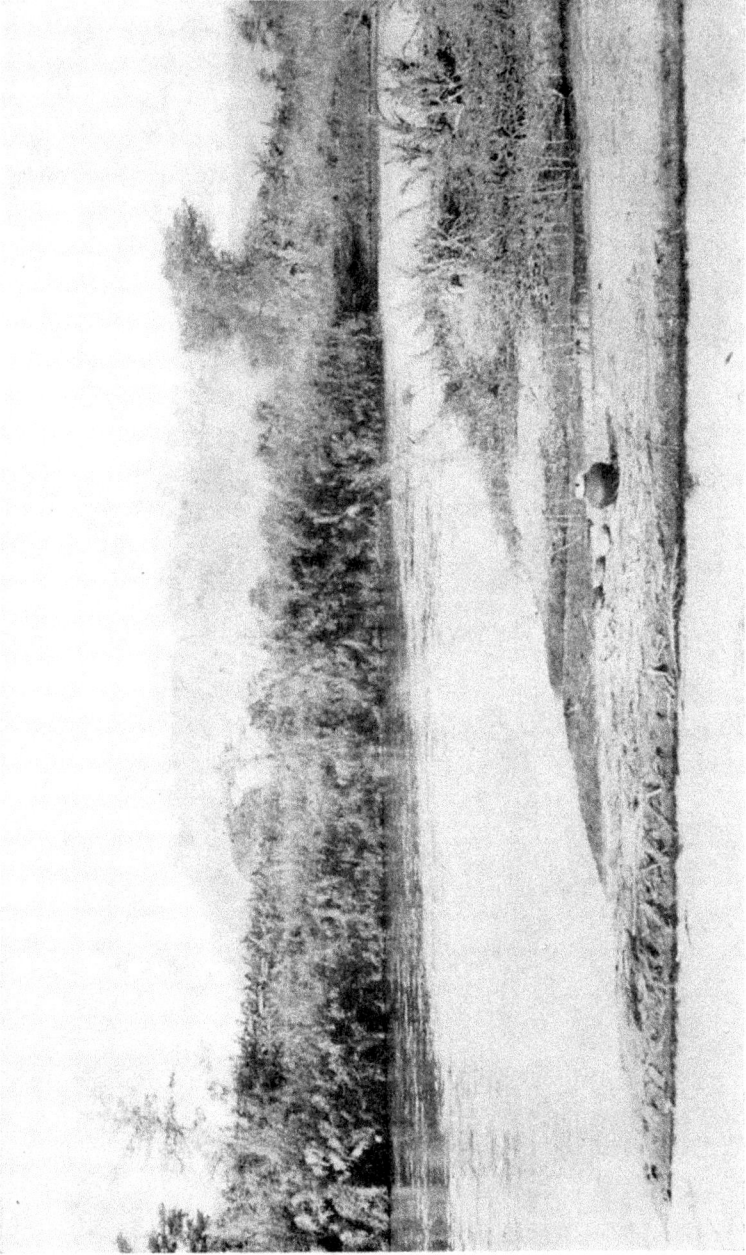

3. MBANDE HILL

4*a*. SACRIFICE AT LUBAGA

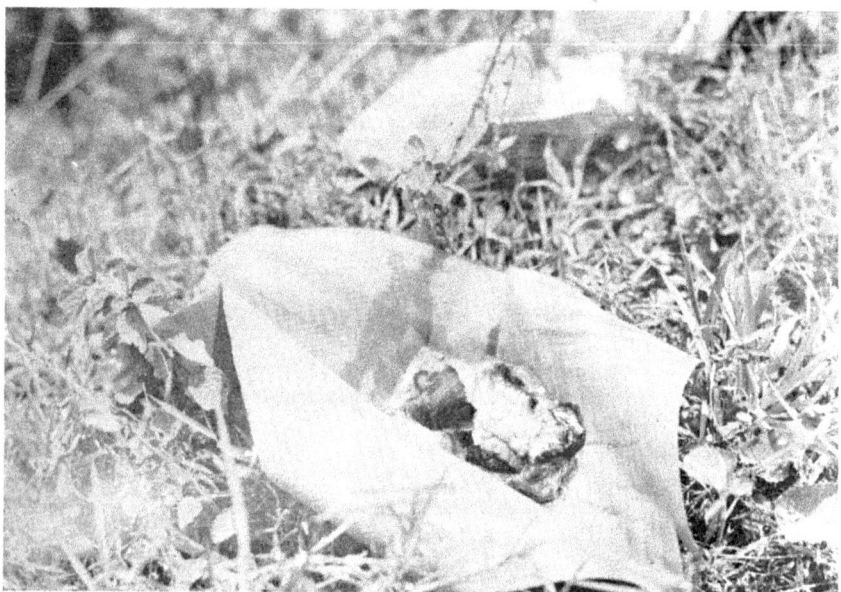

4*b*. THE SACRIFICIAL MEAT

(28) of Mwampondele (27) who had fled from the stool and had died.

The chosen man was secluded in a hut, lying on a litter with his priests, who kept him company (*ukumpanja*), just as a nubile girl is secluded and lies on a litter with her maids, or a young chief with his village headmen at his 'coming out'. Here is the account of Mwasesi, the oldest of the priests of Lubaga (a man of about seventy-five) who saw the installation of the last Lwembe, Mwakisisya (56).

A skin and a head-pad of leaves (*ingata*)[1] are brought by the Kinga. The priests catch the chief and set him on these; and then he cannot run away, it is taboo. I, Mwasesi, would sit on one side of him and my friend on the other, and force him to sit on them. Then we plead with him and say: 'You are the Lion, the Leopard, the Snake, the Banana, the Bean, the Millet, the Cow Pea, and the Lentil.' (Lentils are very important, you know, because it is with them that we celebrate the ritual, and with cow peas.) Then, after a time, he says: 'Leave me', and he goes to find the cow; this cow is just for the priests to eat that night. Then we take him into a certain house, cut leaves and spread them for a litter; and we keep him company there on the litter for some time. Then he sends messages to Mwakyusa (38), to Mwankyuse (33), and to Mwakisambe (30), and the Kinga [i.e. their descendants]. Each chief who is Lwembe's descendant sends commoner priests . . . they gather to induct him into Lubaga, he who was in the house. It is just like the 'coming out' ritual for a young chief.

The Lwembe in his own person, and in a lesser degree his 'sons' who are ordinary chiefs, are identified with the power of growth. Not only must the Lwembe not die with the breath still in his body, or with his hair and nails still upon it, but when he is chosen the priests test whether his reign will be long or short (perhaps whether they can permit him to live or not) by taking a little millet, putting it in a banana leaf and watching to see whether it sprouts or not. 'If it sprouts and grows at once he will live long; if it does not, he will be the priest [i.e. divine king] but will die very soon.'

Because the power of making rain, food, milk and children lay in the body of the Lwembe he was fearful and terrible. 'No one built close to him, it was taboo, no one touched Mwakisisya (56) . . . if he wished to make it rain he would make it rain all

[1] The Kinga priests spoke of a cloth to wear and a stool and an axe which were kept in the inner part of the hut of the Lwembe's great wife and which no man, save a priest of Lubaga, might see.

C

round him and sit at home in the middle in the sun. . . . All the old chiefs inspired fear (*bapala*). It used to be taboo to walk near the house of a chief and approach him unless taken by a village headman . . . nowadays men walk about and enter his home and even steal his food.'[1] The power came partly from his position as the living Lwembe, and partly from the medicines with which he was treated, especially the terrible *ifingila*.

The 'divine king' who came as a conqueror bringing iron is also associated with victory in battle. Still today a brave fighter is saluted as 'Lwembe', and an iron spear is one of the emblems of chieftainship.

The Lwembe was himself a priest—he is often referred to as *unyago*—but he was assisted by commoners. There is a hereditary keeper of the grove of Lubaga named Kissoule who is the descendant of that Kissoule the commoner who fled from BuKinga with Lwembe. It is he who conducts the sacrifices, who daubs the participants with medicines before they enter, and who protects the groves. 'If by mistake the grove was a little burnt then the people here paid a beast to Kissoule, it was his to eat as he liked.' Others of the priests say that Lwembe found their ancestors at Lubaga; they are 'owners of the soil' there, and one of them, Mwasesi, could give us the names of six generations of ancestors who had been priests of Lubaga before him. But the bulk of the commoner priests are not hereditary at all, they are surviving village headmen (or their heirs) of the most recently dead Lwembe.

The success of the sacrifices at Lubaga was held to depend upon the proper co-operation of chiefs and priests: first, on the Lwembe himself (the shortage of food among the Kinga, and of milk among the Nyakyusa, while we were there, was attributed by Kasitile to the fact that there was no living Lwembe); secondly on the commoner priests of Lubaga; thirdly on the commoner Kinga priests; fourthly on Kasitile (86) and certain other priests of Selya; and fifthly on the chiefs of the Nyakyusa and the Kinga who provided the offerings. 'Can a priest celebrate alone?' said Kasitile. 'No, the ritual depends on the chiefs.' The celebrations thus linked together chiefs and people, as well as Kinga and Nyakyusa, and numerous different Nyakyusa chiefdoms. The hereditary Kinga priests live in the country of the Kinga chief Mwakalukwa and

---

[1] This is inconsistent with Kasitile's statement quoted above. The general opinion was that chiefs were more powerful than formerly, but the living Lwembe less so.

'Lwembe listens to him'. 'If Kinga messengers went [to Lubaga] without going through Mwakalukwa's country there would be much hunger. . . . Once Mwemusi and Kyelela [Kinga chiefs] conspired together and sent off men with hoes to Lubaga, without reference to Mwakalukwa. They carried ten hoes. But when they got back disease killed many in the country, and they paid Mwakalukwa and did not do it again.'

It is true that an independent Nyakyusa chief *can* send an offering to Lubaga on his own; it is received by the priests of Lubaga and sacrificed in the grove, and such a sacrifice is held to be in some measure efficient, but drought or sickness in the country as a whole is often attributed to one or other of the participating groups failing to play their part. Moreover, such a failure is thought to be dangerous to the chief or priest who neglects his duties, as we shall see in the case of Kasitile.

The priests of Lubaga ministered to the Lwembe but they had also the right and duty of admonishing him if he did wrong, just as village headmen have the right and duty of admonishing their chief. If the Lwembe broke a taboo 'then Kissoule and the other priests would be very angry and reproach him for bathing and making hunger, and he would pay them a bull in recompense.' Even the 'divine king' was subject to the rule of law. All through the political organization and ritual patterns of the Nyakyusa there is this balance and reciprocity between chiefs and commoners and it is here that the Nyakyusa system differs radically from that described by Professor Frankfort for ancient Egypt.[1] The heroes had brought the gift of chieftainship to the Nyakyusa but it had not ousted another, perhaps older, tradition of democratic leadership; instead, the two were welded in a partnership which, to the Nyakyusa, is so much part of the necessary order of the universe that they speak of commoner priests and headmen as 'wives' of the chiefs. The Kissoule in office is 'the wife' of the Lwembe.

In the grove at Lubaga sacrifices of black cattle and sheep and libations of millet beer were offered by the Nyakyusa, while the Kinga brought hoes, bamboo beer, salt, the sacred drum *ngoma*, and *ifika*, that is, marvels whose nature, Kasitile averred, he did not know himself. The shrine of Lubaga, and the actors and actions connected with it, are miraculous and terrible, terrible even to the actors themselves who tremble when they enter the grove, and

[1] H. Frankfort, *Kingship and the Gods* (1948), pp. 51-6.

dare not greet their children on their return without the safeguard of protective medicines. At a celebration the Kinga priests took medicines, 'powdered medicine which comes from Mwemusi and Mwakalukwa [the Kinga chiefs]', and smeared it on Lwembe's forehead and shoulders 'because the grove is great. If you entered it without this medicine you died'; they gave the Lwembe the medicine 'so that Kyala (*vide* pp. 17-18) might not kill him, that he might show respect and escape'.

Another medicine, *imbinga*, which is red in colour, was brought from BuKinga to smear on the foreheads of the children of the Lwembe and Kissoule, the priest, when these two returned home after celebrating in the grove. Their senior wives 'would smear the *imbinga* on the children's foreheads, when they would turn round calling: "You hit us", and Mwakisiya (56) (the Lwembe) and Kissoule (the priest) would both reply: "No, I am innocent (*mwelu*)." The medicine was smeared on the children because Mwakisisya and his fellow thought: "How can we meet them, how can they look on our bodies, since we are taboo from the ritual." Yes, the words are the same as in the twin ritual, but the medicine is different.' During one of the rituals we attended, Mwakilima (111) begged the Kinga priests to bring him some of this medicine for the protection of his children.

The numinous quality of everything connected with Lubaga can hardly be exaggerated; the Nyakyusa believe that it overcomes even curious Europeans. The most sacred and terrible object of all was the drum which was polished with blood, the blood of children, who, in Nyakyusa thought, had died for the people, that the country might live and be fertile. 'Formerly, when the Kinga came with a drum, they said: "Catch the child of a commoner, fat and strong, hide him in the drum." In the old days when the Kinga came beating their drum, ping . . . ping . . . [single strokes with long intervals] we of the country used to run away and women would hide their children for fear lest they be snatched up and put in the drum.'[1] The child was strangled

---

[1] These statements were made by three different groups of informants independently. All had special knowledge of these matters. The *ilikole*, the sacred drum of the Kinga, differs in shape from the Nyakyusa *indingala*. It is made of *nkuju* wood and ox-hide and is beaten when a ritual is celebrated and to summon men to war. The Kinga do not dance to drums and the Nyakyusa did not do so formerly either, but after the Europeans arrived Nyakyusa chiefs began to buy *indingala* from outside BuNyakyusa, paying a bull for a set—'a mother drum and her children'. Only quite recently have Nyakyusa craftsmen learnt from a Henga immigrant to make *indingala*.

and its body taken to Lubaga and added to the 'medicine for fertility' (*unkota gwa ifugo*) which was sprinkled throughout the country, starting at Lubaga, proceeding to the other sacred groves, and then to the ordinary homesteads. Thus the terror of the grove had objective roots in the fact of human sacrifice, but it is rather a fear of the unknown and miraculous than of death itself; a fight involving casualties was not terrible in the same way as the grove and the throb of the sacred drum.

The Kinga priests travelled 'the road of Lwembe', down the escarpment of the Livingstone mountains from Mwakalukwa's country and across Selya, beating their drum. They stopped to sleep at the home of Kasitile the priest, and poured a libation of beer at 'the places where Lwembe had rested': Isumba, a hill overlooking Kasitile's homestead, Kituli in Mwaipopo's country, and near the homestead of the priest Munyoso.[1] 'He [Lwembe] used to shout on Isumba, the little hill here, then no one would cut the trees on the hill,' said Kasitile. 'It was one of his resting places; he used to come here to tell my grandfather to go and get a cow for Lubaga, and later to tell my father to do so. . . .' The beer is poured at the base of an *nkuju* tree (a variety of *ficus*) at Isumba, in the long grass in Kituli, and at the base of an *nkuju* near Munyoso's homestead. 'They pour [it] out here by the *nkuju*, they beat the drum to say: "We have come", then the people of Munyoso hide their children—that's of old.' Besides the drum the Kinga travelled with a kudu horn[2] (blown in battle in BuKinga) and a sacred drum and horn were lodged in the hut of the Lwembe's chief wife. Before they start the Kinga priests make an offering of millet flour and beer in one of their own groves,[3] and leave there overnight the beer and salt and hoes which they will take to the Lwembe, 'that the aba-Ngulube (9) may see them before they go to Lwembe'.

At Lubaga there were several places of prayer and offering: the trees planted at the installation of the last living Lwembe (*vide infra* pp. 54-5), the trees planted at the installation of a previous

---

[1] Probably grandson of 84 and representative of a junior lineage to which priestly functions had been delegated.

[2] *Ulukilima* in Kinga, *inganga bwite* in Nyakyusa. cf. plate 5*b*.

[3] Nyandala, a Kinga chief, and two priests took Godfrey Wilson to a sacrifice in one of their groves. The form of sacrifice is very similar to that among the Nyakyusa save that the meat-offering is placed in the fork of a tree. The priests had gone very early in the morning 'to tell Bululile (the dead chief) "Do not be angry, a European comes to greet you".'

Lwembe, and the grove of the first Lwembe himself, the last being the most sacred. In it stands a miraculous tree from which, the priests aver, sometimes comes sap like water, and sometimes blood. 'If it is watery there will be a plague of ulcers in the country—running sores—if it is blood there will be dysentery. But as soon as the hoes are placed in the grove, or the black bull is killed, then the sick begin to recover.'

Godfrey Wilson attended three celebrations at Lubaga, and we heard of five others which occurred during our period of field-work. The ritual is esoteric, that is to say, only the representative of Lwembe and his priests participate, and the details are not revealed to others, but its occurrence is widely known and discussed among older men.

The celebrations observed were modified by the fact that no one had been installed as Lwembe since the death of Mwakisisya (56) before 1914. The possible candidates whom the priests had wished to instal had refused—'they feared the grove'; the only one who was said to be willing was rejected on account of his character. The priests gave 'European times' as the reason for there being no Lwembe. 'When the country was ours before you Europeans came' the elected candidate was compelled to accept office. On the death of Mwakisisya, the Kinga priests ordered that his senior son Mwanjala I (77) should take his place, and when Mwanjala I died (three years after his father) his full brother Mwanjala II (78) succeeded. He took a leading part in the rituals observed, but was not an anointed Lwembe. The priests explained: 'We fear, thinking that if a chief is seized [and compelled to sit on the stool] he will complain to the Government and we shall be punished.' During the period of German rule they had been threatened with imprisonment if they continued the ritual . . . 'we feared and stole through the country by night'. . . . And there is still much secrecy about its truncated celebration. Since the journey down 'the road of Lwembe' with the drum traditionally involved human sacrifice, and the Lwembe was smothered when ailing, there is an absolute incompatibility between a full celebration of the ritual and European administration.

The influence of the Christian minority is also considerable. The view of most Nyakyusa Christians with whom we discussed communal rituals is that they used to be efficient, but are so no longer, since men have been taught a better way of approaching God. 'God said: "They are mistaken but in their hearts they are looking for me", and so if there was much heat he would send rain.' But this no longer happens.

At the same time both pagans and Christians tell a myth of how a European missionary, Rev. — Jauer (Mwaisumo), who visited the grove of Lubaga intending to remove the hoes in the grove to demonstrate the falsehood of the ritual, was confounded by a miracle (*ifika*).

Once the missionary Mwaisumo wished to go and see the grove of Lubaga. He was warned that if he entered he would flee because there were many marvels there, and the rain would catch him. He said: 'Oh, I shall go, nothing will happen.' So he went and entered the grove, and he found many hoes, some standing up, some lying down, and some of them had 'eyes'. He seized one to take it away, then there was a crash of thunder, and he was afraid and fled. When he ran out of the grove the rain fell in torrents. It is said that he was so frightened he left his jacket behind. From that time people said that indeed there are miracles at Lubaga.

'European times' is given as the reason for sacrifices being less frequent and regular than formerly. The occasions were, and still are: any period of hunger or scarcity, such as the Kinga regularly experience during the dry season, and the Nyakyusa also complain of at that time; any irregular misfortune such as a failure of the rains, a plague of locusts or an epidemic; and any prediction of hunger or disease by a prophet (*unsololi* or *unkunguluka*). But the chiefs are said to be more reluctant to provide the cattle for sacrifice than formerly, and less quickly influenced by the actual occurrence of hunger or by prophecy that famine is imminent. Nevertheless they still 'treat the earth' (*ukutendekesya umfu*) by sending a black cow to Lubaga when hunger presses.

According to Kasitile (86) and Mwamakunda (his fellow priest) no ritual could be performed in the grove of the first Lwembe when he had no living representative. Formerly, the Kissoule in office and another priest penetrated alone, and there bound a live sheep and left it to bleat until a python took it. 'It is Kyala, he turns himself into a python' (*Jo kyala: ipela sota*). Here Kasitile used *kyala* in the sense of 'the lord' and he was referring to Lwembe. According to another informant, when the heir to any priesthood connected with Lubaga is installed he should sleep in the grove enclosed in a stout wicker hut, and remain there until the python of the grove comes and *licks* him. The case was cited of a priest who had lain captive for two weeks and come home 'very thin', but just when this happened was not clear.

We turn now to the account of the three sacrifices witnessed at Lubaga which illustrates (a) the occasions of celebration, (b) the procedure, and (c) the tensions between the participants. In the ritual described on pp. 35-8, Mwakilima (111) complained that most of the chiefs of Selya did not even recognize his ritual supremacy by sending cattle to kill at Lubaga, but Kasitile the priest retorted that Mwakilima himself, in his capacity as a chief, was slow to provide the cattle for sacrifice required by his own priests.

In July 1935, two Kinga priests, Kikungubeja and Nsyanigwa, came from the Kinga chief Mwakalukwa to Lubaga, with an offering of hoes. A bull, provided by Mwakilima (111) as chief of Lwembe's line, was then killed beside a tree planted at the 'coming out' of Mwakisisya (56), the last Lwembe, on the site on which the house of his second wife, Kitega, was built, and the meat was thrown into the old banana grove close by. At the end of September the same two priests returned (each accompanied by a grandson) bringing bamboo beer and 10s. and a hoe with which to buy a bull to sacrifice again, for the Kinga were suffering hunger and a prophet in their country had gone into a trance and prophesied cold, disease, and hunger, and urged the chiefs to pray. No fault had brought the hunger, they said, but 'the shades wish a cow. The shades say: "Formerly we ate much, now you do not kill cows for us, indeed we wish to eat. . . ." Therefore much hunger affects our country. It is on this account that we Kinga come with a bull and hoes. When the blood of the sacrifice soaks into the earth then the shades are satisfied, and they also receive the meat from the upper foreleg (ijammapa).'[1]

The initiative came from the Kinga who were suffering most severely, but the Nyakyusa were also complaining of scarcity. The weather was very hot and dry and Mwakilima (108) remarked to Kasitile (86) the priest, who had come up to Lubaga for the sacrifice: 'You have killed us with this sun.' He was referring to the unusually small yield of early maize and beans which had been scorched by the drought. Kasitile replied: 'No, all of us [are responsible], the sun has hated us.' Both men smiled.

Five days after the Kinga reached Lubaga (28th September 1955) the sacrifice was offered up. The men concerned gathered in

[1] The sacred cut. cf. Monica Wilson, *Rituals of Kinship among the Nyakyusa*, p. 96.

the house of Mwamalunguka, a hereditary priest of Lubaga (whose ancestor came with the first Lwembe (*vide* p. 8). There were present five chiefs of Mwakisisya's (56) line, including Mwanjala II (78), who represents the Lwembe, but is ailing and has never been installed; two Kinga priests and a Kinga messenger sent to escort them; four priests of Lubaga (including Mwamalunguka himself), Kasitile the priest of Selya, and Godfrey Wilson.

Mwanjala brought a small black bull worth 12*s*., bought with the money and a hoe provided by the Kinga, and sent for a stem of bananas and a flask of fresh milk. A rowdy discussion began about the procedure: 'In the old days we used to pour whey over our hands to wash them, and to wash our mouths, and in the sacred grove we would pour it away. . . .' Then the party went to a small grove surrounded by cultivated land, and Nsyanigwa, the Kinga priest, stopped at the stump of a tree, still alive, on the edge of the grove, saying: 'This is the *umpandapanda* tree [a *ficus* planted at the coming out of a chief] where we used to pour the beer,' but Mwanjala denied it saying 'No, they have hoed over it, the tree was here in the bean patch.' After some dispute they agreed to go right into the grove to sacrifice. The grove is on the site at which the trees were planted at the 'coming out' of Mwaki-sisya (56) the last Lwembe, and the house of his senior wife, Njala, was built. She is buried there, where her swept courtyard used to be, and during Mwakisisya's lifetime the beer used to be poured out beside this sacred tree. The last sacrifice here was when Kissoule was a boy (1885-90), hence the uncertainty as to the place, but just why the beer sacrifices had all been at the homestead of Kitega (*vide supra*) was not clear.

Nsyanigwa (the Kinga priest) asked Mwamalunguka (the priest of Lubaga) to bring over the three calabashes, one of millet beer, one of milk and one of bamboo beer, but Mwamalunguka refused and Nsyanigwa had to fetch them himself. It was the Kinga who had insisted on the Nyakyusa providing millet beer saying: 'If we first pour out our bamboo beer we will go off with all the fertility of the country, let them begin with theirs.' Mwanjala, summoned by Nsyanigwa, came and stood at the foot of the tree while Nsyanigwa poured millet beer first into his hands and then at the foot of the tree, and the priests prayed, Mwanjala and Nsyanigwa in Nyakyusa, Kikungubeja in Kinga:

Oh thou Mwambipili, thou Kissoule, thou Mwamalunguka,[1] thou

---
[1] Three hereditary priests of Lubaga.

Lwembe, this is your millet beer, we complain of hunger, oh thou Mwampondele (27), thou Lwembe.

Then the milk was poured likewise and again they prayed for milk and calves, for children and health:

Here is your milk . . . may the locusts pass, may sickness be slight, may milk be plentiful, may the cows calve!

Finally the bamboo beer was poured out, too, and both the Kinga priests prayed in Kinga speaking of hunger. Mwanjala, instructed by Nsyanigwa, took some bamboo beer into his mouth and blew it three times in different directions, saying, between blowing: 'May the rain come.'

The bull was killed by Mwanjande (?). Nsyanigwa first gave the axe and knife to Mwanjala saying: 'This axe and knife [an unhafted and very old spearhead] I, Nsyanigwa, brought from BuKinga to kill the bull, go and kill it.' Mwanjala asked: 'Shall I not give the axe to my younger brother?' and Nsyanigwa replied: 'Yes, give it to him.' So Mwanjala gave it to Mwanjande who killed the bull with one blow at the back of the head. Mwansasu (a commoner priest) cut up the carcass, collecting the first stream of blood in a pot. Then the sacred meat was taken from the forelegs, that from the right leg being placed on a plantain leaf, that from the left on a leaf of sweet banana. It was cut up and carried by Kitega (heir of 57?), who walked behind Mwanjala and the two Kinga priests, to the tree where they had poured the beer and milk. Mwanjala turned to the group of those sitting talking and shouting and said: 'Friends, a spear will go to the shades [i.e. the shades will be offended by your noise], be quiet', and they fell silent until the offering of meat was made. Then Mwanjala scraped a hollow in the cleared earth at the root of the tree with his foot and threw into it seven or eight pieces. He and the Kinga prayed, while Kitega stood silently holding the rest of the meat:

Oh thou Lwembe, thou Mwampondele (27), stand by us, this is your bull. . . . Give us children, milk, cattle, food; may sickness be slight . . . stand by us.

All this meat was taken from the plantain leaf—the men's portion. At the end, as they walked away Kitega asked: 'What about the women's meat?' And Mwanjala repeated his question. The Kinga replied: 'Are there two sacred places? No! There is no sacrifice to the women here, but to their husbands.' So Kitega took back to the tree the sweet banana leaf, containing the portion for the women.

Meanwhile strips of meat had been roasted and were eaten with roast bananas, while the milk was finished up by the Nyakyusa present. All the millet beer had been poured out, but the bamboo beer that remained was finished, part drunk, part blown from the mouth by the two Kinga boys, grandsons of the priests. Then the rest of the meat was divided up, one back leg being given to the Kinga. But they took the head (their traditional right) as well, without being given it. There was some considerable protest at this: 'Do you take twice?' they were asked. And more protest still when they began to go away with it. Nsyanigwa (the Kinga priest) replied furiously. 'Let it go, let them take it' was the final comment of the local people, but both parties were angry. Two legs went to the chiefs, one to the Nyakyusa commoners, and the breast to Mwanjala.

After the meat had been safely disposed of Nsyanigwa gave his parting instructions: 'You sirs (*batwa*), thank you, thank you. We remember that it was Mwakalukwa (the Kinga chief) who said "Pray for us"! Thank you! We thank you! Now you must build your chief, Mwanjala (78), a little hut in which to sleep with the breast of beef so that the lord (*kyala*)[1] may eat, and in the morning if *kyala* has eaten let him go to his home. This calf I brought, I Nsyanigwa, from BuKinga. Let the knife I brought remain with it too.' Then Nsyanigwa went off and his advice was discussed. Mwanjala laughed and said: 'I have no house to sleep in . . . shall I sleep by myself? Outside?' Several suggested that it was the custom for some other man to accompany him. No one knew who should do so, but someone suggested Kissoule. In fact Mwanjala went home with the breast of beef and did not remain overnight in the grove. But he and the priests held apart from their wives and children. Mwamalunguka (the priest) explained: 'We avoid sleeping with our wives for three nights. It is taboo to go to them. We say, "Let us wash and anoint ourselves and be alone until that lord (*kyala*) has gone out of our bodies, since we were in the ritual". We bathe tomorrow and the next day and anoint ourselves, but avoid our wives for three nights. Also our children are anointed on the forehead with medicine—the young

---

[1] The name *kyala* had not been used in the invocation, and the only references to him in this ritual were the two just quoted.

children, not the married ones with wives. Kissoule and I both have our children anointed now.'

This ritual was not complete because Mwanjala shirked the crucial act of remaining in the grove until a python licked him. The Kinga priests were continually nagging at the Nyakyusa for their failure to provide an acceptable Lwembe, but it is doubtful whether in 1935 Mwanjala II would have been acceptable to any of them since he was old and ailing. It was Mwakilima (111) that men wanted and he steadily refused to be installed.

The next ritual observed at Lubaga was in March 1937. An ordinary commoner of Selya (not a priest) named Kijaja had been prophesying repeatedly: 'I do not sleep, you will not eat the crops you hoe if you do not go to Lubaga.' He was taken to his village headman and thence to the chief Mwaihojo (147) who finally, two years after he had begun prophesying, agreed to find a bull. Word then came to Kasitile (86) who notified the commoner priests of chief Mwaipopo (116) and sent a message to the priests of Lubaga. Kasitile (86), together with three other priests of Selya (Mwalukuta, Nyama, Mwamakunda) and Godfrey Wilson, set off early one morning from Kasitile's house to take the bull (brown streaked with black, called *ingombe isolola*) to Lubaga. On the way they called in at Munyoso's house, where the Kinga stop on their journey to pour a libation of beer (*vide supra*, p. 27). Kasitile asked Munyoso, 'Shall the bull enter?' and he replied, 'Yes, let it come into the house', so it was tied up inside while the party talked with Munyoso. He was sick and did not want to accompany them. The others pressed him, and at first he refused. Whereupon Mwalukuta said: 'Very well, then, we are at your place, let the bull return and we will go another day', in other words, refusing to go without him. 'No, that is taboo,' said Kasitile, 'once the bull has faced towards Lubaga and entered a house here it is taboo for it to turn back. The shades will be angry.' And so Munyoso went with them.

On the way they passed a group of men hoeing hard. One of them called out: 'Where are you going with that bull? Where are you off enjoying yourselves?' 'Ah, you fellows,' answered Kasitile, 'do you ask where we are going? We visit where our fathers always did.' They understood at once. 'Oh thank you, thank you,' they cried. 'You,' went on Kasitile, 'do you call that work? Are you growing your own food? No, you lie still and eat without effort. It is *we* who exert ourselves for you' (implying that their crop depended upon sacrifices at Lubaga). But five minutes later, as if to illustrate the constant co-existence of dogma and science, of economic and ritual effort, Kasitile commented on a very uneven field of millet saying: 'Its unevenness is due to the rubbish heaps. Where they burnt the rubbish the millet has grown well', as indeed it had.

The party went to the house of Mwakisopile, priest of Lubaga, and after a polite interval for greetings and small talk Kasitile proceeded to explain his business. 'The sky has changed its temper towards us, we do not sleep (*Kumwanya kutusambukile, tutikugona*). Therefore I said to myself, "Let me go to my father, let me go to my mother." I have come to ask for bananas, and for maize.' So the host sent messages to Mwanjala III (79) and the priests Mwamalunguka and Kesa. Mwanjala II (78) and Kissoule the chief priest of Lubaga, were away from home. Kasitile had long been ailing (*vide infra*, pp. 121-41) and Kesa asked after his health. 'The sky has changed its temper towards us', repeated Kasitile, implying that his illness was connected with Lubaga, and hinting at the quarrel between the priests and men of Mwakisisya (56) of Lubaga and the priests and men of the chief Mwaipopo of Selya (*vide infra*, pp. 37-8). Mwakisopile (the host) repeated to Kesa the reason for the visit. 'Mwamukinga (i.e. Kasitile 86),' he said, 'and Mwalukuta and Mwamakunda declare they do not sleep. They have come to ask for bananas and maize and children, and that the cattle may increase.' Kasitile added, 'The sky has made us still and silent. We long for the grove: since Mwakisisya (56) died we have wished for it. We have come to beg. I lie down wrapped in mats but the cold will not leave me. So I said to myself, "Let me go to my father, let me go to my mother." I am hungry. Have I food? The earth is destroyed.'

Then Kesa and Mwakisisya (111) replied: 'We are astonished that the people of Selya don't sleep. We have heard nothing about it. I, Mwakisisya sleep all right. And only Mwakalobo (67 or heir) and Mwankuga (94) these two alone of all the Selya chiefs came to me. Most of the men in Selya insult us! Ask them who has remembered that they should sacrifice here?'

Kasitile answered: 'It was I, Mwakisambwe (30, i.e. Kasitile speaks as his great grandfather) who initiated it.'

Kesa: 'Yes, but who agreed to give you an animal?'

Kasitile: 'It was Mwalubange, it was Kajula (i.e. the chief Mwaihojo, 147).'

He also admitted that the people of Selya had insulted the Lwembe, 'But,' he added, 'we have heard that Mwakisisya (111) himself, when someone does not sleep, says "All right", but does not offer a cow.' Thus Kasitile accused the chief of Lubaga who should be Lwembe, to his face, of being reluctant to provide cattle for sacrifice just as the chiefs of Selya were reluctant.

Then Mwalukuta interposed: 'But Kasitile, you admitted that you had injured your father, you had injured your mother.'

Kasitile: 'Yes, indeed it is so, I have injured[1] my father, I have injured my mother.'

That ended the discussion. Kesa fetched bananas and a huge calabash of thick milk for the men of Selya, and Mwalukuta and Mwamakunda started eating at once. Kasitile reproved them: 'What? Do you eat anyhow?' They dropped the bitten bananas hastily. 'Do you not know that you have come here to ask for bananas, to ask for maize? We have come to Mwatonoka (29), to Mwakisisya (56), to Mwanjala (77), to Mwampondele (27) to ask for it. Kyala provided the food.' Then he took up his flask of thick milk and two bananas, and went over to the banana grove at a little distance and prayed aloud:

'You, Mwatonoka (29), you Mwanjala (77) . . . I have come, I Mwalubange (58), I Mwakagile (59) [Kasitile represents their descendants] I have come to beg for maize, to beg for bananas.' Then he came back and joined the party. He sent a large flask of milk over to the local priests; they wanted to refuse and leave all the milk for the visitors, eating only roast bananas, but Kasitile said: 'No, Kyala has provided the food, Kyala has provided it, let us all eat and be satisfied.'

During the meal Kesa and Godfrey Wilson discussed steamships and aeroplanes, and the distance and fares to Europe. Mwamalunguka had been to Mbeya and described the wind of an aeroplane coming down and starting, most graphically. Mwanjala (78) wanted very much to go to Europe to see the country. Then Kasitile said: 'Let us go, friends, the rain is coming', so they got up and left, leaving the bull tied to the bananas; the Selya priests had nothing further to do with that; the Lubaga men would kill it at their own convenience.

On the journey back Mwamakunda apologized to Kasitile for having begun to eat before they prayed: 'I am sorry, Mwamukinga (44, addressing Kasitile by his grandfather's name), you have

---

[1] *Nakendile*: literally surpassed, overstepped, with the implication of injuring.

instructed us, you have taught us the customs, we did not know them, we thought that when the food came that was all.'

Kasitile said: 'Yes, I do it as our fathers did it.' Then they discussed the dispute between Mwakisisya and Kasitile and agreed that Kasitile had got the better of Mwakisisya with the reference to his own reluctance to provide cattle for sacrifice.

Kasitile was determined to extract a cow for sacrifice from the chief Mwaipopo (116) also, and presently he said:

Friends, listen, let us report at home that we used hard words, we insulted Mwakisisya, we said there is nothing left to eat though we are not really starving. What has come over me? Why am I ill? Let Mwaipopo pay a cow.

The following day Mwamalunguka, one of the priests of Lubaga, explained what was meant by the complaint of insults from Selya:

The people of Mwaipopo (116) do really insult us, and since the Europeans have given them a Court they have begun to say that Mwakisisya (111) is a priest, not a chief, but just an old priest (inyago), and we his men are all angry to hear this because Mwakisisya was always the senior. And they do not send us cattle to sacrifice, they say: 'It's European times now, all that is finished.'

But of Kasitile's retort that Mwakisisya himself did not listen to his priests at home, Mwamalunguka said: 'Indeed it is so, that was an excellent reply.'

The party going up to Lubaga and back travelled dry, but on the return journey Kasitile noticed that the road was wet and he remarked, 'The rain follows us again', and it was true, clouds were gathering quickly. An hour and a half after they got home heavy rain began and continued for three or four hours. During the preceding weeks there had been many heavy showers and bright spells, unnoticed and of no particular significance, but the downpour on the day of the sacrifice was immediately connected with it.

Three weeks later the rain had almost stopped and people were talking of drought. Kasitile was quick to link this with the failure to follow up the offering at Lubaga with sacrifices in the groves of the chiefs. On the sixth of April he spoke his mind to Mwambuputa, the senior village headman of Mwaipopo, when both were visiting us.

Where is the rain? [said Kasitile] I am at fault, and my child Mwaipopo (116) also. He ought to provide a cow to kill at Mwaijonga's

(82) grove. According to custom, we should kill a bull here at the same time as one is killed at Lubaga. A messenger from there finds us eating. That was the custom when the chiefs were really chiefs. Now we neglect the rituals. Mwakisisya (111) cut a ripe banana stem for us, but now the bananas are rotting in the homesteads without ripening [owing to our failure to sacrifice]. If our fathers did not sleep they sacrificed cattle, but if we do not sleep we merely offer beer.

Then Kasitile recalled the quarrel between the men of Mwaipopo (116) and those of Lubaga.

Why did you insult Mwakisisya (111) saying 'What remains of your power?' When we built the Court House in Mwaipopo's country, Mwakisisya's men came to help, and some advised that a beast should be sent to Lubaga to seek blessing on the Court, but others said: 'What use is Lubaga?' . . . Mwakisisya cut a banana stem for us and said 'Seek another cow oh thou Mwakagile' (59, i.e. identifying Kasitile with the grandfather of the chief Mwaipopo whom he represented).

This, however, was an invention of Kasitile's. He continued: 'I, Kasitile, have seen a sacrifice at the grove of Mwaijonga (82) twice, at that of Mwaipopo (115) once, and at that of Mwakabule (117) once, but at Lubaga Kyala has received us frequently.' To which Mwambuputa replied: 'Yes, Kyala has helped us.'

Under pressure from Kasitile and the other priests of his chiefdom Mwaipopo did eventually provide a cow for sacrifice at the grove of his father Mwaijonga (82) but the description of that ritual is deferred to a later chapter.

A fundamental conception in Nyakyusa religion is that the proper working of the natural order depends upon harmony of the social order; on proper co-operation between the 'divine king' and his 'sons' the chiefs, between priests and chiefs, and between them and the whole community. If the Lwembe or a rain-maker is offended, that causes drought or flood in the area of his influence. When there is heavy rain in Selya it is said, 'There is anger at Lubaga' or 'There is anger at Lwembe's place'. Mwanjala II (78) talking of how angry he had been over an insult remarked, 'Had it been the wet season there would have been a torrent of rain.'

And not only does quarrelling between chiefs and priests bring public misfortune; it reacts upon their own health. How Kasitile linked his ill-health with the quarrel between Mwakisisya (111) of Lubaga and the men of Mwaipopo (116) over the Court, and Mwaipopo's failure to provide cattle for sacrifice has just been

5a. PRIESTS OF LUBAGA (KINGA)

5b. KINGA PRIESTS WITH HORN AND DRUM

indicated (*vide supra*, p. 35). And, as we shall see later, he also suspected that his quarrels with the Kinga priests and with the commoner priests of Mwaipopo's chiefdom made him ill.

Chiefs, and even the 'divine king' himself, lived in fear of the legitimate anger of their people, more particularly of their village headmen and priests, believing that such anger would bring them sickness, and this belief gave headmen and priests a very strong hold over their lord. How it worked was illustrated by an incident at Lubaga.

Mwanjala II (78) remarked to Mwakilima (111): 'I sent to summon Mwasesi (a commoner priest) for the ritual tomorrow but he refused saying: "I shall not come." He is angry because he was not called to the ritual at your home, nor was he told formally when the Kinga came, or when Mwaipaja [G.W.] came.' Mwakilima (111) asked: 'Will you pay him?' [i.e. admit your mistake and offer him compensation]. Mwanjala replied that he would, and Mwakilima expressed disgust. One of the Kinga priests who was listening broke into the conversation: 'Ignore him if he refuses to come. If it were us we should leave him and celebrate without him, but you Nyakyusa are all witches, and you fear to ignore a man who refuses to come to a ritual saying that he will bewitch you. You are cowards, you are!'

At this Godfrey Wilson asked if there were no witchcraft in BuKinga. The Kinga priest replied: 'There is some, but if the chief gives orders to celebrate a ritual and someone refuses to come we ignore him, and celebrate without him. You Nyakyusa *pay* a man for doing wrong. A man refuses to come when he should and then you *pay* him! If you are afraid of witchcraft why not finish the ritual and send his portion of meat to him afterwards?'

Another priest objected: 'Then he would say it was too small a piece.'

The commoner priests then could control even the Lwembe (for Mwanjala II acted in the place of the Lwembe though he was not installed), but at the same time the mystical power of the Lwembe was feared both by ordinary chiefs and commoners. Mwaijonga (82), who ruled before the European occupation, insulted and fought Mwakisisya the Lwembe (56), and killed some of his men, because 'Lwembe had spoiled the year', but he sent back the cattle that were seized.

In the old days it did not matter killing the Lwembe's men (in war), but no one dared to take his cattle, they feared lest he would spoil the year and send too much rain, and a plague of ulcers, and cause the cattle to

D

die. . . . People feared very much because the Lwembe had medicines for smearing on his body, which could cause rain, sickness, food, ulcers, anything.

And they feared lest they might get ulcers if they killed one of Lwembe's men 'on the road'—i.e. a traveller. In short, Lwembe's mystical power afforded the first feeble beginnings of a 'king's peace' in a land of warring chiefdoms, where strangers were fair game.

(c) MBANDE

Mbande is a hill on the plain of north Nyasaland with a commanding view of the surrounding country and well suited to defence. The west side is precipitous and below the scarp edge there used to be a marsh; to the north the hill is protected by a wide reach of the Lukulu river. It is a sacred place and for many generations was the home of the 'divine king', the Kyungu. Like the Lwembe he was the living representative of a hero, and was selected by a group of hereditary nobles from one of two related lineages, the office alternating (if suitable candidates were available) between the two. They sought a big man,[1] one who had begotten children and whose sons were already married, not a young man for, the nobles said, 'young men always want war, and destroy the country'. He must be a man of wisdom (*gwa mahala*) and generous in feeding his people.

The Kyungu's life was governed by taboos even more rigorous than those surrounding the Lwembe. He must not fall ill, or suffer a wound, or even scratch himself and bleed a little, for his ill health, or his blood falling on the earth would bring sickness to the whole country. 'Men feared when Kyungu's blood fell on the ground, they said, "It is his life".' 'If he had a headache his wives (if they loved him) told him not to mention it, they hid his illness; but if the nobles entered and found him ill they dug the grave and put him in it, saying, "He is the ruler (*ntemi*), it's taboo for him to be ill". Then he thought: "Perhaps it is so" (with a gesture of resignation).'

Great precautions were taken to preserve his health. He lived in a separate house with his powerful medicines. His food was prepared by boys below the age of puberty lest a menstruating woman, or a youth who had lain with a woman, should touch it and so bring sickness upon him; and his numerous wives were

---

[1] *Unyambala unwamu.* It implies both big physically and important.

immured in the royal enclosure—a great stockade—and jealously guarded, for any infidelity on their part was thought to make their husband ill, and with him the whole country.

When the Kyungu did fall ill he was smothered by the nobles who lived around him at Mbande, and buried in great secrecy, with a score or more of living persons—slaves—in the grave beneath him, and one or two wives and the sons of commoners above. And in the midst of all this slaughter the nobles brought a sheep to look into the grave that the dead Kyungu might be gentle (*mololo*) like the sheep!

The living Kyungu was thought to create food and rain, and his breath and the growing parts of his body—his hair and nails and the constantly replaced mucus of his nose—were believed to be magically connected with the fertility of the Ngonde plain. When he was killed his nostrils were stopped so that he was buried 'with the breath in his body'; while portions of his hair and nails and of his nasal mucus were taken from him beforehand and buried by the nobles of Ngonde in the black mud near the river. This was 'to defend the country against hunger', 'to close up the land, to keep it rich and heavy and fertile as it was when he himself lived in it'.

His death was kept secret—a relatively easy matter since he lived in seclusion—and one of the nobles (*Ngosi*) impersonated him wearing his clothes. After a month or two when the nobles had decided whom to choose as the new Kyungu, the luckless man was summoned to Mbande: 'Your father calls you.' 'Then he came with his companions and entered the house to make obeisance; they seized him and put the sacred cloth on him and set him on the stool "Kisumbi", saying, "Thou Kyungu, thou art he", and he became the Kyungu. Then they struck the drum, Mwenekelwa, and everyone knew that the Kyungu had died and another had been installed.' Men feared greatly to be seized as the Kyungu, just as they feared to be seized as the Lwembe, because the life of a divine king was short. Ngonde historians quote a number of cases of sons of the Kyungu who fled to escape being set on the stool; once they had sat on it they dared not flee lest they die.

Though[1] the early Kyungus had lived on the stony top of Mbande none of them had been buried there, for 'the ground was

---

[1] The following section is quoted, with additions and amendments, from Godfrey Wilson, *The Constitution of Ngonde*, pp. 29 ff.

too hard to dig graves in'. They and their successors were all buried in the valley, each in a different spot. Over their graves trees were planted and grew up to form a ring of sacred groves round Mbande. Each grove has a name and the Kyungu who is buried there is usually referred to, not by his own name, but by that of the grove where he lies. . . . We traced sixteen groves in the plain surrounding Mbande and the nobles who pointed them out remembered participating in celebrations at all except that of the last Kyungu. The ruling Kyungu and the spirits of his dead predecessors were believed to form one divine company, the anger of any one of whom had terrible effects, and both living and dead were placated with offerings.

In time of drought the nobles of Ngonde would go to a diviner to inquire who it was who was angry; they would mention all the names of the sacred groves of the Kyungus in turn and he would tell them that it was so and so. They would inform the living Kyungu and he would give them a bull or a sheep, together with some beer—they would take one of the pots of beer from his own house, brought by his people as tribute. And he would give them some flour and cloths also. Then they would go with them into the grove and build a miniature hut. Next they would kill the beast and hang some of the meat up on a tree—the rest they would eat later outside the grove. Then they would tear up the cloths and fasten some of the pieces on to the hut in the grove— an action they would explain as 'giving him cloths'. And finally, they would pour out some of the beer and the flour. Nearly always, in time of drought, they would thus build a hut and make an offering in the grove of the Kyungu whom the diviner had mentioned.

But occasionally, if one of the chiefs had recently insulted the Kyungu, they concluded that it was the living Kyungu himself who was angry. They would go to a diviner and mention all the names of the dead Kyungus, but he would refuse to accept any of them: 'No . . . no.' And at length he would tell them that it was the living Kyungu who was angry because so-and-so had insulted him. Then there would be no sacrifice at the grove at all, but the nobles of Ngonde would go to the one who had insulted the Kyungu and charge him with it, asking him what he meant by thus killing them all, would not the whole land starve? And so the wrongdoer would take a cow to the Kyungu who, thereupon, would address the nobles of Ngonde, saying: 'If it was my anger which brought the drought then it will rain (for I am no longer angry). But if the rain does not come then it cannot have been my anger, it must have been someone [of the dead Kyungus] whom you forgot to ask about.' 'And if, after that, the rain came soon, then it was not likely that anyone would insult the Kyungu again.' If, however, it did not rain, then the nobles of Ngonde would approach the Kyungu once more and ask why it had not rained. He would say that he did not know, that he himself was certainly not angry, and they must have forgotten someone, they had better go and divine again. And so they would, and then the diviner would tell them that it was so-and-so (one of the dead Kyungus) and they would go and sacrifice in his grove.

Thus to insult Kyungu was not only treasonable, it was blasphemous, and the whole plain was believed to be cursed with drought or disease in reply. An 'insult' might mean any neglect of the obligations of the chiefs and nobles and commoners of the plain to their lord.

The people of Ngonde hoed large fields as tribute to the Kyungu and if they failed to do so 'he grew angry and poured all the water out of the pot in which he kept his rain stones' (*vide infra*, p. 114) and 'the sky dried up'. Then the chiefs called their men to hoe. . . . 'They hoed and hoed and hoed and their wives planted, then the rain came in a torrent. . . . Kyungu created much rain.'

Or if an elephant hunter neglected to send the Kyungu one of the tusks of any elephant he killed he would not kill another. 'The country beneath was angry . . . the shades of the dead Kyungus . . . they were angry saying: "Why do you stint our child?" '

The rainfall in the Ngonde plain is less than half what it is in the Nyakyusa valley and anxiety about rainfall was constantly shown in the communal rituals; elephant hunting was also a matter of concern in a way in which it was not among the Nyakyusa and this too is reflected in rituals; but there was also the preoccupation with health and fertility, as in the prayers at Lubaga. In the groves circling Mbande the nobles prayed: 'May the sterile bear children, may the cattle and fowls increase, may the children sleep and not cry at night, may the witches not injure anyone.' And as we shall see, it was health and fertility that men had in mind when they cleared out the ashes each year after the break of the rains.

Towards Christmas time, when the first maize and the first

pumpkin leaves were ready to eat, an elaborate first-fruit cere-
mony was formerly carried out. The new season's food was
offered first by the nobles of Ngonde in the grove of the previous
Kyungu, the one who had last died.

The great chiefs would do so next, each at his own sacred grove (the
grave of his own predecessor in the title). And after them everyone,
both chiefs and people, each at his father's grave. All offered first
fruits to their own shades. And finally they would themselves eat, each
with his chief wife. But they would not eat beforehand for fear of
angering the shades.

In time of tribal war also the Kyungu and nobles of Ngonde
led the people in prayer. All chiefs and nobles were summoned
from the plain and the great ones entered the Kyungu's house to
receive their instructions:

When he had finished speaking he would tell them to go and pray.
So they would leave his house and gather all together, all the chiefs,
and the other men, and pray. The premier noble of Ngonde would
begin asking each of the sacred groves of the Kyungus in turn to bless
them in the fight. And then the great chiefs would pray after him.

This organization of religious ritual in the Ngonde plain was
both a factor of and itself determined by the general political
structure. Many details of the secular power of Mbande and of
the lesser authorities were dependent upon their religious functions, but the reverse is equally true. Among the Nyakyusa,
where the hierarchy of chiefs had scarcely any secular significance,
the organization of religious ritual was far less elaborate. Cattle
were sent to Lubaga by the chiefs to be sacrificed for rain and
health; but the 'clearing out of the ashes' was done by each
chiefdom separately; there was no general first-fruits ritual at all;
while, as war was never waged on a tribal basis, prayers and
sacrifices for military success were always undertaken by each
warring chiefdom alone.

The majesty (ubusisya) of the Kyungu was cultivated in a variety
of ways. He smeared himself with ointment made from lion fat,
and his bed was built up with elephant tusks and lion pelts. He
was enthroned on the sacred iron stool called Kisumbi, he had a
spear, Kamisa, and Mulima, a porous piece of iron 'like a mouth
organ' used to make rain, all handed down from the first Kyungu.
His zebra tails, set with medicines in horn handles, were waved in

war and during prayer to the shades, and he also had the famous drum on which the blood of a child was poured:

The Kyungu had a drum, called Mwenekelwa, which sometimes refused to sound when struck, then they asked: 'What does it wish, friends?' and they killed a sheep and poured the blood over Mwene-kelwa; if it refused to sound when they struck it again, they killed a cow and poured the blood over it and if it still refused to sound when they struck it again, they said: 'What does it want now? It wants a man.' And they took the child of a commoner and cut his throat and poured the blood over the drum and struck it and it sounded loudly. If the drum did not sound when struck it was as if it had boomed an order; its silence was like a prayer. The drum was to show the majesty (*ubusisya*) of the Kyungu, that all the little chiefs at a distance might say: 'Something is happening, let us hear what it is.' Then they all gathered and were told to bring ivory. . . . They needed the blood of a man because their Lord (*Kyala gwabo*, i.e. the Kyungu) had fastened up the drum saying 'I myself am war, there is no other war' . . .

The corpses of those sacrificed to the drum, like those condemned to death, were thrown over the scarp edge of Mbande, to be sucked into the marsh beneath.

Towards the early Kyungus their subjects expressed the feelings of worship and terror appropriate to an irascible divinity.

At Mbande the nobles of Ngonde would sit round praising the Kyungu —the drums went *kinde! kinde!* And they would praise him in antiphony: 'Oh, Kyungu! . . . Great Father! Great Father!—burier of men!—Great Father! Great Father!—Great Father!—O Mpeta![1]— Great Father! Great Father!—O Kiposa[1]—Great Father! Great Father!—O Kyabala![1]—Great Father! Great Father! O Striker and Stabber! Great Father! Great Father! O Mwenende! Great Father! Great Father! O Mpolombasambo! Great Father! Great Father! Dweller in the hot sun!—Great Father! Great Father!—O Fish-eater! O Banana-eater!—Great Father! Great Father!'

The general form of this praise-song was identical with that of the prayers in the sacred groves and so it is literally true to say that the nobles of Ngonde worshipped the living Kyungus.

But the majority of their subjects only worshipped from afar in fear and trembling. At Mbande no ordinary commoner was ever conducted into the sacred enclosure, but only the territorial nobles and the elder chiefs, and they only occasionally; while when the Kyungu travelled through his country all men save the

[1] These names are obscure.

very oldest fled from his approach. Even in speech fearful cir-
cumlocutions were used to refer to his journeying—'The country
is on the move'—'the great hill is moving'—'the mystery is
coming'. It was taboo both for the old men who stayed to
see him, and for those who entered the sacred enclosure, ever to
greet him in the usual way. Falling down and clapping the hands
was the only greeting for the Kyungu.

From the wives of the Kyungu also men fled in terror, fearing
lest they be compromised and thrown over the cliff of Mbande,
and this both added to the atmosphere of terror which surrounded him and was an expression of it.

Of the effects of personal relationships upon public events we
heard much less in Ngonde than in Selya for we lived there for a
much shorter period, but there were indications that, as in
Selya, public misfortune was traditionally attributed to quarrels
between the nobles of Mbande and within the family of the
Kyungu. One fearful drought was thought to have been caused
by the exile of Kyungu's son, Mwakasungula,[1] and men tell how
the rain came down in torrents on his return. The nobles also
asserted their power of calling on the shades of the Kyungu to
punish him when he did wrong, and rebuking him over beer
telling him, 'It was we who caused you to be ill, don't do it again'.
Since he was killed by his nobles if he really fell ill their power
over him was inexorable.

(d) PALIKYALA

PaliKyala is a cave at the north-east corner of Lake Nyasa
where sacrifices are made to the hero, Kyala (2). It is on the
border between Nyakyusa, Kisi, and Kinga country; the chiefs
are Nyakyusa, but of Kinga extraction,[2] while many of the
commoners are Kisi. Nyakyusa is generally spoken as the first
language, Kisi as the second, and Nyakyusa, Kinga, and Kisi all
sacrifice to Kyala. As indicated in the myth already quoted (vide
supra, p. 8) the location of the shrine has changed from one
cave to another; according to one version, Kyala was driven out
by Europeans; according to another, 'the Lake rose and roared
and destroyed all the pots in the cave and the roar was heard in
the mountains by the Kinga' and after that Kyala moved.

The ritual differs from that at Lubaga and Mbande in that

---

[1] Godfrey Wilson, *The Constitution of Ngonde*, p. 26.
[2] They are not of the lineage of Lwembe.

Kyala has no living representative—in the myth he had no descendants—but only a priest. However, the priest is sometimes referred to as 'Kyala' as were the early missionaries who preached about Kyala.[1] The present priest (1936) is a young man who, by his own account, would be a Christian were it not for his public responsibility in providing food for the country. His grandfather, Mwakinyasa, was a Kisi who came as an immigrant doctor from Ikubajila in Kisi country to the south, and was the first of his family to hold office at PaliKyala. Before that the chiefs of the line of Mwampasa themselves celebrated the ritual. According to Mwampasa's descendant, the present chief Mwandula, 'We planted food and the crops failed, but when "the owner of food" (Mwakinyasa) came with many medicines it grew, there was much food in the homesteads, hence we said: "Kyala has indeed loved this man, let us give him the duty of sacrificing", so the chiefs gave him cattle of his own and said: "Let the ritual come out of our bodies and go to Mwakinyasa." ' It was Mwakinyasa who (according to his grandson) introduced a variety of crops— beans, maize, cowpeas and groundnuts—to the people of Ikombe; before that they grew only bananas and *mapemba*,[2] so the myth of the hero who brought benefits is linked to the new line of priests. But there is no tradition that the priest of Mwampasa's line was once a 'divine king' like the Lwembe and the Kyungu.

Those who sacrifice at PaliKyala are the local chiefs (de-scendants of Mwampasa), the Kinga chiefs Mwakalukwa and Kyelela (to whom Mwampasa was related), and various chiefs of the Nyakyusa plain as far west as Mwandisi (107) near Mwaya. The Kinga priests bring bamboo beer, hoes, sheep, and occasion-ally goats or cattle; the local people offer white fowls, flour, cattle, and, traditionally, pots, which are produced in quantity near by, and which were being sold at the market at Ikombe when the Europeans first arrived in the country.[3] The Nyakyusa of the plain send black (or black and white) cattle and sheep. According to the Kinga priests they themselves offer black animals in Bu-Kinga when they want rain—black clouds—and white animals when they want sun and a clear sky. At Lubaga only dark animals are offered, but at PaliKyala white fowls and black, or white (or

[1] F. Fülleborn, *Das Deutsche Njassa- und Ruwuma-Gebiet*, p. 317.

[2] *Mapembe*—maize in Penja, but here it is contrasted with *ifilombe* (maize).

[3] Joseph Thomson, *To the Central African Lakes and Back* (1881), v. I, pp. 262-3. The missionary, Dr. A. Merensky, saw hatchets and choppers, as well as pots, on the floor of the cave. F. Fülleborn, *op. cit.*, p. 320.

black and white) animals are killed, with the same symbolism as in BuKinga.[1] 'We kill a white sheep in the dry season that the sun may shine—if we killed a black sheep in summer the wet season would last all the year.'

The Kinga pray for fertility of the fields, that illness may pass, that they 'may sleep at home'; the local people[2] for fertility of the fields and that the pots they make (and on the sale of which they largely depend) may not crack in the firing. The more distant chiefdoms of the Nyakyusa plain sacrifice only in drought or plague—the last sacrifice remembered was during a plague of locusts about 1915, but the Kinga chief Kyelela sent a cow in PaliKyala in July 1937.

Like the grove of Lubaga, Kyala's cave is fearful. There is a story of two men who took a length of creeper from near it to tie up their canoe, and when they got home both went mad. Godfrey Wilson's guide, a young Christian, refused to enter the cave on the grounds that his pagan half-brother had once entered and taken away a potsherd and 'when he got home he went mad'.

[1] Merensky appears to have been misinformed on this point, *op. cit.*, pp. 321-2.

[2] The potters are primarily Kisi, but neighbouring Nyakyusa have taken to this lucrative trade.

CHAPTER IV

THE RITUAL OF CHIEFTAINSHIP

(a) THE 'COMING OUT'

THE ritual which arouses the greatest excitement in BuNyakyusa and in which every man, woman, and child participates, is the 'coming out' when the two heirs of a chief are acknowledged as rulers, and the government of the country is handed over to them and their village headmen.[1] This ritual occurs but once in a generation, when the chief's senior sons are between thirty and thirty-five years old; they, and their slightly older contemporaries and juniors 'come out' together. Should one, or even both heirs of a chief die after their 'coming out' and before their sons are grown up, the ritual is not celebrated again—it cannot be, for it concerns not individuals but a generation. Instead the young chiefs are replaced by their younger 'brothers', full or classificatory. And should a village headman die he also is replaced by his heir; the office does not lapse. Therefore there are two types of change in status: the great communal ritual when the old men retire and their sons take office, and the family ritual when a dead man is succeeded by his younger brother or his son. An *individual* may inherit from his father, succeeding to his office and moving into his homestead at any time, and when he has done so he is treated formally as a member of his father's generation; but the celebration throughout the chiefdom of sons succeeding fathers only takes place thrice in a century. Each chiefdom celebrates separately. There is no attempt to synchronize with neighbours.

It was usual, traditionally, for two sons to succeed their father, and divide his country between them. The division was foreshadowed at the father's 'coming out' when he married two senior wives and settled them in different sections of his country; but it sometimes happened that a chief had a favourite for whom he built separately, and whose son went through the 'coming out' with his brothers and became independent, unless he was defeated in war and subjugated. Even a son who had no expectation of a

---

[1] Neither of us saw a 'coming out' in full. Godfrey Wilson saw the conclusion of the coming out of the heirs of Mwangoka (24) in November 1935 and in April 1955 I was able to observe the territorial changes brought about by Mwanyilu's (117) 'coming out' in December 1953.

separate inheritance sometimes went through the ritual because he might later be required as a chief, and the son of a conquered chief who had retained limited authority over a small area might be permitted to 'come out' with his senior brothers also. The common pattern, then, was for two sons to 'come out' as principals, but for a variety of reasons one or more 'younger brothers' might join them.

In Ngonde, as opposed to BuNyakyusa, several brothers normally went through the ritual as principals and the reason given us was that power should be distributed. They would say, we were told, 'If we bring out only two they will be boastful and ill-use their people, let them be many therefore, then, if a man has a quarrel with his chief, he can flee to another. . . .' In BuNyakyusa any tendency to tyranny in a chief was effectively curbed by his village headmen; but it is possible that headmen never had as much power in Ngonde as they did in BuNyakyusa.

An analysis of the genealogies of Nyakyusa chiefs shows that very often one half-brother lost power to the other, but occasionally several brothers (e.g. seven sons of Mwaipopo 26) got independent chiefdoms, and a junior brother (e.g. Mwakyusa 38) might attract a larger following of men than his seniors. Mwakyusa led his men from the hills to the more fertile plain and drove out the Kyungu of Ngonde from the lake-shore north of the Songwe river.

The 'coming out' was traditionally the occasion when authority was handed over by the elder generation to the younger. The old chief retired and he was *expected to die shortly*. In Nyakyusa theory he died because his men no longer loved him: 'A chief did not live long after the "coming out" of his sons; he died because there was war and people would complain: "He is too old, when we fight we are beaten, he had better die, perhaps the heir will help us." He died of the "breath of men".' But, as will be shown, his headmen had the duty of smothering a chief who seemed likely to die, and they were much more ready to do this after the 'coming out' of his sons than before. It was right that the sons should come out before their father's death, but not right that the period of coregency should be extended, for the division of authority between old and young was uneasy. When the old chief did die his headmen became the priests (*abanyago*) responsible for the sacrifices in his grove, and the young men were solely responsible for the defence of the country and the administration of justice.

Since the 'coming out' of his sons spelt not only retirement, but a speedy death to a chief, he was not unnaturally reluctant to hasten it and, we were told, chiefs would try to defer it, but were pressed by their village headmen to celebrate, and had eventually to accept their advice. Indeed we heard of one chief whose illness was attributed to the 'breath' of his men, angry because he refused to hold the 'coming out' which was due.

Nowadays the situation is radically altered by the fact that chiefs continue to live long after the 'coming out' of their sons, and the administration treats the old chief as the sole authority, or the old men find good reasons for not holding the celebration at all.

Before the ritual there is much speculation and excitement throughout the chiefdom, and private discussions between the old chief and his village headmen about suitable candidates for office. They look for men of wisdom (amahala),[1] skilled in settling disputes, modest (for boastfulness is judged intolerable in a Nyakyusa age-village as it is in an English public school), and given to hospitality. A leader must feed his men and to do so he requires to be relatively wealthy, therefore the poor have little chance of office.

When the old men are agreed among themselves they summon all the young men to the capital. They come dancing and swaggering with all their cattle, and there the old headmen seize, one by one, those they have chosen as village headmen for the next generation, beginning with the senior headman for each heir, then the second senior for each, and so on. Usually eight are chosen, four for each young chief. We get a glimpse of what it means to one individual in the following statement by the second headman of the chief, Koroso (173):

I made fire at the 1910 'coming out'. I can't tell much because we who were caught were in fear and trembling. I knew beforehand, because my brother was told to come from Ipyana [mission], but he was a Christian and the missionaries refused to allow him to become a village headman—they feared the medicines. He ran away and came here—he wanted to be a headman and the old men wanted him, but then he changed his mind and went off to be a soldier, and so they took me.

Probably word of who have been chosen as village headmen

---

[1] For a discussion of the content of amahala, cf. Monica Wilson, Good Company, pp. 89-90.

often leaks out, but in theory the young men must not know, and those seized always put up a show of resistance before being bundled into the hut of the senior heir's mother. Once there, no man dare flee lest, like a Lwembe fleeing from the stool, he should die. The two heirs are seized also and carried into the hut with their headmen. A litter is spread for them, and they remain there in complete seclusion, required to 'talk softly' and avoid quarrelling, guarded by the 'doctor of the coming out' and forbidden to wash except that each of the chiefs and his senior village headman washes with medicines in the doorway of the hut. Each chief also lies down with a commoner and is covered with a black cloth which, according to Mwandisi (the old blind chief 107) is a symbol of clouds and therefore of plenty. 'It means, may it be heavy—cloudy—above, may food be plentiful; may both heirs bring fruitfulness.' The commoner who lies with the chief is 'one body with him', 'his wife', and continues through life to share with him certain medicines. Some said that the senior village headman performs this function for his chief: others that it is another man altogether. The whole matter is very secret and our information is limited. The period of seclusion varies. Mwanyilu (177), who 'came out' in 1953, remained in the hut a month, and he complained most bitterly of the inconvenience of not washing for so long. During this time the young men are admonished by their fathers' senior village headmen, and told of their faults and their future duties. According to Mwambuputa (Mwankuga's [150] senior headman who was responsible for bringing out Mwanyilu), he said: 'Listen to the people: they are the real chiefs! Be hospitable! Greet people politely! Don't beat your men!' And the other senior headman, Kakuju, said: 'Do not beat your men, respect them! Feed your people on milk, meat, chickens, beer! Fear your people!'

Then the great moment, from which the ritual takes its name, arrives. Very early in the morning a crowd gathers and a junior kinsman of the chief knocks on the door and shouts: 'Come out! War has come!' Each heir, followed by his senior headman, rushes out and grasps the 'spear of chieftainship' held ready at the doorway for him, while the headman grasps a medicated zebra tail. The spear has a little horn of medicines bound to it 'to show that the chief has come out', and brandishing it is 'comparable to carrying the chief aloft. We show his greatness to the people and acclaim him.' 'The spear of chieftainship is strength, manhood.' Some say that it is not the chief himself who grasps the spear but his senior village headman who pauses in the doorway calling the war cry and rejoicing. However that may be, the spear represents the authority of a ruling chief. At the 'coming out' of Mwanyilu (177) and his junior brother Mwabungulu (178), both were secluded and rushed out of the hut, but for Mwabungulu there was no spear since the chiefdom of their father was not divided into independent units.

The heirs separate, each going to where his village is to stand, whether it be pasture land or the site of a former village. The young men build temporary shelters for themselves and proceed to the most important rite of all, the making of fire by friction, using a lion bone as the trough of the drill and a reed as the shaft. Each of the two young chiefs starts the process, then his senior village headmen take over, one twirling the shaft and the other holding the trough. It is difficult to make fire with the bone and reed and great importance is attached to success; the senior headman may even be replaced if he fails, for it is taken as a sign that his headmanship will be a failure. If he succeeds, he is known in future as *ulifumu gwa lupegeso*—the headman of the fire-making. All the old fires throughout the chiefdom are put out and each appointed headman, in order of precedence, takes fire from his immediate senior and calls to his men: 'You of such and such a village come to me' and gives fire to them. The men, though crowded together in one or two shelters, split into small groups, each with its own fire, to cook. This is interpreted as a symbol of the ending of the old chieftainship and the establishment of the new. 'That fire means a new chief has come, he brings new fire, we throw away the old fire in the houses. . . .' 'The old chieftainship is coming to an end, the new has come. The fires are put out in all the homesteads, those of the young men and those of the old men, they make new fire which is taken to every home. . . .' 'But why fire?' we asked. 'Because of old . . . we chiefs came with fire, the commoners had not yet got it, they ate raw food only. When we came we slept in men's houses and we lighted fires and cooked food. Men were astonished and said: "Ha! What's this?" They were burned so they said: "These are chiefs because they brought this fire." It is this they remember still.' 'Fire *is* lordship (*ubutwa*)', therefore a junior chief who goes through the ritual with his brothers does not make fire with his headmen; only those who are to rule do so. In other contexts the lighting of fire by friction is a symbol of potency,[1] and we suggest that this also is an element in the ritual of the 'coming out', for the fertility of the chiefdom is thought to be bound up with the virility of the chief.

There are a number of stories about the way in which Mwakyusa (38) surpassed his brothers and one of them tells how each brother made fire and set alight the pasture land (for traditionally parts of the pasture land were fired each season to provide fresh grass for grazing in the early spring), and the fires started by the elder brothers soon died out, but that started by Mwakyusa 'burned for a whole month'. This is interpreted as an omen of his greatness as a chief: fire, potency, lordship are inextricably linked.

At the 'coming out' all things are made new. No matter how crowded the country the young men must move to new sites and the shelters in which they live must be new, though, as will be shown, they do not necessarily move to *unoccupied* country. On their new site the young men live as bachelors, milking their cows and cooking for themselves on their new fires the meat of the cattle they seize, the bananas and grain brought by their wives and mothers. Meat is abundant, for the young chief now rules and has the right to take what cattle he chooses, even from the villages of the old men in his country. 'It was as if there were war, the young men seized cattle, food, and women', and though they did not fight their fathers directly, as the Meru did, they clearly asserted their power. And, as so common further south, the accession of a chief was the occasion for raiding the neighbours: the young men, we were told, went forthwith to test the efficacy of the magic spears and the medicines with which their chief and headmen had been treated. Or the chiefs might lead a battue to clear the country of wild pig, as Mwakatumbula (Mwambete 162) did directly after his 'coming out'. Well fed and exuberant, the young men dance and display their cattle, and entertain visitors lavishly, for every chief seeks to attract men to his country by his hospitality.

Then they set up the sign and memorial of the chieftainship: they plant cuttings of two species[2] of *ficus*, *indola* which is much used as a shade tree, and *umpandapanda* from which bark-cloth is made. Close to these the first house of the chief and that of his senior village headmen are built, and the trees also mark the

---

[1] Monica Wilson, *Rituals of Kinship*, pp. 124, 143.

[2] When writing *Good Company* I mistakenly thought that two cuttings of the same species were planted. Cf. *Good Company*, p. 27.

6. YOUNG CHIEF WITH HIS TREES

7. HEIR TO A CHIEFDOM
(*Mwanyilu in 1936*)

future boundary between the two halves of the chiefdom, where it will split the next generation. They serve as beacons[1] and are cited as evidence both of the 'coming out' and of the division of land in any later dispute. At the same time the trees are symbols of chieftainship and with their growth the success of the reign is mystically linked. According to one account, 'four headmen fetch the cuttings and the young chief stands between them (*vide plate* 6) and tells the trees to grow well, and the others say: "We are planting you likewise, we are at the ritual of establishing a new chieftainship, you are a symbol for our chief, spread branches that our young headmen and other people may rest in your shade." ' A doctor assists at the planting, burying at the roots a live white sheep and medicines, which, it is said, later turn into the lions or leopards which protect the trees from the impious (*vide infra*, p. 58); and he sweeps beneath the trees, a symbol of what the senior headman must do in future, for it is his duty to 'watch over the trees'. In Nyakyusa thought, village headmen are an integral part of chieftainship—it cannot exist without them—and the trees symbolize *both* the chief and his lady and the two senior headmen. The same informant (well known as a doctor for the 'coming out') told us: 'It means we are planting the chief and his lady; *umpandapanda* is the herd to herd *indola*, which is the more important. *Umpandapanda* is the woman, it may dry up, but *ulupando* (*indola*) never does; it is the chief, it is familiars (*ulupege*). but *umpandapanda* is not', and a moment or two later, 'the *ulupando* is the senior village headman, *umpandapanda* is the junior headman'. The strength of the chief is associated with the growth of the trees. If these trees go dry the reign will not be successful, the chief will be defeated in war. If they flourish and grow the reign will be successful, the chief is a ruler. The *indola* planted for Mwaijonga (82) is shown proudly by his great-grandson, and Mwambete (162) who had a long reign and an enormous family boasted of the size of his *umpandapanda*—'a great spreading tree'. Ideally the young chief should, in due course, sit in the shade of his *indola* with his headmen, to settle disputes.

After the trees are planted the young men build their senior headman's house and the doctor sets up his hearth bricks, burying medicine beneath them also. The marriage of the chief follows.[2]

---

[1] cf. D. Kerr-Cross, 'Crater-Lakes north of Lake Nyasa', *The Geographical Journal*, v, IV (1895), p. 117.

[2] According to most accounts, but *vide infra*, p. 56.

E

He, like many of his men, may have been married long before the 'coming out', but his ritual wedding to the mothers of his heirs follows it, and from the time of his seclusion, until his marriage, he, and all his men, should live as bachelors. The brides are chosen by his village headmen and in theory they are carried off by force, whether betrothed or not, but nowadays, since the Administration discountenances forced marriages, the headmen arrange matters with the girls' families beforehand, very privately, but still they come with a show of force to carry off the brides. Girls are chosen who are approaching puberty and they are taken to the house of a commoner contemporary of their future husband. There they live until both have grown up and the puberty ritual can be celebrated. It follows the usual course except that the neighbours of the man in whose house the brides are secluded play the part of the girls' families, cooking for the groom's party at the prescribed feasts. The chief washes with both girls, thereby acknowledging them as his senior wives; the marriage bed is prepared with medicines and there is great rejoicing. The following morning someone knocks at the door of the nuptial chamber crying: 'War has come', and the chief and his brides rush out to the pasture land, just as the parents of twins do at the end of their ritual.[1] Then[2] a long narrow stone (ulufiga) is set with medicines in the earth, beside the chief's trees as a symbol of his marriage (ikimanyilo kya bwegi) to the mothers of his heirs. 'The stone is the chief' (ilifiga ili jo malafyale). Hearth-bricks (amafiga) are then set up for each bride with medicines buried beneath them, and they are given fire from that ritually kindled by their husband and his headman. Finally they are given medicines to drink in order to develop in them 'the dignity of chief's wives' (ubusisya bwa bwehe).

No marriage is complete, in Nyakyusa eyes, until cattle have been handed over, and though the chief's brides have been carried off by force, cattle—more than double the normal number—are given to their fathers. The village headmen of the retiring generation should provide these cattle and they or their heirs are recompensed when the eldest daughters born of the two wives are

[1] cf. Monica Wilson, *Rituals of Kinship*, pp. 158, 169.

[2] Mwanyilu's marriage apparently preceded the planting of his trees and the phallic stone was erected at the same time as the trees were planted, but the marriages of the sons of Mwangoka *followed* the planting of their trees. The order of events seems to vary, and differences are explained as due to the order of the doctor in charge of the ritual. 'Different doctors have different customs.'

married. Thus, yet another bond is forged between chief and headman, for he who provides marriage cattle is 'father' to him who marries, and the chief's wives acknowledge this by avoiding the village headmen of the senior generation as they do their father-in-law. Once the chief's ritual marriage is complete the sex taboo is lifted and such of his men as are already married are joined by their wives. In theory, though not nowadays in practice, the taboo is observed until the marriage of the chief.

All through the ritual of the 'coming out' the idea of a new beginning is expressed—a new site for the villages, new houses, new fire, new power for the young men. The events of this ritual, the seclusion, the lying on a litter, the prohibition on washing, washing with medicines in the doorway of the hut, the admonition, are directly parallel to the events of the rituals of death and puberty which, we have argued in a previous book,[1] are dramatizations of death and rebirth. There seems little doubt that the 'coming out' is yet another celebration of this theme. The young men enter an enclosed house—that of the senior's mother— and 'come out' (ukusoka) renewed as a child 'comes out' (ukusoka) of the mother's womb. No Nyakyusa informant volunteered such an interpretation, but, when it was suggested, it was eagerly accepted as expressing the real meaning of 'coming out'.

(b) THE CHIEF'S MEDICINES

Reference has already been made to medicines used by chiefs and by village headmen at the 'coming out' and we must now examine them more closely. The great medicines of chieftainship are ifingila and their function is to create amanga, i.e. spiritual power, and ubusisya, i.e. dignity, majesty, in order to make the chief fearful 'so that men obey him'. The medicines are comparable to robes of office for they are designed to give their user assurance and fill the commonality with awe. The Nyakyusa also think that chiefs and headmen should be 'heavy' with 'pythons in their bellies' which give them the power to see and fight witches. Without such a 'python' a chief or village headman cannot fulfil his duty of 'watching over the country by day and by night' and if a man is not born with one he may develop it through the proper use of medicines. This notion has been examined elsewhere.[2] The ifingila medicines are also thought to give courage and ferocity (ubugasi) in war, with luck in seizing enemy

[1] op. cit., p. 205.   [2] Monica Wilson, Good Company, pp. 97-102.

cattle and protecting one's own, and to attract men to the country.

The two senior sons of a chief are given powdered *ikingila* to drink from early childhood; at the 'coming out' they lie on it and drink it again with their village headmen, some is buried beneath their ritual trees, and the chief's homestead is treated with it periodically. One form of *ikingila* is made of the heart of a lion and the heart of a leopard, together with the scrapings from a charred root, and one of its qualities is to create lions or leopards which guard the trees under which it is buried. 'They make anyone who has cut a branch of one of the trees for firewood tremble at night, he trembles and returns the wood; they do not kill, but they stay roaring there until he repents.' Now part of the dignity (*ubusisya*) of a chief is that lions and leopards attend him; they roam his country; they are his familiars (*imbege*). 'The sons of Lwembe' lack the fearful power of their great ancestor who 'rode a lion like a donkey', but they are believed to command familiars which clear the country of the wild pig that destroy men's gardens, and protect the sacred groves by terrifying any sacrilegious person who dares chop wood where he should fear. But they do not kill men or cattle. That is what distinguishes them from 'God's lions which kill cattle even by day' and the man-eaters made by sorcerers to destroy those they hate. There is no hint of lycanthropy—our informants denied emphatically that chiefs, dead or alive, turned into *imbege*, but they 'follow the chief' when he travels.

A second *ikingila*, sprinkled on the chief's mat when he is secluded, and drunk with his two senior village headmen, is made of red, black, and shining white or yellow pebbles, which are ground up and mixed with *imbinga*, a medicine brought by the Kinga, but the symbolism of these ingredients remains obscure.

The greatest of the *ifingila*, used only for the chief himself, is *inyifwila*, a terrible substance with power perilously like that of witchcraft. When either of the senior wives of a chief gives birth to a son a little is hidden in the litter on which she lies; it is put into the litter on which the heirs lie at the 'coming out'; and into the sacred tails and trumpets which are carried into battle. Like other medicines of chieftainship, *inyifwila* is used to give the chief majesty (*ubusisya*), 'that people who meet him may fear him'; that he and his warriors may appear fierce; that they may be 'heavy and strong' in war; that when the trumpet is blown it may 'make the enemy fearful and sue for peace'; and that even men who have left his country may return to him. And it is so powerful that the dose must be carefully adapted to the individual. If a chief is already 'heavy' with an inherited python he is given the merest fragment, but a gentle fellow thought to be 'light', 'empty', is given more, that his words may carry weight. Too much will make a chief harsh (*nkali*)—'he will always be beating men'—and he must be given an antidote to calm him down. Too much in the tails causes them to 'fly through the air at night, gleaming, and throttle the cows'. This is the danger of *inyifwila*, that it may act like the pythons in the bellies of witches and kill men and cattle. Controlled by a chief it is held to be reasonably safe, though Kalobo, Mwaipopo's (116) second wife, who was grumbling because no tail had been lodged in her house was told that she did not know how lucky she was for '*inyifwila* is very fearful—it enters the belly, it makes itself into familiars'.

The use of *inyifwila* is forbidden to commoners. In Ngonde, with its hierarchy of chiefs, it was the danger of attempting to equal one of superior rank that was emphasized. 'If a commoner sprinkles *inyifwila* on himself saying, "Let me surpass my fellows", and he meets a chief (who is entitled to use it) then he dies immediately because he said to himself, "I also am a chief" '; and 'If an Ngana chief dances and sprinkles his spear with *inyifwila* . . . and then meets Kyungu, he dies.' In the more democratic atmosphere of BuNyakyusa chiefs were 'very angry' if commoners used it, but it was the danger of its acting like witchcraft and throttling men and cattle and, eventually, its owner, that men spoke of most. We heard of half a dozen men—among them the most successful trader of Selya—who were reputed to use it 'to surpass their fellows' and 'get rich' and one case actually came to Court. Mwaipopo, the chief (116), raised the matter himself:

Why does this thing go about at night? I have seen it myself, it shines, I know it. It is that with which the doctors treat us chiefs to make us impressive [i.e. *inyifwila*]. Do you not know, you commoners, that we chiefs have prohibited its use in our countries? Ask your fellow Mandala! He is bad, he planted this thing, it kills you people.

So two village headmen went and called Mandala who lived near Ngulyo, and brought him to Court. There he was asked: 'Why did you keep this which kills people?' Mandala denied vehemently saying, 'I have not planted this.' But Mwaipopo replied: 'Why does he deny it? He told me once: "I have a thing which kills people!" ' Then, turning to the man: 'Go and fetch it out into the light.' Mandala went and we heard that he brought out another medicine, not the one asked for, he brought it to the headmen and Mwaipopo. Mwaipopo (who, being a chief, knew *inyifwila*) rejected the one Mandala brought saying: 'This is not it.' Then Mandala brought out another and again the chief rejected it saying: 'This is not the one we want.' Then he brought out a little bag made of bark-cloth. They sought a doctor to clear it out. All this happened in secret; we heard of it but did not see it. But in Court Mwaipopo turned Mandala out of his country 'because he had admitted that he was wicked', and Mwaipopo reminded the other chiefs in Court of a previous case of a man in Mwangomo's country who had used this medicine.

Inyifwila is made out of a python 'as thick as a man's thigh' which has been killed by crawling over razors. In Ngonde we were told:

A certain snake they call *ngone* is killed in the hills to the west. They build a hut, closed, with a man inside ringing a cow bell and razors all over the roof. The snake comes and crawls over the roof, trying to get in and so dies. Then the doctors come to 'close it up'. When they have done so they cut it up for medicine—*inyifwila*; some is brought to Kyungu direct . . . some is taken to the doctors, and it is the doctors who give it to the chief.

A similar story was told in BuNyakyusa but they got their *inyifwila* from the Sangu and Hehe, to the north and east, not from the west, and in their account the trap was baited with a goat, not a man, and it was the blood of the python (*isota*) shed on the surrounding grass and on the trap itself which was used for medicine. To test the medicine the doctors gave a little to a chicken; if the chicken died the medicine was satisfactory; and the remains of the chicken were burnt and the ashes used as tested *inyifwila*.

'That snake is awful (*nisya fijo*), no one approaches to kill it. No! If it were speared everyone would die.' And because the python which is so terrible is thought to be linked with the rainbow it, too, is disliked. 'We fear the rainbow very much, we say it appears when a python looks up to the sky; if we are near a river we run from it for pythons live near rivers. . . . No, we are not mistaken, it is so.' The essential quality of the python is *ubusisya* (fearfulness, majesty, dignity) and this is what is required in rulers and is thought to be transferred to them in the medicine brewed out of python blood.

It will be noticed that the central mystery of Lubaga and the sources of the most powerful medicine are the same, and the medicine is akin to witchcraft. The shades, medicines, and witchcraft are distinguished and are thought to operate independently, but they are all manifestations of a mystical power which is logically one, though none of our informants saw it as that.

We referred earlier to the function of the chiefs' medicines in giving courage in war and luck in raiding. Certain emblems of chieftainship are carried in war: a sacred spear, a bamboo trumpet (*ililonge*) or a great war-horn (*ingangabwite*), and several giraffe or zebra tails (*imiswigala*), and all of these have little horns filled with *inyifwila* attached to them. Of the trumpet it was said: 'You hear it and your heart swells and a great trembling comes over you and you fight.' 'The chiefs forbid them to be blown now because their blowing always brings war.' Each of the senior village headmen is given a tail at the 'coming out' and he went into battle with it bound on to his upper arm. A notable warrior was sometimes given one also. To lose a tail in battle was comparable to losing the regimental colours and there are epics of their loss and recovery. If the leader who carried it saw that he was surrounded he would try to pass it back, or he might hide it on the ground:

then that night they would go back to the spot and they would find it because it shone with a light and made a bubbling noise, *burukut, burukut, burukut.* . . .

In the old days the medicine [in the tails] was frequently renewed; for there was war, and it gave the headmen the power of dreaming of the course of war. . . . But now, since you have brought peace to the land, no one renews it, and it has gone rotten.

However, the tails in Mwaipopo's chiefdom *were* thus treated in December 1937, and we saw it done. The four tails, with six tiny medicine horns and a calabash of medicated ointment, were formally handed over to the care of Kalinga, Mwaipopo's (116) chief wife, having previously been in the care of his mother. Mwaipopo himself was there with two kinsmen and the three commoner priests Kissogota, Njobakosa, and Ngulyo, but not Kasitile (86) since he was 'father-in-law' to Kalinga and could not meet her, though he was informed of the ritual. Kalobo, the second senior wife, looked on. Kalinga poured out the ointment and Mwaipopo and Kissogota smeared it over the tails which were then put out with the horns to dry in the sun. Mwaipopo suggested getting Mwaisyelage, the doctor, to treat them further, and the others agreed saying: 'Let Mwaipopo find some-one, that the earth may be good, that it be heavy.' Njobakosa had spoken earlier of the cattle giving much milk after the treatment of the tails. And they went on to discuss the fact that the young chief Mwankuga II (151) had begotten no child by the wife inherited from his elder brother (150) whose place he had taken. Thus the function of the chief in creating plenty and fertility was in the priests' minds, and there may be some link between the virility of the chief and success in war—one inform-ant spoke of the chief's senior wives jumping over the tails immediately after the consummation of their marriage—but of this we are not certain. What is common knowledge is that the tails are 'for seizing cattle', and they are associated with 'manure and blood'. We were told at the conclusion of the ritual: 'Formerly we should have gone tomorrow, after this treating of the tails, to fight.'

Besides medicines for majesty, courage, and popularity as rulers, chiefs use medicines to protect themselves against the fearfulness of the groves in which they sacrifice, medicines to 'close the country to hunger', to make their capitals grand, and to cause thieves who have stolen, to walk round and round until caught.

Medicines are regarded as essential to authority, victory, and successful rule, and the kind used and the dose given are adjusted to the status and character of the individual. 'Village headmen do not drink the most important *ikingila*; they drink a lesser one, *imbinga*; the senior headman is given most, the junior less.' And the chief's wives do not drink *ikingila* at all, but only a powder suitable for them. But the use of these medicines has its dangers. The chief, like other people who have been drinking protective medicines, does not eat the new crops grown on fields fertilized by ash without fortifying himself. The danger is said to come from the burnt rubbish heaps, because medicines for defence against witches and sorcerers are burnt in them and, as we have seen, certain of the medicines which the chief uses create a power akin to witchcraft. He tastes the new millet ritually in June, the cow peas in September, and pumpkin leaves in November; and he also tastes the 'new earth' at the break of the rains in October or early November. 'We chiefs fear that the medicines we have drunk will

turn round in the belly; people say the earth will go bad in us.'
'A child who has drunk medicines will be ill, the smell of the new
food or the wet earth goes to the belly.'

The chief eats the first fruits and medicines with the commoner
who lies down with him at the commencement of his 'coming out'
and 'is his wife to taste with him the first fruits and powdered
medicines' and is 'fearful' like the medicines. He is identified with
the chief's body and may be compared with the *isithununu* of the
Pondo chief[1] or the *insila* of the Swazi.[2] His function is to protect
the chief against the medicines themselves.

(c) DEATH AND BURIAL OF A CHIEF

Both because of a chief's descent, and because of his use of
medicines, mystical power resides in his body.

In the old days a ruling chief was not allowed to die, but was buried
while still living, because they feared that if he became unconscious
before death he would take away all the food with him, and great
hunger would come on us. Men feared *ifingila* medicine in his belly.
They said: 'If he dies naturally many of his people will die. . . . He
should go alive.' And formerly they buried him with the son of a
commoner, also alive, for they said, 'Let him enjoy the company of
his man on the road.' When a chief was sick before the coming out of
his sons they tried to keep him alive if possible, but if he was clearly
going to die then they buried him like this; after the coming out they
hastened his death—but only if he were ill. That was why the chiefs
fear the 'coming out' of their sons so greatly. Had Mwaipopo lived
in the old days and his heir been alive he would have been buried
during his last illness.

When a ruling chief was sick the village headmen sent the chief's
wives away and looked after him themselves. Then, if they thought he
would, or should, die, they tore off all his nails, those of his toes and
those of his fingers, and pulled out his hair, and put them in a pot.
After that they buried him by night still alive, with a live person, the
child of a commoner whom they had seized very secretly. The pot
stayed in the house of the senior wife of the chief who had died, and
they said, 'It is the chief, we are with him still.' This was the sacred
pot for the sacred beer.[3] They kept silence about the death for a month
or perhaps two months, saying: 'Let the chief go away first.'

And when a younger brother, a junior chief, died, though he died

[1] M. Hunter, *Reaction to Conquest*, p. 390.

[2] H. Kuper, *An African Aristocracy*, p. 78.

[3] Kasitile flatly denied this, *vide infra*, p. 64.

naturally and was buried dead, and no human was buried with him, yet they buried a live cow with him in imitation of the custom of the senior, because the junior was also a chief, and the cow was like a person. And now in European times the ruling chiefs are buried with a cow, not with a man, in imitation of the custom of the juniors; but still they are buried at night.

Kasitile denied that chiefs were buried before death, but he admitted that they were smothered.

When the chief was very ill we priests came, Njobakosa and Ngulyo, and I. We took his nails and his hair, we tore them off while he was still alive, he started up and we hid ourselves that he should not see us. Then we attended to him.

Here he made a gesture of stopping up the nostrils. That is, they hastened his death as soon as the nails and hair had been stripped off.

And we dug the grave; we buried him by night, when he had died, when he had gone, with a live cow; we did this at night for it was taboo for people to see the burial of a senior chief. We killed a cow in the sacred grove and we ate it, we the priests, before people heard that he had died. The chief Mwakagile (59) when his death was approaching said: 'My body is sick.' After waiting two days, the village headmen said, 'This illness has defeated us', and they tore off his nails—yes, before he died. If they had waited until after his death, would not the *ifingila*, the power of chieftainship, have passed away? But they did not smother him, he just died. . . . His nails and hair were put into a little reed, which they hid beneath an *umwali* (*Chrophora excelsa*) tree at the village headman's, the *umwali* which grew at the homestead of Njoba-kosa [the grandfather of the present Njobakosa]. They buried it at a commoner's place, as if to say: 'We commoners are the earth, we have taken the power of growth (*ifugo*) from the chief, those nails and the hair are the power of growth of the country (*ifyala fila newili fyo ifugo lya kisu*).

Kasitile took Godfrey Wilson's hand and explained: 'Because, Mwaipaja (G.W.), when you cut these nails of yours do they not grow again?' 'Yes, they grow again.' 'Well, then, where does their growth come from? Does it not come from the body?' 'Yes.' 'Well, so it is, the village headmen take the power of growth (*ilifugo*) from the chief, his nails and his hair.'

On another occasion Kasitile explained that formerly the relics had been kept in a pot in the house, but that when Mwaipopo (116) succeeded

Njobakosa [the grandfather] ran off with them to Mwaihojo in the hills, where he died so that they disappeared and were never returned to his fellow-priests. Therefore they bury the relics by the *umwali* tree, at his old homestead, lest someone run off with them again. . . . The hair and nails of the chief are buried there, the earth of the chief will always be heavy. All this is very secret. . . .

Mwandisi (107, the old blind chief) told us that

When a chief dies they take his nails and hair and put them in the house of his wife who buries them with medicine for fertility of the soil (*ifugo*), then at the time of planting the village headmen come and take that medicine to plant the food with. This was done on the death of the chief Mwakalukwa (141) and the chief Mwakalinga (142) and others for, it is said, the chief goes off with our fertility (*imboto yetu*).

Thus, though our informants differed slightly about the details, they were agreed that the power of growth lies in the nails and hair of a chief, and these must be taken from him while he is yet alive, and later used to fertilize the earth.

The burial of a chief's son with a live black calf we saw for ourselves, and the wailing was delayed until after the burial. A distinctive funeral of this sort is accorded to all the sons of a ruling chief and his senior daughter, but not (we were told) to more distant kinsmen. The other mark of a royal funeral is the slaughter of many head of cattle to accompany the deceased and to feed the mourners. At the death of the chief Mwakyembe (99) over 300 head were killed, and Mwaipopo (116) killed thirty head at the funeral of his mother. Since a chief has many wives and daughters he has many affines all of whom must bring cows to kill, and he also has a large herd himself on which to draw. To fail to feed his people at a funeral is to fail as a chief. The whole country mourns for two or three weeks, no one going to work in the fields, or occupying themselves with ordinary business. All smear themselves with mud, as if they were kinsmen, and even the men bind their bellies tightly with mourning belts 'that they may not tremble'.

(d) THE CHIEF AND THE 'BREATH OF MEN'

Fruitfulness, the power of growth (*imboto*), lies in the chief's body and the village headmen have no share in it; they only tend it, taking care that it does not disappear with the dead. But the headmen share with the chief and the priests the duty of 'watching over the country by day and by night', and power (*amanga*) to see the enemies of darkness (that is, the witches) is thought to come to each priest or village headman from a python in his belly. No one can fulfil his duties as a ruler and defender unless he is 'heavy', but to have a python inside one is *also* the mark of a witch. Pressed on the point the Nyakyusa hold that a chief or village headman only has one python whereas witches have several, but this distinction is not maintained consistently, and many of our informants were agreed that the power of witchcraft and the power to see and fight witches were one and the same. The essential distinction lies in the use to which the power is put; wrongly used it is 'witchcraft' (*ubulosi*); rightly used to defend the village or to punish evil-doers it is 'the breath of men' (*imbepo sya bandu*) and how any particular case is labelled depends upon the viewpoint of the speaker. The victim of a misfortune and his kin will indignantly attribute it to 'witchcraft' when other people regarded it as due to his wrongdoing and a punishment brought about by 'the breath of men'.

Each village headman, together with those of the village who are 'heavy', is thought competent both to defend those of his village whom he judges innocent against witches from outside or within, and to punish wrong-doers, by bringing upon them the chill of fever. Hence those who have angered their neighbours and believe themselves to be attacked by 'witches', take refuge in another village.

The power of witchcraft is believed to be inherited, rarely acquired; but the power of defence is both inherited and increased by drinking medicines, and there seems little doubt that the medicines drunk by chief and village headmen at the 'coming out' to create in themselves *ubusisya*—majesty, awesomeness—also develop *amanga*, the power to see and fight witches. Indeed, one of our Christian informants insisted that *ubusisya bo bulosi*— 'awesomeness *is* witchcraft'.

These ideas have been discussed in some detail elsewhere.[1] Here I am only concerned to show the importance of the belief in 'the breath of men' in the relationship between chief and village headmen. Not only do village headmen have the ultimate power of life and death over their chief, but they are thought to bring illness upon him if he acts unconstitutionally or disregards their advice, or fails in his duty of providing beef for his men. He may

[1] Monica Wilson, *Good Company*, pp. 91-135.

play one village against another and go to sleep in that section of the country which supports him, but he dare not anger all his headmen. In the same way a village headman dare not anger the main body of his men. In short, public opinion is an effective sanction because those in authority believe that the disapproval of their fellows may bring a fever or paralysis upon them. One of our Christian informants was insistent that, were it not for the belief in the 'breath of men', pagan chiefs and headmen would act tyrannically.

The situations in which a chief or headman fears the breath of men are very varied. We have already referred to the chief who thought his illness was due to his refusal to hold the 'coming out' for his sons when advised to do so.[1] Mwaipopo, before whose court a very bitter land dispute between two of his villages had been brought, refused to give judgement and was careful to sleep in the village that had possession of the land, and therefore less cause for anger.[2] Kasitile, the hereditary priest of the chief's lineage who counted as 'a chief' as opposed to 'a commoner', thought he had angered the village headmen of his generation (who had become priests) by not providing meat for them (*vide infra*, p. 125).

The headmen are responsible for the health of their chief and it is they who go to consult an oracle if he is ill and take him to a doctor. Mwankuga II (151), heir to Mwaipopo's chiefdom, had not begotten a son by any of the wives he inherited from his elder brother who had died. His village headmen[3] went to consult an oracle and were told that it was the wrath (*imindu*) of his father; so they reported the matter to Mwaipopo, who sent a junior kinsman to consult another oracle. The diagnosis was confirmed and Mwaipopo gathered his younger brothers and prayed and told the shades that he had no quarrel with his kinsmen. Then he told the village headmen to take Mwankuga to a doctor for treatment, but this they did not do, so that Mwankuga went to consult a doctor on his own. According to Kasitile it was because the headmen had not taken Mwankuga that the medicine did not work. 'They should take him to the doctor and be present in dreams, to watch over him in dreams.' What the headmen were angry about was not revealed—there was no obvious cause.

---

[1] *op. cit.*, pp. 134-5.   [2] *op. cit.*, pp. 188-90.

[3] Mwankuga I who died had 'come out' before Mwankuga II inherited from him, but Mwaipopo (116) continued to rule as chief and draw a Government salary.

As we have seen, the chief's fearsome medicine *inyifwila* is thought to be very dangerous, and too much in the tails may cause them 'to fly about throttling men and cattle', but a chief is never accused of working witchcraft; it is inconceivable to the Nyakyusa that he could be. If the tails have got out of hand they are treated by a doctor 'to close them up'; no one suggests that the chief should get rid of them. It is commoners, 'black people', who are witches —cannibals, the eaters of raw flesh—as opposed to chiefs who, since the dawn of history, have killed cattle for meat and cooked their food like civilized men. But the distinction does not extend very far; junior kinsmen of the chief are 'commoners' and may well be accused of practising witchcraft.

There was a delicate balance of power in the Nyakyusa constitution between hereditary chief and commoner headmen and the belief in the power of medicines and of witchcraft was an integral part of it. The chief provided fruitfulness by the power of his own body and his medicines; all men depended upon him for their well-being—food, cattle, children, success in war; but he in his turn depended upon the goodwill of his men led by their village headmen; without it he shivered and fell ill, only to be buried by them 'with the breath still in his body' lest the power of growth disappear with his breathless corpse.

Something of the quality of this mutual dependence and fear is conveyed in Kasitile's account of his own illness quoted in Chapter VIII.

(e) THE NECESSITY FOR HARMONY

The welfare of the chiefdom is thought to depend upon harmony between the chief and his village headmen and priests, and also between the chief and his kinsmen. Any friction between them may result in public misfortune as well as sickness to the individual at fault. The quarrel of Kasitile, the priest, first with the Kinga priests, and then with the commoner priests of Mwaipopo's chiefdom was believed to affect the crops and the weather, as well as Kasitile's own health (*vide infra*, pp. 124-41), and Mwaipopo's failure to tell Kasitile formally of the death of their kinsman led to rain which spoiled the funeral dance. A quarrel between the lineages of two chiefs which should have sacrificed, together was said to have been followed by a very poor millet crop (*vide infra*, pp. 79-80, 118, 136).

How the personal relationship of a chief with his kinsmen is thought to affect the whole country was illustrated in Mwaihojo's chiefdom where the people were plagued by wild pig destroying their gardens. Mwaihojo (147) had a longstanding quarrel with his half-brother, Mwakyonde (148), whose country he had seized after their 'coming out'. Mwakyonde became famous as a doctor, and he was a great raconteur and beer-drinker, a regular Silenus, the boon companion of many influential men, whereas his brother was cold and irascible; so although he had lost his chieftaincy, Mwakyonde had considerable power. In February 1937, four lions were seen in the adjoining chiefdom of Mwaipopo (116), and we heard pig squealing as it was killed. Angombwike (whose father lived near Mwakyonde in Mwaihojo's country) explained to us: 'People say that these are Mwakyonde's lions. . . . Lion-makers have bundles of twigs which they put into the long grass, and which turn into lions. Long ago Mwakyonde made lions and they came and killed all the pigs, and the country (Mwaihojo's) was at peace, but he quarrelled with Mwaihojo and put his bundles of twigs into his box and locked it up. Then the country was filled with pig, and buck, and elephant, and all the crops were spoiled, and so it is still. Now Mwakyonde has begun to be friendly with Mwaipopo (116); they enjoy each other's company and drink beer together, and so he is making lions again in Kipungu, the land where Mwaipopo is hoeing, to kill the pig for Mwaipopo. They say Mwaipopo has given him a country in secret.' Now Mwaihojo claimed as his the forest country, which Mwaipopo's men had begun to colonize, therefore to aid Mwaipopo there was an effective slap at Mwaihojo. The lions came into Mwaihojo's country—we heard them repeatedly close to our camp—but they did not clear the pig.

Then, in March, Mwakyonde was supposed to be using a new medicine he had obtained to scare off pig from the fields. We asked him about it. 'Oh, it has failed. The pigs are still there eating. I've done everything I should but without effect. I think that the pigs are possessed by the shades (*sili nimindu ingulube*).' 'Why?' we asked. 'Because my elder brother (Mwaihojo) and I are not on good terms (*tutikwangala kanunu*) the shades are angry.'

So the destruction of men's gardens was traced to the quarrel between the chief and his brother.

CHAPTER V

SACRIFICES AT THE GROVES OF CHIEFS

(a) THE PLACE, OCCASION, AND FORM OF SACRIFICE

A CHIEF is buried near the trees planted at his 'coming out' and around the grave a thicket grows up. It is taboo for men to cut saplings or brushwood there and since trees grow very fast in the climate and soil of the Nyakyusa valley, the thicket soon becomes a grove, and there sacrifices to the dead chief are made. The priests look for the stone planted at his marriage, and place the offering beside it. How long a chief is so honoured depends on how conspicuous he was as a ruler or warrior, and perhaps also on whether the sacrifices are judged to be efficient in producing rain and health or not. Mbyanga and Kabale, two groves which are particularly honoured, were the shrines of founders of expanding lineages. At Mbyanga was planted a cutting of a tree which sprouted from the grave of Mwakisambwe (30) who had first occupied the country in which Mbyanga is situated. He is often spoken of as having been 'buried' at Mbyanga, in fact he was carried back ten miles to Lubaga, whence he had come, for burial. But he is worshipped at Mbyanga and we attended a sacrifice there for which his great-great-great-grandson, Mwaihojo (147) the chief, provided a cow, and Mwaihojo's grandsons ate the holy food. In contrast to this, the grave of Mwaipopo's (116) younger brother, who had once ruled a country but was defeated in war and whose sons had died, was completely neglected; no one sacrificed there. We knew more than a dozen chiefs' groves at which sacrifices were made, and there must have been a great many more in different parts of BuNyakyusa.

Since every ruling chief normally had two heirs, sacrifices involved co-operation between independent chiefdoms—two chiefs at the grove of their father, four at that of their grandfather, and so on. But if there is friction between the chiefs, some branches of the lineage cease to participate, saying that the connexion is 'too distant', and celebrate at the groves of their nearer ancestors only. This happened at the sacrifice of Mbyanga which we attended (*vide infra*, pp. 79-81). The sanction for co-operation is the belief that quarrelling between kinsmen annoys the shades and

8. COMMUNION WITH THE SHADES

9. SHRINE IN THE SACRED GROVE, MBYANGA

may nullify any ritual, but often it is not strong enough to over-come the fissiparous tendencies of the lineage. In theory a celebra-tion at the grove of a senior should precede that at the grove of a junior and sacrifices at Lubaga would be followed by sacrifices at the groves of the 'sons of Lwembe' in order of seniority, but this does not happen in practice nowadays and we doubt whether it ever did, since a hierarchy was not organized and maintained by a central authority as in Ngonde. In 1935 a celebration at the grove of Mwaijonga (82) preceded one at the grove of his great-grandfather Mwakisambwe (30) by a month, as we shall see.

Sacrifices are made when a drought or flood occurs, or a plague of locusts, or an epidemic among men or cattle; when fishing is poor in the chiefdoms of the plain, or war is imminent. They occur most often during the 'winter' in the hills, when a malaria-sodden people feel the chill of damp mists and cool south winds, and in October, just before the break of the rains, when the country is parched; but they are not confined to these periods. In theory the village headmen and the priests who 'watch over the country' foresee *coming* misfortune in dreams, and avert it by making the appropriate sacrifices. And they are helped by ordinary people who are dreaming repeatedly or falling into a trance or fit, and prophesying evil and jabbering of 'a black cow, a black cow' or some other appurtenance of sacrifice. But in practice the prophecies generally occur when there is hunger or plague in the land, or an omen (such as a python or a ground hornbill behaving oddly) has been seen.

The dreamers are *abasololi* or *abakunguluka*, and, as these names indicate, they are believed to have descended into the land of the shades. *Ukusoloka*[1] means to go down into something, like the roots of a tree into the earth, and *ukukungula ingungula* means to pluck a banana flower which (as was shown in *Rituals of Kinship*) is a symbol for a corpse and is buried; so the *abakunguluka* are those who have been buried in the earth. '*Abakunguluka* go to the land of the shades and return. . . . An *unkunguluka* plucks up the "blessed grass" (*ikisajelo*) in his swept courtyard and goes beneath and sees.[2] . . . He goes down into the earth beneath and takes the chief to the land of the shades when he dies, and he also sees the witches. . . .' More rarely, the *unsololi* or *unkunguluka* is

---

[1] *Ubusolola*=a breach presentation, the implication being that the infant's head is in *busyuka*, but children born in this way are not necessarily prophets.

[2] cf. Monica Wilson, *Rituals of Kinship*, pp. 77, 212.

F

said just to become aware of future events without any dream.

Abakunguluka are distinguished from those who suffer from fits or fall into trances (*abakom' amalago*), but a woman in a trance may also prophesy and induce the chief and priests to celebrate a ritual, for it is thought that she too is in communication with the shades. Men say 'The shade has entered her' or 'Kyala catches hold of her that she may speak of the matter'. This type of prophecy is something new among the Nyakyusa. Mwandisi (107) told us that 'it did not exist in BuKinga whence we came', but had been introduced from the south, through Ngonde, and it is mainly confined to women, whereas the *abakunguluka* are men.

There are many tales of famous prophecies. Nsamba (90) claimed that his father (63) foretold that 'there will come a white thing on the Lake, and it will land on the shore. That will be the man who will make peace', and Mwakalinga (142) who died fighting the Germans is said to have foretold his own death.[1]

Dreams and revelations of the possessed concerning public matters are reported to the local village headman and referred to the other headmen and priests, and a prophecy is accepted as valid only after formal discussion. As we shall see, Kasitile was sceptical about the revelations of one man who was repeatedly 'possessed', perhaps because he threatened to become a rival in interpreting public misfortune. If there is doubt, suspicions are confirmed or problems elucidated, by divination.

When they judged a sacrifice necessary the village headman and priests went to their chief saying, 'We do not sleep', and it was his obligation to secure an animal for sacrifice. He might provide it out of his own herd, but very often the duty of 'finding' sacrificial cattle was delegated to a junior line—the ruling chief gave cattle to a younger brother charging him and his heirs with the function of providing sacrificial cattle when necessary. Today all the chiefs are reluctant to expend cattle on rituals whose validity is questioned, and there is often friction between the senior and junior lines over who should 'find' the cow or bull required. Their reluctance is illustrated by the following passage from Godfrey Wilson's diary:

Mwaya (on the lake shore): 22/12/34
It is still stormy; there has been wind and heavy rain for four days. People are saying: 'We are hungry. It is very bad. We need light rain

[1] According to Mr. Harkin's informant the Sarabwe eruption was foretold a year before it occurred. *Tanganyika Notes and Records*, 40 (1955), p. 21.

for planting, but now all the fields are muddy, we can neither hoe nor plant.' Five days ago there was no rain but locusts, and people did not plant for fear lest the locusts should eat the rice and maize as it sprouted. Kissoule tells me: 'Kyala is very angry. . . . Mwandisi (107, the priest-chief) wants to pray to put things right, he has sent Mwalulabosya to ask Mwakisisile (170, the ruling chief) for a cow. Mwalulabosya and Mwakalobo went and the chief agreed saying: "I have not got one now, but I will look for one!" Then Mwalulabosya sent me (Kissoule) to fetch it, but the chief refused saying: "I am busy now." Then Mwandisi (107), who is blind and infirm, went himself, but still there is no cow.'

The priests who minister to dead chiefs, like the priests of Lubaga, are of different types. The senior village headmen of a dead chief are responsible for conducting sacrifices at his grove in co-operation with his heir, and when a headman dies his office is taken over by his heir. Where a grove is much honoured this continues for generations and the heirs of one of the village headmen become hereditary keepers of the grove, each incumbent of the office assuming his name. Secondly, there are chiefs of a junior line, who become hereditary priests on whom the ruling chiefs depend for their prayers, but these priest-chiefs do not actually attend the sacrifices; the celebration is delegated to commoner priests and junior kinsmen. Mwandisi (107) mentioned above, Kasitile (86) and Nsamba (90) were all priest-chiefs of this sort. Kasitile prayed at his own home, blowing out water before any celebration in Mwaipopo's country, and he was given the chine of any animal sacrificed on behalf of the country. If this were not done 'all the cattle in the country would die . . . it is the most important part of the meat'. The commoner priests who conducted the ritual always shared the head of the sacrificial beast and the breast went to the chief. With priest-chiefs, as with commoner chiefs, the name of the first incumbent of the office (or an early and famous incumbent) may become a hereditary title, e.g. three generations of priests in Selya have been known as *Kasitile*.

The essential elements in the ritual are: the sacrifice of a black bull or cow in the grove; the offering up of the blood and pieces of the sacred meat from the forelegs, together with the beer, on the earth close to a sacred stone and near a sacred tree; an invocation calling on the shades to come and feast, and petitions for rain, fertility, and health. One piece of meat is thrown down for each name mentioned: 'We give this meat to you so-and-so.' 'May the children sleep, may we all sleep, may it rain, may there be much food, may milk be plentiful.' Then follows a communion in which young 'grand-children' of the dead share the sacred meat and beer. 'The shades eat together, they break off firewood there from the tree, they rejoice, some clap their hands to give thanks.' Finally, a hut is built for the shades and half-formed bananas and sweet milk are left in it to 'ripen'. It was thought that if the sacrifice were accepted they did so miraculously quickly and the milk increased in quantity, the bananas in size. Among the Kukwe a white and grey cock and a hen were offered as well as the cow or bull. An account of two of the sacrifices we attended will make this clearer.

(b) SACRIFICE TO MWAIJONGA

In July 1935, two days after the Kinga had sacrificed at Lubaga (*vide supra*, p. 30), the chief Mwaipopo (116) came to tell us that he was going to sacrifice at the grove of his father, Mwaijonga (82). Ngulyo, heir to Mwaijonga's second senior headman and now his priest, came with the chief, and he remarked,

Kasitile (86) summoned us some time ago. He and Njobakosa and Kissogota[1] and I thought that the hunger was very great indeed, and Kasitile sent us to tell Mwaipopo (116) to look for a cow and sacrifice. Then Mwaipopo agreed, because the hunger is indeed very great; he has not yet found the cow; when he has, we shall inform Kasitile and then kill it in Mwaijonga's grove.

Mwaipopo 'found' the cow at once for next morning Kasitile told us

Mwambene (Mwaipopo, 116) came with Ngulyo yesterday to say he had found the cow. This evening, after sunset, because there is a moon (second quarter) I shall pray at my place with water; and Mwaipopo will pray at his homestead also with water. Tomorrow morning they will kill the cow. I shall not be there—I never go—I stay at home and they [i.e. the shades] find me at home.

The same evening (10 July 1935) Godfrey Wilson went to Kasitile's homestead just after sunset. Kasitile took a calabash cup hanging under the eaves saying: 'No one ever drinks from this cup, it is for praying only. At my death it will go to my heir to use for prayer.' He filled the cup from his wife's water-pot, and then

---

[1] Heirs of two other village headmen of Mwaijonga, also priests of his grove.

plunged into it a glowing brand from the fire. Then he went to a low tree in the middle of a cultivated field where the byre of his senior brother (85) had been. He took a root of 'blessed grass' with him, and as he stood before the tree he took a couple of bites of the root and two sips of water. Then he blew out the water in a cloud twice and he spoke for twenty minutes and mentioned thirty-five names or more: 'Thou Mwakanjoki (60), . . . thou Kalesi (18), Mwakalebela (19), . . . Mwakisisya (56) and Mwampondele (27), . . . Kikungubeja, Silobwike, Kyamba Kitali, Nsyanigwa,[1] . . . Mwaipaja (21.) He talked about the punishment of 'Mwakagile their child' (i.e. of Mwaipopo (116) who was here identified with his grandfather) . . . 'Kyala is there . . . he sees Mwaipopo. He says "Do this ritual, I am rejoiced".' At another point Kasitile added the name 'Jesus' to a list of ancestors. He prayed for food, children, and cattle. . . . 'Give us bananas, millet, maize, may children be born in the morning and in the evening, may cows calve in the morning and in the evening.' He spoke of the old sacrifices of Mwalubange (58) and others which had been accepted . . .

Now Mwaipopo has found a cow, he has learnt his lesson, he has agreed; receive him tomorrow, grant him food, give food to all in Selya . . . to Mwaisumo (62), Mwaitende (61). . . . You are proud (*uli namatingo*) to send so much hunger. . . . When I went down to the plain men asked me 'Are you taking all the food with you?' I said 'Yes', but now I have come up, the earth has come up. You alone remain and hold back. I ask you to send food again. I alone remain of all the contemporaries of Mwaijonga (82). I alone am Kasitile. All the people of Kyungu (16), of Mwakyusa (38), all know I am Kasitile. I alone remain. The birds say, the snakes say that I am Kasitile. There is trouble all round in BuNdali, BuSangu, BuKinga, but we thought here there would be no trouble in the country of Mwakilima (111) and Mwanjala (77), but there is. They have sacrificed, the Kinga have come to Lubaga. Mwakisisya (111) has begun, Mwakagile [i.e. Mwaipopo, 116, here identified with his grandfather, 59] sleeps with hunger, receive him tomorrow. I 'treat' the earth, all treat their earth, all over the country.

Next morning early the chiefs and priests met near Mwaijonga's grove which is some hundreds of yards from Ipinda, his senior village, where his *indola* tree still stands.[2] The talk turned on the

[1] These four are the Kinga priests with hereditary titles, who serve at Lubaga.

[2] Why the grave was not beside the *indola* tree as it usually is was not made clear to us.

weather, and the ritual. 'We prayed yesterday at Ipinda, Mwai-popo and all of us, we prayed and prayed. Did you feel the cold as much as usual last night? Did you hear the banana leaves rustle as usual?' 'No.' 'Well, Kyala has heard our prayer.'

At 7.45 a.m. they moved into the grove. A black cow had already been killed. 'We killed it at cock-crow, while it was still dark, we were all there. Mwambene (the chief Mwaipopo 116) handed the axe to Mwanyoso (his junior kinsman *vide* p. 84) who killed the cow.' Bananas were brought and all roasted them and ate, waiting for the other priests, Njobakosa and Kissogata. After a discussion about certain persons who had not come because the last time they got no meat, one of them said: 'Don't talk of what is forbidden in the sacred grove, don't let's make a noise; no, we pray to Mwakagile (59). . . . If we quarrel and make a noise the shades will not hear our prayer.' James (119), Kasitile's heir, was there but not Kasitile (86) himself. Someone asked whether Tandale ought to be summoned. But one said: 'We have never asked this Tandale to come here; we used to ask his father.[1] . . . Tandale lives in the boys' village. He has not the position of Ngulyo and Kissogota,'

Mwaipopo: 'Why do you argue about this today and not before?'

After an hour's delay Njobakosa arrived, and shortly after him Kissogota, who apologized, saying: 'I am late because my child has just died.'

Kissogota and Ngulyo flayed the cow, letting the blood pour out on to the ground. There was some discussion over the division of the meat, and they cut out the chine, saying: 'We send it with the tail to Kasitile—if we sever the tail we have spoiled it.'

Ngulyo took the sacred meat (*isyammapa*) from both forelegs, and with Kissogota's help he chopped off twenty-three small pieces. The rest of this meat was left for the children. At 10.10 all gathered to go to the grave. A sacred stone (*ulufiga*)[2] was found under a tree. Mwaiteteja (Mwaipopo's junior kinsman) cleared the undergrowth with his bill-hook and dug a hole close to the stone, then he threw the meat which Kissogota was holding on two leaves, placed the leaves on top and filled in the earth. Five or six men spoke:

[1] Tandale the senior had buried the previous chief, Mwaipopo I (115).

[2] It was not clear whether this was the one planted at Mwajonga's coming out or not, since his *indola* was some hundreds of yards away.

Here is your cow, your food. We pray to Kyala. May theft go away. Give us food and beans and millet, may we eat and be satisfied. . . . It is said that the sweet potatoes are scarce now, help us. You Mwaka-bule (117), Mwakomo (112). . . . This is your cow Mwaijonga (82). This is your meat. I shall seek another also which we shall give you like this.

NGULYO: May the locusts go away. It is you who have caused theft because there is hunger.

KISSOGOTA: At night since we eat scraps of food our bellies are disquieted . . . may we be satisfied. People are eating millet porridge;[1] when food is plentiful they say it's horrible. When someone eats millet porridge he dies, it kills a man. We pray to him, this Kyala, because we do not know him, so we say: 'You Mwaijonga (82) drive away the hunger. Give all of us, Mwaipopo's people, food, and hear us all.'

Mwaipopo's young sons (not the older ones) ate the rest of the sacred meat (*vide* plate 8). Other boys who approached were chased away: 'They thought because their friends were getting meat they would too.' Then the remainder of the carcass was divided: two legs went to the chiefs, two to the commoners, the chine to Kasitile, the breast to Mwaipopo (the chief) who gave half to his sons and half to his daughters—his wives may not eat it. The head went to the priests Ngulyo and his fellows—and some entrails were sent to Seba, widow of Mwaijonga (82). There was some discussion about the disposal of the head: 'Let it be put in Ngulyo's house', they said. Mwaipopo commenting later, explained:

We leave the head in the house of a commoner near the sacred grove in order that the shades can come and eat it. So also with the chine. . . . Kasitile leaves it so that his shades may eat it. We throw the meat by a tree which was planted long ago. He whom we have buried looks towards it, he sits facing the tree and the meat is thrown beside it.[2] He sees the meat we throw. We offer the meat of the upper forelegs (*ijammapa*), this is the sacred meat, the rest we eat ourselves. The blood pours out on to the ground, it goes beneath, which means that the owners, the shades, receive it, because they are beneath. The shades say: 'We are angry because you have not given us cows to treat the grove, we are angry and send this hunger. Treat the grove frequently!'

Kasitile also discussed the ritual with us later and he remarked:

---

[1] Millet is ordinarily used only for brewing beer. The Nyakyusa regard millet porridge as very distasteful and eat it only during extreme scarcity.

[2] We omitted to ask why, in this case, a hut had not been built in the grove.

I kept the chine for two nights in my house. The shades came to eat—
they left practically nothing. Had I not been ill I would have asked
you to come and see since you say they do not eat. . . . The shades
come and see that we are celebrating the rituals.

The whole ritual was esoteric. Only the chief with eight of his
agnatic kinsmen, four of his young sons (but not his grown-up
heir or young grandson), and four priests participated, and we
two anthropologists were permitted to look on. Peeping small
boys were chased off. The shades were addressed in a conversa-
tional tone and, except during the invocation, the priests and
chiefs chatted to one another, but arguments and raised voices
were taboo. The boys who ate the meat were told:

See, we your fathers are sacrificing, we are making plenty of food.
Follow the custom of your fathers when it is your turn to sacrifice.
Learn how to do it.

The same evening Kasitile prayed at his tree again. He explained:

I would not usually pray at all tonight, it is finished. Mwaipopo and
I prayed yesterday, today the ritual is finished, but that boy of mine
[his heir, 119] does not visit me, he's not been to see me and he did not
tell me that he was going to the ritual. . . . I am going to pray to tell
my fathers not to be startled, to tell them I am not angry, to tell them
to send only a little rain, not a lot, to tell them to accept the sacrifice.

He went to the same place, and chewed the root of 'blessed
grass' and blew out water as before. He prayed to about thirty
persons, especially to Mwamaloba (85, his elder brother) and
Mwakanjoki (60, his father), and also to Mwakagile (59), Mwaijonga (82), Mwaipasi (81), Mwakabule (117), Mwamwifu (84),
Mwafungo (83), Mwakipesile (118), Mwakapala (?), Lyambilo
(12), Mwalubange (58), Mwamukinga (43), Mwaihojo (147?),
Mwaitende (61), and Kyala (2). No mention was made of the
Lubaga chiefs this time, or of sons of Mwaipaja (21) or of 'Jesus'.

You have received your child Mwakagile (116, identified with his
grandfather 59), Mwaijonga (82), you have received the chief, this
boy of mine (119) is quarrelling with me, do not be upset, he is a fool,
a fool, but let him be . . . go and call your brothers to eat, you Mwaijonga (82), you Mwaipopo (115), and all your younger brothers; call
Mwakagile (59) and Mwakanjoki (60) . . . Mwalubange (58) go to eat
with your younger brother, let us find food, millet, bananas, children,
milk . . . let there be a little rain only, not too much . . . people believe

that I can speak, that when I speak food comes tomorrow; let it be so.

Three points call for comment here. First, it will be noted that if the crops failed Kasitile had a scapegoat in his heir who was quarrelling with him. The sacrifice was performed correctly but a quarrel between any of the leading actors could destroy its efficacy, and Kasitile made it clear that he was being very forbearing with a difficult 'son'.

Secondly, a great many names were mentioned in the prayers, but they were not mentioned in any discernible order. This is obvious if the prayers are compared with the genealogy facing p. 3 And since Kasitile was a famous priest, acknowledged to be an expert in ritual and tradition we must conclude that the order was not thought important: all that was required was to mention the names of dead members of the lineage, including even one (Mwakabule 117) who was junior both to Mwaipopo and Kasitile who were sacrificing.

Thirdly, what did Kasitile imply by his reference to the moon? (p. 74). We omitted to ask Kasitile himself, but a number of informants insisted that there is no necessary connexion between the celebration of a ritual and the phases of the moon. However, rain is expected with the *waning* moon, therefore rituals which are intended to produce rain are usually performed with the waning moon, and the sacrifice to Mwaijonga in which sun and warmth were sought, was performed with the waxing moon. This may or may not be what Kasitile had in mind.

Everyone agreed afterwards that the rituals had been effective for the weather grew slightly warmer. Before the sacrifice at Lubaga on 7th July, the temperature was 62° F. at sunset, but from the 9th onward the cloud cleared, and by the 14th the sunset temperature was 68° F. Whether or not the Kinga priests living high on their mountains with a view down the Lake whence storms come are weatherwise, and time their visits carefully, we do not know. Certainly any change in the weather after a celebration is interpreted as a direct answer to prayer.

(c) SACRIFICE TO MWAKISAMBWE

A month later a sacrifice was made to Mwaijonga's great-great-grandfather Mwakisambwe (30) in the grove Mbyanga. The chief Mwaipopo was not concerned this time, but the senior line of Mwaihojo (147) and a junior line who had traditionally the responsibility of providing cows for celebrations at Mbyanga.

Mwalukuta, the hereditary priest of Mbyanga, had been pressing the chiefs to sacrifice for some time. He had sent messengers in March, April, May, and again in July, saying: 'At Mbyanga things have gone back, it is bad, see hunger kills!' At last, in August, Mwaihojo agreed to provide a cow if Mwaitende of the junior line finally refused. Mwalukuta, the priest of the grove, explained:

We went to Mwaitende (121, identified with his grandfather 61) and asked him to sacrifice. He said: 'No, I am not coming; do the work there at Mbyanga yourselves.' We said: 'Why do you refuse to come, to return a cow? Our grandfathers gave you a cow, why don't you return it? They gave you cows on the understanding that you would bring them back, one by one, and kill them in the sacred grove here. Why do you refuse to return them?' It has always been the custom for the junior brothers to find cows for sacrifice. Their seniors give them wealth and appoint them priests to bring cattle to the sacred grove. But in European times they refuse to come, each man kills at his own place. . . . I must go and tell Kasitile (86) and also Kifubuka, or rather his son—the father refuses to come he had a lawsuit with Kasitile. . . . Kifubuka used to kill the cow, then Kasitile said Makuli should kill the cow, but now Makuli has refused to come so I go to fetch Kifubuka [the younger]. Makuli was a chief who ate the meat. . . . Mwaitende (61) used to send the cow to him and Mwaluseke to bring to Mbyanga . . . as he now refuses to send the cow they say: 'What should we bring?' and have refused to come here.

There had been another spell of cold weather and the temperature on the night of 8th August was down to 59° F., but fine weather was visibly approaching from the Lake. On the 9th the ritual was to have been held, but not everyone had been formally summoned and it was put off to the 10th.

Only eight men came, Mwalukuta I, the priest of the grove, and his younger brother Mwalukuta II, two other priests (Nyama and Mwakasukula) and Mwakyonde (148), younger brother of Mwaihojo the chief who provided the cow, and three other young men of the chief's lineage. One of the young chiefs was wearing a red cloth and was scolded by Mwakyonde for doing so: 'It's taboo in the sacred grove.' 'Why?' 'Because it's like a rainbow.'[1] And he took it off.

The mother of Nyama brought a bundle of saplings for building the hut for the shade, and Kisisile, the senior wife of Mwaihojo the

---

[1] The rainbow is a symbol of misfortune. cf. p. 60.

chief, brought a bundle of firewood. Mwalukuta I was not expected to enter the grove and he went off soon. His brother and Nyama took a little basket of maize and millet. The chiefs stayed on the edge of the grove and the three commoners entered alone. Mwalukuta II and Nyama built a little hut five feet from the 'grave' with the saplings brought by Nyama's mother. 'We put firewood and food and a little calabash which we have prepared in it, it's for the shades.' The calabash contained millet, maize, pumpkin seeds, ground nuts, and cow peas; and a stem of bananas was put beside it. Mwalukuta swept the 'grave' which was marked by a few small trees, and Mwakasukula killed the cow, which must lie facing east to BuKinga. Mwalukuta spoke the invocation: 'Thou Mwakisambwe (30) . . . Mwakihaba (45) has gone back, but Mwamukinga (44) is here still. . . . Mwakihaba says, "I am no longer a relative, I have gone out." ' Then they took the sacred meat from the forelegs of the cow: that from the right leg was buried near the 'grave', that from the left by an *nkuju* tree (a species of *ficus*) forty paces away. The priests ate some roasted meat and intestines with bananas, and the rest of the meat was divided between them and the chiefs. The head went to Nyama's house and was kept for three nights. The priests explained that they are forbidden to bathe for three days or lie with their wives, but on the fourth day they eat the head and after that they bathe and resume married life.

Eighteen days after the sacrifice Mwalukuta went to look and found the stem of bananas which had been left in the little hut had ripened, and the earth on the grave had been disturbed. This was a good omen. But later his legs began to trouble him—he could scarcely walk—and it was said that certain priests who should have been called to the ritual had not been summoned and were angry and had cursed him. He fled to a distance and sought a bull to kill for his fellows.

(d) SACRIFICE AT KABALE

The form of sacrifice among the Kukwe is very similar. We never saw a sacrifice at Kabale—our friends assured us that they had been dropped before 1935—but a description by two of the leading priests of the grove of Kabale demonstrates the similarity between the rituals there and in Selya. The only points of difference were that the Kukwe sacrificed fowls as well as cattle, and granddaughters shared the sacred food with grandsons.

In this grove of Kabale three chiefs in particular gather together, Mwakilulele (67 K) and his brothers Mwakalukwa (68 K) and Mwangoka (24 K) [or his son], with the younger brothers Mwakamela (66 K) and Mwakilasa (69 K) in whose country the grove is situated. The senior, Mwakilulele, initiates matters; it is he who calls his fellows saying: 'Let us pray in the grove.' Then Mwakilulele seeks a black cow and Mwangoka seeks a black bull, Mwakilasa brews beer and brings two fowls, a black and grey cock, and a black and yellow hen. So they go to the grave with their children, young boys and girls and the junior chiefs who have lost their positions as ruling chiefs—sons of Mwangomale (4 K)—and their village headmen. In the grove they pour some of the beer over the sacred stones and kill the cattle and take the liver and fat round the stomach and the meat from the upper forelegs (*ijammapa*) and cut it into small pieces and put it on two leaves, sweet banana and plantain. Then they take little pieces of meat and throw them on the ground and pluck out the feathers of the fowls. They praise the shades saying: 'Receive the fowls and beer and meat, may there be fertility of the fields that all the crops may be plentiful.' . . . 'Help us Kyala, thou Ndolombwike (?), thou Kajubili (?), you created·us, together with our fathers. Help us that illness may be slight, that we may increase and be many, that all the fowls and cattle may increase and that the fields may be fertile.' When they pluck out the feathers of the hen the praises are for the wives of the chiefs who have died. Then they pick up little pieces of meat and eat them with young children; it is taboo for wives to eat it. Boys drink the beer which is in the calabash cup—they receive it in their hands—and the girls finish the beer in the large calabash. Then the men drink the rest of the beer and divide the meat. . . . The calabash cup and the large calabash and the head are left in the grove overnight . . . then the large calabash and the cup are taken home and hung under the eaves—it is taboo to put them in the house—women must not approach them. When they have finished and come out of the grove rain pours down immediately and they rejoice saying: 'Kyala has helped us' . . . or 'the fathers have heard'.

Pouring out the beer on the ground and throwing down little pieces of meat, and sticking feathers into the ground means: 'May the fathers beneath receive them, may they bless the crops so that they flourish and food be plentiful. . . .' Children finish the food because they are like the shades—when the children have eaten they say the shades have eaten. They roast the meat at a distance because if they roast it close to the place of sacrifice no shades come there for the smoke drives them off. . . . The large calabash and cup and head which stay there symbolize fertility (*mboto*), so that when we eat they may help us and the food may not fail. The taboo on women—wives—eating the sacrificial meat (the *ijammapa*) and drinking the beer in the calabash

SACRIFICES AT THE GROVES OF CHIEFS   83

and cup is because this food is sacrified to their fathers-in-law. Those who are not sons of Ngomale do not drink the sacrificial beer or eat the meat either, because they are of other lineages. A *black* cow is used in the grove because groves are always fearful and darkness falls if something improper is done. So it is said that the blackness of the cow matches the fearfulness (*ubusisya*) of the grove.

Besides the sacrifices at Kabale and to their more immediate ancestors, Kukwe chiefs sent offerings to the BaNgumba, earlier occupants of the country. Mwamunda explained:

My grandfather prayed in the grove which is across the river on mission land, in the forest; it was the grove of us BaNgumba; we were owners of the soil, the Kukwe chiefs found us here. If ever a chief sent my grandfather and his fellows to pray there they went with an unripe stem of bananas, and sweet milk, and unripe maize, and small sweet potatoes; then they prayed and came home again and the next day, when they went to look they found the stem of bananas had ripened, the maize had hardened, the milk was thick and the sweet potatoes large; everything which was unripe had ripened. Then they said Kyala [that is Kyala and the shades] had stood by us. . . . We spoke of Kyala even before the Europeans had come. . . .[1]

They say that very long ago we BaNgumba, we sons of Kasyapula, had not yet got fire, the chiefs brought it. It is this they commemorate in the 'coming out' ritual. We, the owners of the soil, were always here, the chiefs came and built, and when others came the firstcomers fled. They are like you Europeans who fight wars; we owners of the soil think only of hoeing.

(e) MODERN CHANGES

It is quite clear that, though sacrifices to the heroes and at the groves of chiefs were still made while we were among the Nyakyusa (and more frequently than our friends at first admitted), the cycle was attenuated. Not only had human sacrifice probably ceased but the chiefs were reluctant to part with cattle. . . . Kasitile (86) said one day:

Since you [Europeans] came into the country the rituals have disappeared. Mwaipopo (116) never thinks of the rituals now. . . . It is cold and there is hunger; I went to Mwaipopo and told him to tell his

---

[1] According to the records of the first missionaries, sacrifices on Rungwe were to *Mbamba* but the same passage refers to *Mbamba or Kiala* meaning God. It is not clear whether the two names were equated by Kukwe informants or by the missionary himself, who was in touch with missionaries elsewhere in the district. (*Journal de l'Unité des Frères*, 1894.) I am indebted to the Reverend Paul Fueter for drawing my attention to this valuable Journal.

priests to sacrifice to his father and elder brother so that fertility may return and men may eat sweet potatoes, but he does nothing.

A conversation between Kasitile and Mwanyoso, his fellow priest (*vide* p. 76), was also instructive on this point:

The soil has changed, we are not like those of old, we are different. Mwakisambwe (30) had power; when he prayed the thunder crashed and rain fell in torrents. In the old days when the Kinga came they came with drums and we all feared them, what they said was done— they did not have to say much—just a few words and it was done. But now they spend all their time explaining things and talking and we do not do anything. . . .

MWANYOSO: I have sent people time and again to Mwaijande (?) for a cow, but he just insults us. . . . I have asked Mwaihojo (147) about celebrating. . . .

KASITILE: What did he say?

MWANYOSO: I don't know . . . if he is wise . . .

KASITILE (*breaking in*): Well, you had better admit that the chiefs do not respect you—the chiefs say: 'It is European times now.'

G.W.: What do they fear? The Government does not affect the ritual, does it?

KASITILE: They are unwilling to part with the cows which I take for sacrifice, they do not like to lose their cows. In the old days they feared, and when we said: 'We do not sleep, celebrate in the grove', they agreed quickly, for they feared that we, their men, would move to another chiefdom.

(f) THE FIRST FRUITS

No communal ritual of the first fruits is celebrated among the Nyakyusa as in Ngonde,[1] but after the millet harvest a little grain is collected from every homestead and later brewed into beer which is offered to the shades of the chief. In Mwaipopo's country the offerings of millet were collected by the priest, Ngulyo, who, with his colleagues Kissogoía and Njobakosa, took it to Kalinga, senior widow of the late chief (113). She was custodian of a sacred pot inherited by the chief from his predecessors, in which the offerings of millet are stored, and this is the pot which, according to some informants, also contained the power of growth—the nails and hair torn from the dead chief (*vide supra*, pp. 64-5). When the new crop was reaped Kalinga almost emptied the pot, refilled it with the fresh grain, and brewed beer with the old. There had once been a sacred winnowing basket used in preparing the beer, but

[1] Godfrey Wilson, *The Constitution of Ngonde*, p. 42.

it was stolen by Ngoni raiders. When the brewing was ripe, the chief sought a calabash of curds and Kalinga cut a stem of bananas, and the priests ate and drank in her hut, together with junior kinsmen of the chief's family, but not the chief himself. As they drank they prayed:

Oh thou Mwakagile (59) give us millet, may it be plentiful, and may the milk be plentiful and may the bananas grow.

One pot of beer was due to Kasitile, the priest, and he would leave it overnight in his house.

The shades come and drink a lot, only a little beer is left in the morning. . . . then the bananas flourish and there is much fertility in the homesteads. . . . The sacred pot gives fertility of the soil to the whole country.

A very bitter quarrel flared up while we were in Selya because Kasitile came upon Ngulyo and his colleagues drinking the sacred beer without their having sent him his pot, or even notifying him of the brewing. The repercussions of this are discussed in chapter IX.

NOTE

Chiefdoms do not have names which continue indefinitely. They are referred to by the name of the ruling chief or one of his illustrous ancestors, and often several different names are in common use for one chiefdom. To simplify the map we have assigned a number to each chiefdom held by a segment of the Nyakyusa or Kukwe lineages (*vide* genealogies, pp. 3, 27), and these numbers are plotted on the map. The map is based on that of Mr. R. de Z. Hall (sometime D.C., Tukuyu) and includes all, or almost all, the Nyakyusa and Kukwe chiefdoms recognized by the Administration.[1] The Penja, Nyiha, Ndali, Lambya, and Saku chiefdoms on the fringes of the valley are indicated, but not plotted. The map does *not* include all chiefdoms recognized in some fashion by the Nyakyusa themselves, e.g. Mwabungulu (178) 'came out' in 1953 and has been established at some distance from his elder brother with his own senior headman, but he is not recognized by the Administration as a chief and therefore his domain is not included on the map as a separate chiefdom.

[1] Two names listed by Mr. Hall are omitted, Ali Bin Omari because he is an immigrant and Mwakalinga of Kimbila because he is the son of a commoner appointed as headman by the German Administration, and not a member of either royal lineage.

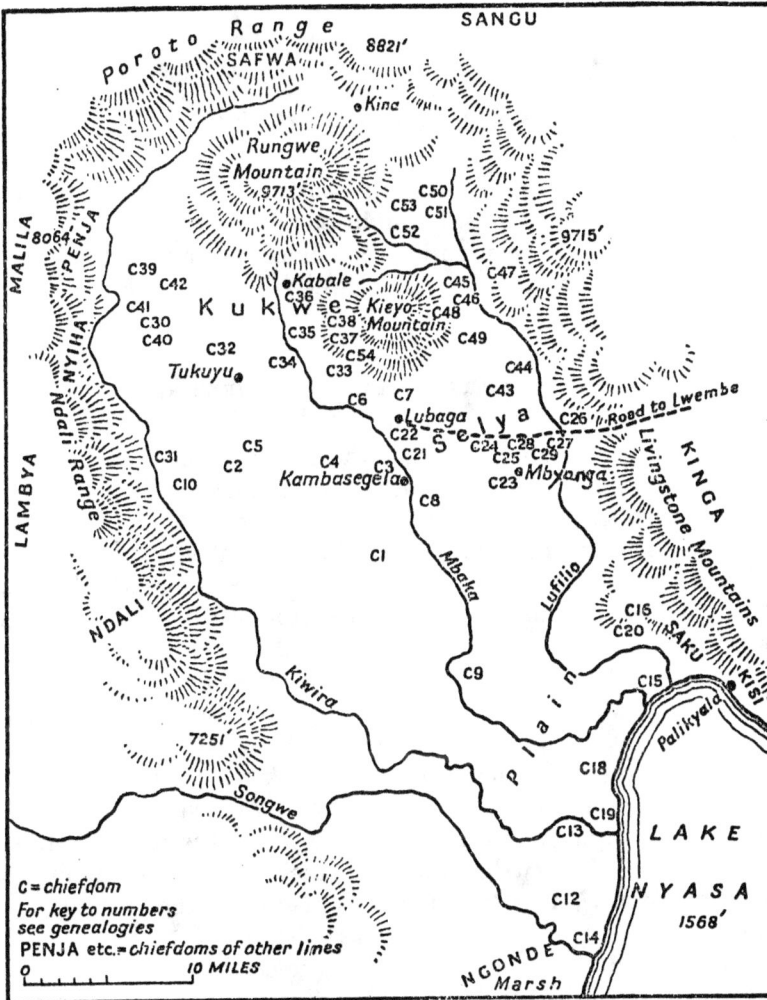

Map II. Nyakyusa valley showing location of chiefdoms

CHAPTER VI

LAND AND POWER

THE crux of the chiefs' 'coming out' was a redistribution of power and of land, and we must pause in our description of the ritual cycle to discuss the relation between chiefdoms and villages and the land, and to consider more closely the balance of power between successive generations.

(a) THE TERRITORIAL ALIGNMENT OF CHIEFDOMS AND VILLAGES

Tradition makes it clear that the heroes came to a sparsely occupied country and that their descendants gradually spread out as their numbers increased. The settlers chose to live on hillocks overlooking the surrounding country. Lubaga and Mbande, the seats of the two 'divine kings' are commanding sites. The grove of Kabale, where the ancestors of the Kukwe chiefs first established themselves, is on an eminence rising from the plateau, and Kambasekela (near the Mbaka bridge) on which the early chiefs Mwaipaja (21) and Mwaipopo (26) were buried is a hill very like Mbande, overlooking the plain.

Unlike most of their neighbours the Nyakyusa show a preference for cleared and cultivated land, planted with bamboos and the oil-bearing *unsyunguti* trees (*Trichillia supp.*)[1] as well as the great *umwali* (*Chorophora excelsa*) which, in their view, adds dignity to the homestead.[2] A study of the trees planted at the 'coming out' and the sacred groves in Mwaipopo's chiefdom (C 24)[3] shows that for four generations the ruling chiefs (descendants of Mwaijonga 82) have established their principal villages within a quarter of a mile of one another, and for seven generations the descendants of Mwakisambwe (30) have lived within two or three miles of one another (*vide* plan, p. 101), though there were acres of fertile land

[1] I am indebted to Mr. P. B. Nightingale, Forestry Officer, Tukuyu, for giving me the botanical names of these and other trees.

[2] cf. Monica Wilson, *Good Company*, pp. 77-8.

[3] C followed by a number is the reference number of a chiefdom as listed in the genealogies of chiefs.

available which are only now being settled. Colonies are established, but usually by junior sons, the seniors remaining near where their fathers built; e.g. the descendants of Mwakasangule (22) remained near Lubaga, but Mwakisambwe (30) the junior heir moved to Mbyanga about 1750 and his senior great-great-great-grandson Mwaihojo (147) lives close to Mbyanga still, while Mwaijonga (82) the junior heir settled two or three miles away. Mwakyusa (38), a junior son not strictly an heir at all, but personally very popular, was defeated by his elder brothers and driven from the hills to the plain, where his descendants now live. It is not an invariable rule that the junior should move away— for example Mwambete (162) of the junior line lives close to Kambasekela where his ancestor Mwaipaja (21) is buried, and not Mwakibwele (182) of the senior line—but most often it is the junior who moves. The tradition is that the junior heir of a chief leads off his men as colonists at his 'coming out', and this may indeed have happened in the past, but the area of colonization in Mwaipopo's country (which we have observed over twenty years) was first opened by private individuals moving into unoccupied savannah forest land in search of virgin soil for cultivation, and lush grazing. The chief Mwaipopo asserted his claim to the area first by establishing a household there with some of his junior wives, and then by sending the son of a subordinate house (who could have no claim to inheritance of the chieftainship) to live there. Nsusa, the second village headman of Mwaipopo's heir Mwankuga (150), also settled in the forest and acted as headman of the men there, but whether his move was primarily to lay claim to the land or because he had quarrelled with his chief, Mwankuga, and the other village headmen, was never very clear.[1] Then in 1953, at the coming out of Mwankuga's heirs, the junior Mwabungulu (178) was established in the colony, and is regarded by the people as 'chief' of that area, though he is not recognized as a chief by the Administration.

When a colony is established several miles are left uncultivated between it and the parent chiefdom. Mwabungulu lives five or six miles from his senior brother Mwanyilu (177) and there is an area without homesteads between them. It seems that, traditionally, each chiefdom was surrounded by a belt of uncultivated land used as pasturage, and very often at the 'coming out' both brothers merely extended their villages on to the adjoining pasture land

[1] cf. Monica Wilson, *Good Company*, pp. 268-9.

leaving a strip of pasture between them, but when the area became crowded the junior heir would establish a colony at some distance. With the increasing density of population, and of the acreage cultivated by each family, the buffer strips between chiefdoms are disappearing.

The more closely related chiefs are the nearer their chiefdoms are likely to be, as will be apparent if the map on p. 87 is compared with the genealogies I and II, but the pattern of splitting and expansion was continually modified by conquest and absorption. For example, the descendants of Mwaipasi (81) of the junior line have no chiefdom, and the descendants of Mwamwifu (84) were defeated and absorbed by Mwaipopo II (116), and the junior house of Mwakisambwe (30) appears never to have established itself. His second son named in the genealogy, Mwamukinga II (44), was a full brother of the senior heir Mwamukinga I (43), not the heir of the second house. And of the descendants of Mwankyuse (33) only one heir appears to have established himself in each generation.

Although a chiefdom was surrounded by pasture land with unoccupied savannah forest beyond it, when the heirs 'came out' their fathers moved. The old men gave the senior heir a site in the centre of the country, not exactly where his father had lived, but somewhere near the senior village of the past generation, and the old men moved aside to make room for the new village. The old men's villages diminished in size for many members had died and not all the heirs had come to live where their fathers had lived, and the homesteads were built on the periphery of the young men's villages. Traditionally most of the cultivated land was reallocated at the 'coming out' also, but that no longer happens. Nowadays, even where the 'coming out' is celebrated, the old men continue to cultivate until their death most of the fields they cultivated before the 'coming out', vacating only their homestead sites and adjoining gardens. The dominance of the younger generation is reflected in their compact villages, forming wide, straight avenues, in central positions in the country, while the villages of older men are often split, and their homesteads scattered without order. The avenues are felt to contribute to the dignity of the ruling generation and the older men are content to withdraw that their sons may 'display themselves' (ukumoga).

Age, territorial, and kinship grouping interlock in a complex fashion. Each village is occupied by an age-set and men are emphatic that age and friendship, not kinship, are the basis of a village, but the villages of fathers, sons, and grandsons commonly, though not invariably, adjoin one another, as Bujege, Igembe, and Lupando, or Lupondo, Njisi, and Iringa in Mwaipopo's chiefdom (*vide* plan, p. 101). Each section of a chiefdom comprises half the ruling generation, and interspersed with their villages are those of their fathers and sons. Men are identified by the name of their village, section, and chief; the village name defines their age-set, the name of section and chief their generation. The section name is always that of the senior village which leads it. Generation succeeds generation in office when their heirs 'come out', but the relative position of villages (age-sets) within a generation remains constant. Since chiefdoms traditionally split each generation at the 'coming out' the men of the retired generation who remained belonged to one section only; those of the other section of their generation were members of another chiefdom. The territorial arrangements reflected in the plan of Mwaipopo's chiefdom on p. 101 are modified by the fact that the chiefdom has not split for four generations. In generation I Kibonde was the portion of the junior heir, Mwafungo (83), but he died young and his land and widow were inherited by the senior brother, Mwaijonga (82). The son of this leviratical union, Mwakipesile (118), went through the 'coming out' in generation II along with Mwaijonga's heirs, Ijonga (114, representing her full brother 115), and Mwakabule (117). Mwakipesile inherited Kibonde and Mwakabule inherited Kituli, but both were later defeated in war by Mwaipopo II and their land incorporated in his chiefdom. Mwakipesile's heir, Likosyela, and Mwakabule remained as subordinate chiefs. Though the girl Ijonga celebrated the 'coming out' in place of her unborn brother she could not rule, and Mwaiteteja, son of Mwaijonga II (younger full brother of 82) acted for her. He was finally defeated by Mwaipopo II and fled to the periphery of the country. Kabula was his village, and he was subordinate to Mwaipopo, not independent.

In generation III the chiefdom did not split because by that time the British administration was in control, and the territorial division remained much the same, Igembe and Njisi becoming the senior villages in place of Bujege and Lupondo, with Mwankuga (150) and Mwaseba (152) as the young chiefs. Kibonde,

Kituli, and Kabula still remained somewhat detached. In generation IV the second heir, Mwabungulu (178), has moved out to the
forest and the area occupied and ruled by Mwaijonga and Mwaipopo is still one, with a division between Lupando and Iringa.
Kibonde is fully absorbed into Lupando, and Kituli and Kabula
into Iringa—no descendants of Mwakipesile of Kibonde and
Mwakabule of Kituli went through the 'coming out' with Mwanyilu as chiefs. Kibonde, Kituli, and Kabula are subdivided
into age-villages of three generations, but these are not shown
on the plan. They are spoken of by outsiders by the inclusive
names.

To a European the most surprising fact about the age-organization is that a young man of the ruling generation may still choose
to move into the homestead of his deceased father or elder brother.
We knew one young man, who had been spoken of as a possible
village headman at the coming out of Mwanyilu, but shortly
before the 'coming out' he chose to move into the homestead of his
deceased father in Lupondo village (where his father in turn had
inherited) even though he might have inherited his father's
wealth in wives and stock and returned to his own village of
Masoko, after completing the ritual of death and inheritance. Our
informants insisted that, though the young men might rule, the
older generation were the more honoured, and in inheriting from
his father this man was classified as a member of his father's
generation. Nevertheless many young men do *not* choose to move
into the village of the father or elder brother from whom they
inherit, and the villages of old men decrease in size and finally
disappear altogether.

The relation between kinship and territorial grouping cannot
easily be indicated by plans and genealogies for though in theory
each village consists of 'sons' of a village of the previous
generation (as shown in the table facing p. 91) there is considerable movement from one village to another, and the members
of any adult village usually prove to have come from a number of
different villages, though a boy's village consists of sons of adjoining villages. The table of members of three of the villages of
Mwaipopo's chiefdom illustrates this (*vide* pp. 224-6). An analysis
of genealogies showing where different members live gives much the
same picture. Though the shortage of land in the coffee-growing
chiefdoms of the hills and the rice-growing chiefdoms of the plain
is tending to obliterate the age-village organization, the old

system is still the accepted form in Mwaipopo's chiefdom; the advantages of separating kinsmen in different villages are explicitly stated, and the contrast between the Nyakyusa and their neighbours in this respect emphasized. 'Certainly we do not live with kinsmen here but the Kinga do.' 'It is not good for a son to live close to his father, they will quarrel.' 'When we move to another village we consider friendship not kinship in selecting it.'

(*b*) THE BALANCE BETWEEN GENERATIONS AND SECTIONS

The ritual cycle of the 'coming out' and the sacrifices in the groves helped to maintain a balance of power between generations, as well as between chiefs and commoners. At the 'coming out' of Mwanyilu (177) in 1953 it was Mwabuputa, the senior village headman of his father, who took the leading part. He was described as 'the greatest man in the country' who 'brings out the chief' and his manner indicated that he was well aware of his power. During the reign of Mwaipopo (116) the power of his father's village headmen, Njobakosa and Ngulyo, was apparent at every ritual. Spiritual power was shared between chiefs and commoners, but exercised ideally by a virile chief of the ruling generation and the experienced headmen of the retired generation.

Those chosen as senior village headmen at the 'coming out' are commonly older than the young chief, but village headmen are thought of as surviving their chief—it is they who were responsible for smothering him, and performing the sacrifices in his grove. The headmanship is an *office* and so long as the office is necessary an incumbent is found for it, in the person of the heir of the original holder who is so closely identified with the deceased that most precise inquiry is often necessary to establish whether a given individual is the original holder, the succeeding heir, or a later heir, successor to the successor. The Ngulyo who officiated at the rituals in 1935 was the heir of the original Ngulyo (some said the *grandson*, not the son) and he was criticized by Kasitile as being 'a young man who knew nothing'. The principle, so familiar in Central Africa, of a perpetual office[1] emerges, among the

[1] I. Cunnison, *Kinship and Local Organization on the Luapula*, Communications of the Rhodes-Livingstone Institute No. 5 (1950), pp. 14-15; J. C. Mitchell, *The Yao Village*, Manchester (1956), p. 122; A. I. Richards, *Land, Labour and Diet in Northern Rhodesia*, O.U.P. (1939), p. 24; 'Some Types of Family Structure among the Central Bantu, in *African Systems of Kinship and Marriage*, p. 224; J. Roscoe, *The Baganda*, London (1911), p. 3.

Nyakyusa, when sacrifices are continued in the grove of a dead chief such as Mwakisambwe (30), for an indefinite number of generations, and the heirs of his senior village headmen serve as his priests, taking the name of the first holder of the office. Most of the priests of Lubaga held perpetual titles of this sort. The conception of the *corporation sole* is familiar enough in the western tradition, but European observers in Africa are sometimes confused by the use of a personal name and the almost complete identification of each holder with his predecessors, as well as by the practice of treating certain kinship relationships as if they were offices.

Generation was determined among the Nyakyusa by association with a chief. There was no name for those who 'came out' together other than that of their chief, who was the focus of the ritual. On the other hand, however, a 'coming out' concerned a whole generation, and it could not be held out of season. If the heir died he was replaced by a brother, as were Mwaipopo I (115) and Mwankuga I (150). If a chief had no male heir of the right age in his senior house his daughter might represent an heir. For example, at the coming out of the sons of Mwaijonga, it was a *girl* Ijonga (114) who performed the leading part in the ritual which fell due before the birth of Mwaipopo I (115). When Mwaipopo I was born and grew up he assumed office, but he died young and was replaced by his younger brother without a further celebration. Because the 'coming out' was thus linked to the maturity of a whole generation we have felt some confidence in assigning approximate dates to the arrival of the heroes. The period between each 'coming out' we estimate at thirty to thirty-five years, though the higher figure is probably more nearly correct. There must in fact have been some flexibility in the timing of the 'coming out' to account for the differences in the number of generations of ruling chiefs in different segments of the lineage. Some of the differences may be due to errors (e.g. it is possible that 70 is an elder brother not the father of 98, and that a generation has been omitted between Mwakapeje (54) and Mwakage (75), but even where there is little possibility of error the number of generations does not always tally.

In theory a man always belongs to the generation succeeding that of his father, irrespective of his age, provided he has not inherited from a man of the previous generation and taken his status, but in practice, since men often have sons of very different ages, they sometimes build in villages of different generations. When it comes to the selection of village headmen, however, care is taken to ensure that they are indeed sons of men who came out with the previous chief, and a village like Katumba which comprised both younger brothers and sons of Mwankuga's generation breaks up, some members 'coming out' with Mwankuga's son, others acting as 'fathers'. Within a village all the members are equal subject to their headman, but a hierarchy of villages is clear.

The pre-eminence of the two senior village headmen of a chief is marked. They alone make fire with him at the 'coming out'. They alone are handed war tails with which to lead their men in battle. Each is responsible for one half of the country and a dispute not settled by the headman of the village of the defendant is reported to the senior headman in whose side of the country the village lies, and he brings it before the chief Each senior headman has his own village, the two senior villages of the country, in which the royal ladies live; the senior wife married at the 'coming out' is established close to the senior village headman, the second wife close to the second senior headman. A chief may establish wives in a number of villages, and some at least of those he inherits from his father continue to live in his father's old homestead 'to sweep the graves', but his capitals (*ifitangalala*) are the two senior villages of the country in which his two senior wives and two senior village headmen live[1] and the names of the capitals are used not only for the senior villages but for the half sections of the generation they lead. The importance of the two senior headmen is apparent even when their generation has handed over political authority to their sons. At the sacrifices we have described Njobakosa and Ngulyo, heirs of the senior headmen of the chief Mwaijonga (82) officiated, and at the 'coming out' of Mwanyilu (177) it was Mwambuputa and Kakuju his father's senior headmen who organized the ritual.

Each village established at a 'coming out' is a clearly defined unit with its own land, and leader, and name, but villages are also segments of larger units, the half-section of the chiefdom under a senior headman, and the whole chiefdom under the leadership of

[1] Mwanyilu (177), though he had two senior headmen, established his two senior wives in *one* house, close to the house of Kilasile his most senior headman. This was explained as a temporary measure 'because they were young', but it is not the traditional pattern, and may be linked with the fact that the splitting of the country each generation is no longer accepted as the inevitable pattern.

the chief himself. The members of each village co-operate in some measure in cultivation and herding and they form a defensive group against attack 'by day and by night'—i.e. against armed raiders and witches.[1] But there is no great elaboration of ritual for single villages. Such village rituals as occur are connected with defence against witchcraft and involve driving out a supposed witch, or receiving back a member who has fled from fear of witchcraft, or protecting the village fields against witches.[2] Most communal rituals are organized on the basis of the chiefdom or group of chiefdoms, and villages or sections participate as segments of the chiefdom.

The principle of generation and that of section hold one another in check. All those who have 'come out' together have a strong sense of unity as opposed to the generations of their fathers and sons, but every generation is split into two sections each led by an heir of the chief, and these sections have a certain territorial solidarity. It is common in Africa for organized age-groups to cut across kinship and territorial groups. The Nyakyusa peculiarity lies in the territorial unity of age-sets which occupy villages, and the manner in which the fissiparous tendencies within a chiefdom have a constitutional outlet in the rivalry between the sections of a ruling generation which become independent at the 'coming out' of the next generation.

The combination of the hereditary and selective principles of leadership among the Nyakyusa is also somewhat different from that among their neighbours. With many Central African people the heir to the holder of the office of village headman or chief is *selected*, and the most capable member of a given lineage or lineage segment appointed.[3] Among the Nyakyusa succession is precisely defined and there is no selection of a suitable heir except to the supreme and greatly feared office of 'divine king', but the selective principle is given full scope in the 'catching' of leaders for the young men's villages at every 'coming out'. It is this combination of the hereditary and selective principles which binds together chiefs and commoners and successive generations. The rules of

---

[1] Monica Wilson, *Good Company*, pp. 44-66, 91-127.

[2] *op. cit.*, pp. 52-4, 109 ff., 154-6, 270-4.

[3] I. Cunnison, 'Headmanship and Ritual of Luapula Villages', *Africa*, xxvi (1956), p. 11; M. G. Marwick, 'The Social Context of Cewa Witch Belief', *Africa*, xxii (1952), pp. 219-22; V. Turner, 'Ndembu Village Structure', *Africa*, xxv (1955), pp. 123-4; J. C. Mitchell, *The Yao Village*, Manchester (1956), pp. 157-63.

inheritance ensure that a limited number of young men are absorbed into the senior generation and live with the older men, sharing their activities and from time to time holding office as headmen or priests of that generation, and the selection in each generation of young men who are *not* the sons of village headmen, or chiefs, or headmen of the past generation, ensures that commoners without office are constantly recruited to the hierarchy of rulers. In short, power is distributed.

(c) RITUAL AND SECULAR BONDS

As in so many societies, economic and ritual links extended, traditionally, further than political links.[1] Selya was dependent upon BuKinga for iron and the Kinga came to fruitful Selya to pray for fertility. The priests who came to pray brought the hoes. The many independent chiefdoms of Selya and the Mbaka valley acknowledged the spiritual overlordship of the Lwembe by sending sacrifices to him, and it was through the network of hereditary priests like Kasitile, Mwamakunda, Mwalukuta, and Nyama of Selya, and the Kinga priests Kikungubeja, Nsyanigwa, Kyamba Kitali, and Silobwike that wider bonds were maintained. Mwaipopo (116) when he was granted a Court which gave him the secular leadership of Selya, failed to make any acknowledgement of Lwembe's traditional power, and it was Kasitile who later urged him to do so. The western chiefdoms of the Nyakyusa still buy medicines and bark-cloth from the Ndali to the west, and have done so for many generations, but no common ritual links them as it does Selya and the plain with BuKinga. The trade was of lesser importance than that to the east, for it does not seem to have included iron, though the Nyiha who share a common culture with the Lambya, the western neighbours of the Nyakyusa, are known to have been skilled smiths.[2] With the Sangu to the

---

[1] cf. E. Colson, 'The Plateau Tonga of Northern Rhodesia' in *Seven Tribes of British Central Africa* (ed. Colson and Gluckman).

A comparison with the frontier in West and South Africa where economic and religious expansion compelled the establishment of Government is instructive. Cf. W. K. Hancock, *Survey of British Commonwealth Affairs*, vol. ii, part ii, pp. 162-8.

[2] D. Kerr-Cross, 'Geographical Notes on the Country between the Lakes Nyassa, Rukwa, and Tanganyika', *The Scottish Geographical Magazine*, vi (1890), p. 289. Elton's suggestion that some of the Nyakyusa iron came from the west is discounted by Cotterill. J. F. Elton, *The Lakes and Mountains of Eastern and Central Africa* (1879), p. 371 and map, cf. J. Thompson, *To the Central African Lakes and Back*, vol. i, p. 272.

north the Nyakyusa were continually at war; they did not trade or pray with them. Thus we conclude that participation in a common ritual is, in the Nyakyusa case, directly linked with a common origin and essential trade.

The divine kings, Lwembe and Kyungu, were regarded as having power over certain areas, a power closely linked with rainfall. Indeed, one informant argued that the chiefs living around Masoko had never sent sacrifices to Lubaga, 'because when it rains at Lubaga the rain does not come as far as Masoko'. He was mistaken in his facts—the chiefs of Masoko did at one time send to Lubaga as Mwambete (162), chief at Masoko, himself admitted—but the argument points to a conception of super-natural power tied to a rainfall area. This notion was not, how-ever, applied consistently.

The balance between secular and mystical power has altered during the past ten generations. The founding heroes, Lwembe and Kyungu, came as conquerors and must surely have led their men personally; but early in the history of Ngonde the Kyungu was secluded, and power was exercised almost exclusively by the nobles (*vide supra*, pp. 40-46); and the Lwembe also was, at one period, 'not seen by ordinary men' and led a life hedged about with taboos. There is sharp contrast in Nyakyusa tradition between the active chiefs who were warriors, and arbitrators, and worked hard in their fields[1] and the 'divine king' who lived in seclusion. As we have seen, the chiefs often delegated ritual functions, with the taboos involved, to a junior kinsman such as Mwamukinga (44) or Mwakihaba (45) (*vide* pp. 79-81, 114) whose heirs succeeded to the office. It is even possible that the first Lwembe at Lubaga (Mwakalebela 19) took over ritual functions from his senior brother, Kalesi (18).[2] The present tendency is for the development of secular power and its separa-tion from mystical power. The Kyungu is no longer a god but an administrator: the heir of the Lwembes sits as an elected repre-sentative of chiefs on the Local Council. In the traditional Nyakyusa society ritual played an essential part in maintaining the balance between generations, sections, and social strata, and in

---

[1] In 1955 a young chief was bitterly criticized by his men because he 'never had a hoe in his hands' whereas his father and grandfather had (to our personal knowledge) been diligent in hoeing.

[2] But according to one excellent informant, Mwakisambwe (30) lived secluded while Mwakilima (31) 'fed men'—i.e. entertained.

linking scattered political units, but that function is disappearing with the growth of trade and a centralized political authority. District Commissioner, Rural and District Councils, and Co-operatives supplant the 'divine king', and limit the power of local chiefs much more narrowly than he ever did.

NOTE

It should be realized that (i) the names of the two senior villages of a generation are well known and clear cut, but those of subordinate villages are more fluid. Furthermore a village often has subdivisions, distinguished by its members by name, but known to outsiders only by the general village name. (ii) A village may acquire a new name at the 'coming out'; the senior village of Mwanyilu's generation used to be called 'Mpuguso' but 'came out' as 'Lupando'. (iii) Some villages die out altogether, e.g. Kyemo II. (iv) Some villages straddle generations. Katela in 1955 is in the same sort of position as Katumba in 1935. It includes eight sons of Mpunga who belong to generation III, but also fourteen sons of men of Masoko who 'came out' with Mwanyilu. In the case of Katumba the members who were sons of men of generation III moved to younger villages and 'came out' with Mwanyilu, among them being his senior headman Kilasile, a man of over forty. But Kilasile's contemporaries who were sons of men of generation II could not 'come out' with Mwanyilu, at least not as a group—and the members of Katumba attended the 'coming out' as 'fathers'. Boys join a village of contemporaries but may move later to a village of younger men who are of their own structural generation.

At the 'coming out' of Mwanyilu and Mwabungulu five village headmen were 'caught' and secluded with their chiefs. They represented five clear-cut villages. Kilasile and Sikambombo, Mwanyilu's two senior headmen who made fire are leaders of Lupando and Iringa respectively; Pauliki and Batungulu their juniors are leaders of Bujisi (or Ipoma) and Mfumbi (or Isuba), and Mwanjotile the single headman of the junior heir, Mwabungulu, has his own village of Nkuyu established on newly settled land in the forest. The young men of Kibonde were included under Kilasile's authority, and those of Kituli and Kabula under Sikambombo's. The names Lupando and Iringa are well known as those of sections of Mwanyilu's chiefdom, but the names Bujisi and Mfumbi are not: the young men of these villages still use the names of their fathers' villages, Ipoma and Isuba, though there is a clear territorial separation between fathers and sons. Taxes are collected under the names of Igembe, Ipoma, Kibonde, Njisi, Isuba, Kituli, and the three forest villages, Kilosi, Kiloba, and Nkuyu.

CHAPTER VII

CLEANSING THE COUNTRY

Sacrifices to the heroes and the shades of the chiefs are holy and private—only a handful of priests and chiefs may enter the groves and the details of the rituals are not discussed with other people. But there are other celebrations in which everyone participates; these are the rituals for cleansing the community—'throwing out the rubbish' (*ukujola ikikungu*)—more specifically the *ashes* from all the hearths.

In Ngonde the cleansing is organized for the whole kingdom, from Mbande, but among the Nyakyusa each chiefdom acts independently. Traditionally, we were told, the *ukujola ikikungu* was an annual celebration, observed at the 'new year', after the break of the rains, but it could also take place if there were much sickness in the country, or plague, or prophecies of evil to come. It was celebrated (in an attenuated form and by a section of the community only) in Ngonde in July 1937, to cleanse the country of a plague of rats, and in September of the same year a somewhat similar ritual was performed in Porokoto's chiefdom because a fearful omen had been seen—a ground hornbill had eaten a chicken. The annual celebrations had been dropped both in Ngonde and BuNyakyusa before 1935.

As has been shown in the *Rituals of Kinship* the Nyakyusa believe that too close an association with the shades is dangerous; all the family rituals are designed to drive them away, to drive them out of the bodies of the mourners, or menstruating girls, or parents of twins; and the purpose of 'throwing out the ashes' in all the homesteads is essentially the same. The shades 'come to warm themselves' at the hearths of their descendants, they 'bring sickness to the hearths' and so the old ashes are cleared out and new fire is lighted. The phrase *ukujola ikikungu* is used in Ngonde for clearing out the litter (*ulufumbo*) after a burial, or an initiation ritual, and for shaving after a ritual, as well as for clearing the ashes from all the hearths in the country.

It is also thought that domestic fires are contaminated by witches who may have cooked the human flesh they steal over their victims' own fires. In Ngonde it was the connexion between the shades and the hearths which was stressed; in Porokoto's country people talked mostly of the witches; but it seemed clear that both conceptions were present when men murmured: 'The hearth bricks are bad' (*amafiga mabibi*) and they sought to cleanse them by clearing out the old fire and lighting new. 'To clear out the ashes means they take away all that dirt, the dirt which the witches have brought and the shades; it is the cause of illness.' When witches are thought to be active there is also a public complaint, and a public warning is given 'to whom it may concern' to desist.[1] This occurred in the ritual after the ground hornbill had eaten the chicken. Above all, men must admit their anger to one another: 'they fight that the homesteads may be peaceful'. The theme so familiar in Nyakyusa rituals—that quarrels must be confessed if they are to be composed—recurs yet again. Though we distinguish the rituals for 'cleansing the country' from sacrifices, on the ground that the whole community participates in the 'cleansing' while the sacrifice is esoteric, the two are closely linked, and a sacrifice commonly precedes or follows the cleansing. We turn now to the detailed accounts of celebrations for 'cleansing' in Ngonde and among the Kukwe.

(a) THE RATS

In Ngonde they used to clear out the ashes at the new year, at the first hoeing (in December) after 'the break of the rains'. They feared that death and disease would spread through the land if they continued living with the old fires, that the shades in the earth, both the shades of chiefs and of commoners, would be angry. Let them drive the shades away and hoe in peace. They always remembered to do so each new year; for the old men used to keep these things in mind continually, they never forgot. The Kyungu would summon the whole country to clear out the ashes; and then they would hoe in peace. And at other times, too, if prophecy came on someone, they would clear out the ashes again. 'It is to drive away the shade with the sickness that he brings. We throw out the ashes and firebrands because he has come to warm himself over the fire in our houses, we throw out the pots and winnowing baskets because he has come to see us eating; let him go there (to the grove) and eat what he asked for—we say the shades ask for food—let him eat hens, perhaps a sheep. We say the shades bring sickness to the fire, hence we throw out the ashes and make new fire with a drill.'

The nobles of Ngonde approached the Kyungu and he gave

---

[1] cf. Monica Wilson, *Good Company*, pp. 109-13.

H

the order to clear out the ashes; messages were sent to the great chiefs and the senior territorial nobles of the plain, and they told their juniors. A sacrifice was made in one of the sacred groves of the Kyungus and all fires in the whole Ngonde plain were put out. And then

> all the chiefs from every country near Mbande and the nobles and all the village headmen and all the ordinary men and women, too, went to Kyimbwe where we threw away the sickness of all the country.

At Kyimbwe, which is the crossroads in the bush, they threw away the ashes of their old fires, and some of the pots and baskets in which food is served; while those few people who could not get to Kyimbwe threw them away from their own houses on the same day as the others. At Kyimbwe new fire was made with a fire-drill by the nobles of Ngonde who

> ran with it without looking back and the people danced alongside them and speared one another! . . . They said, 'Let us dance, let us fight that the homesteads may be peaceful'. . . . 'Let us throw out the ashes that death may leave the homesteads and they be at peace.' It is to bring out war from within (*ukusosya*).

The symbolism is the same as in the rituals of kinship when kinsmen gather to admit their quarrels and press one another to speak out, so that they may cleanse themselves of anger.

The new fire was distributed to the whole plain in order. Great chiefs and senior nobles took it first and passed it to their juniors, chiefs passed to village headmen, and in each group the common people got it from their own ruling noble or their own village headman.

In July 1937, while we were visiting Ngonde, there was a plague of rats[1] which threatened the food supply, and Bungulu, the wife of a chief and well known as a prophetess, went into a trance and revealed that the rats were caused by the anger of the previous Kyungu and could be got rid of only by a ritual 'throwing out the rubbish' and sacrifice. Her husband reported the matter to Mulwa, the premier noble of Ngonde, to whom the present Kyungu, Peter—at one time a Church member—had long since handed over all responsibility for communal rituals. Mulwa called four of the leading chiefs who were pagan and a number of

---

[1] Nothing new in Ngonde. Lord (then Captain) Lugard suffered from them in 1888: F. D. Lugard, *The Rise of our East African Empire* (1893), vol. i, p. 127. In 1937 the country swarmed with rats: in our own camp we killed 70 to 100 each night.

commoners, and they went together to the grove of Mwangalaba, the last Kyungu (elder brother of Peter), with a white hen and sacrificed it there, and prayed saying:

Mwangalaba go thou to Mwakasungula your father and let him go to Mwangonde, and he to Mwagemo and he to Kiposa and he to Mpeta and he to Mwendemange and he to Kyabala and he to Syola and he to the Kyungu who lived at Mano and he to Ngulube (9) and Lyambilo (12). May he stand by us, may we sleep, may the rats disappear and illness also, may we sleep. Then when we had finished the invocation [I quote Mulwa] we extinguished the fires in all our houses; in the houses of the chiefs, and of Kyungu's great wife Namwilan'ombe, and of us commoners, we threw water on the ashes, but each took some ash, and a firebrand to the crossroads at Kyimbwe where we collected them all and left them to rot; there we threw away the rats saying: 'Let them fly away to Ngulube (9), let them fly away with the wind, let us sleep.' Then we ran to the pasture land to make new fire with a drill. We all took fire there in the bush, each a firebrand and lighted new fires in our own houses and in the house of the Kyungu, that is of his great wife. We arranged it with our wife Namwilan'ombe, because Kyungu had said 'Work with your husbands there'.

'Throwing away the rats' consisted in enclosing a live rat in two winnowing baskets, opening them at Kyimbwe, and flourishing them first in one direction and then in another, releasing the rat in the process. This had been specifically ordered by Bungulu, the prophetess.

(b) THE GROUND HORNBILL

In the country of Porokoto (49 K) there was much illness and many deaths (some, at least, from typhoid) during the dry season of 1937, and when a ground hornbill—always a bird of ill-omen among the Nyakyusa—mysteriously attacked a chicken in Syokela village, everyone was horrified. Mwamunda, a village headman, explained what had happened:

The headman of Syokela came with two men to Bwilile (senior village headman of his side) and said: 'Tell the chief that a ground hornbill has eaten a fowl at our place. We ask what this means. And also we do not sleep, we are ill.' Then Bwilile told me and we went together to the chief who said: 'I have heard, let us discuss it.' So we gathered at Nsyani's and the headman of Syokela stood up and said: 'My fathers, and friends, and children, and you chiefs, we have come to ask: have you ever before heard of a ground hornbill eating a fowl? (With an air of intense questioning.) We have not, but perhaps you have?' Then we all denied having heard of such a thing; we had no idea what the portent meant and said: 'Let us consult an oracle.' The chief agreed. . . . Then men went to the doctor and the oracle said: 'It is because you have not celebrated at Mwakan'ata's (30 K) place since his death;[1] you must kill a cow and clear the grass at his place. This ground hornbill is your father Mwakan'ata; seek a cow and celebrate and pray, then you will see what will happen.' They told the chief this and he said: 'Must I find a cow then?' But it is we village headmen who have done wrong because some of us said: 'What's a cow for? Let us just pray; why should we throw away a cow?' Others of us said: 'Yes, let a cow be found', but the chief listened to those who opposed killing a cow. So we went and prayed without eating anything.

The ritual was put off three times; the first time the people were summoned men of one village had not come; the second time men of another; the third time a headman was missing and also the women had not been called. Finally, on the morning of 28th September, men and women and children gathered on the pasture land just beyond Ilolo village (where we lived). The men and boys sat, with their headmen, by villages, each forming a segment of the great circle round the chief, while the women all crowded together some distance behind him. . . . 'We all go, except the Christians.'

The chief Porokoto, rather nervous in his manner, stood up and addressed the company after one of the headmen had said pointedly: 'We are all women, a man stands in the middle, it is he who speaks.' For women never pray, blowing out water, and commoners in this situation do not pray, only the chief.

POROKOTO: The reason I have called you together is this: there is no peace in the country; there is much cold, many people are shivering with fever, let us drink water and drive away Kyala. This concerns all the homesteads; the cold [i.e. fever] is finishing us. What do you say Mwamunda? [to the headman].
MWAMUNDA: Thank you! We rejoice that you chiefs have remembered. May we sleep well, may there not be illness, may the cold pass, may the children grow well, and all the crops. Indeed we are all in great trouble. Kyala help us, may we be pure (*tujebelu*)!

Then the chief called on one village headman after another to speak; and his elder brother, Mwasalemba, also spoke.

---

[1] Porokoto was already sceptical of pagan ritual and has since become a Christian.

MWAFULA: Indeed, may the illness not be great, may the children not cry by night, may the cattle increase, and the fields be fertile, and the fowls also increase. May children sleep. Our fathers always confessed in the house. Now we are shocked at what is happening.

MWANTIMWA: We say thank you, chiefs, you do not forget us. Let the sickness pass and go away, may the cattle sleep, and you women, may the children grow. May the fields be fertile; may there not be envy of one another. We are sorry because there is much illness. Our fathers say 'Why have the chiefs turned round?'

MWAMULENGA: Chief, we beg you, we thank you, indeed there is sickness. Is there anyone who says in their quarter there is much sickness (more than elsewhere)? Do we say something about sickness?

MWAMUNDA: No, Mwampiki, all of us who have come here are sick.

KILONGO: Yes, we are all rotting.

Mwaikambo commenting on this explained:

If there is sickness one may admit and say, 'It is I, I was angry on account of such and such.' Yes, indeed, they confess openly, because he who sees in his belly (=knows in his heart) that 'It is I who have done this' trembles when his fellows speak many words thinking, 'Perhaps they have seen me.' So he confesses. When he confesses he escapes, they only grumble at him saying, 'Don't do it again.' If someone admits the others say, 'It is he, but we have punished him.' I think that even in the old days he was not driven out, because they hope that, if he has confessed, the illness he caused will go away.

MWASALEMBA: Have you ever before heard of a hornbill eating a hen? We are horrified. Even the prophets did not speak of such an event.

ANOTHER: Indeed, it has never before happened, we are glad that our chiefs have taken the initiative with these words.

ANOTHER: For this custom is old, it began long ago in the time of our fathers. It is the custom to give hope in the homesteads, that we may grow strong.

MWAMPIKI: Always, if the chief is ill it is said, 'Where are you, oh people?' All the homesteads watch over the chief when he is ill. [Mwaikambo commenting: It is said that people have the work of watching over their chief that no one may bewitch him, hence when he is ill they reproach people saying: 'Where are you?' Let the old customs be observed now (implying that they have left all the old customs and hence there is much sickness in the country).]

ANOTHER: There are some who say 'Let so-and-so die that I may move into his homestead. Let envy which brings sickness also go away.'

ANOTHER: If sickness appears let us tell the chief that we may all express astonishment together, asking where the illness has come from, then it will be light, if we all grumble together. [Mwaikambo commenting:

They say that complaining drives away illness, even though the witches are not seen, and do not confess saying, 'It is we' yet they are ashamed thinking 'People have caught me' and they desist.]

MWAMULENGA: Catch anyone you see in your dreams. If someone is ill should we not all gather?

MWAMUNDA: Countrymen, give thanks that there are the chiefs.

And the company assented.

Then there was a discussion about the direction in which the chief should spit and people run. One pointing towards Tukuyu said: 'We always looked that way.' Another said: 'We always reached the boundary.'

Mwafula (a village headman) came with his young son carrying a calabash of medicated water. Porokoto took a sip and spat out eastward, 'in the direction of the grove of Kabale, to the shades.'

Mwamulenga shouted: 'Now we have prayed, the sickness is finished, we are present and watch over the homesteads. If we see anyone bringing sickness we will catch him and crush him on the sleeping mat.' There was a roar from the crowd, then all rushed yelling 300 yards or so eastward to the edge of the fields, and back again. Porokoto ran a little way with them, his malacca cane raised, then stopped, looking self-conscious, and strolled homeward. Everyone else scattered, chattering and laughing. On the way back we were greeted: 'You have prayed! Did you catch witches? Whom did you catch?'

Mwasalemba, senior brother of Porokoto and an expert in ritual, added one or two points in explanation:

In the old days we threw out the ashes, but we have not yet done so this time; we begin with the ritual on the pasture land and throw out the ashes afterwards. In the old days we threw them out of all the houses and put in fresh fire, new ash, saying 'Thou Kyala, thou shade, receive us, let us sleep here, we throw out the ashes, let sickness be slight.' Those who are angry now are our shades—those of the chiefs— they have gathered with the shades of the commoners. The medicated water means: 'Thou shade, you fathers, may we sleep, use this water for us if we are ill, may we be strong.' The water goes to the shades with these words.

Q.: Why must the women come?

M.: They call the war cry, we run swiftly, the women follow calling the war cry which means, 'You shade, we call the war cry for you that we may be pure—without anger—in our bellies, make us strong also, thou shade, may we also be pure in our bellies, this is your war cry . . .' The running and calling the war cry is to mock at him, to drive him away. We run with him, we leave him over there, we return and bring him in. We drive him off because he brought sickness; when we have done so we return and bring him again that we may be pure—without anger—and he also may be pure. We are with him all the time; we never throw him away. We always have the old one in the belly, an infant is he, and if I die I am with him, this earth (pointing to the earth of his homestead) never goes away, it is he. So if the crops fail when I have hoed I say: 'The shade is angry, this earth.' (*Papo nkulu tulinagwe bwila munda, mutukeke jo jujo, nalenga mfwile ndinagwe—umfu ugu gutijonga nakamo jo jujo—papo lenga ndemile nikuti 'unsyuka akalele umfu ugu' bo fisitile.*) Yes, in the death ritual also we drive him away with his sickness, and bring him back, always the old one.

After the ritual all have normal intercourse with their wives, but the night before there was no intercourse. How should we do evil on the mats when we have not yet blessed the shade? But when we have blessed him then all of us lie on our mats again. To lie together is to overstep the ritual, the shades are shocked and say, 'How can you do this? You agreed yesterday to bless the shades and you do this, why?' Then later, if a woman bears a child which cries at night, people say, 'You overstepped the ritual, pray for the child.' Or perhaps the woman is barren. We liken the water and the war cry to what we do on the mats—the water is the shade's and the war cry is his, it is his work. When we have spoken to the shade he comes into my belly—then I come together with my wife again.

This interpretation by Mwasalemba indicates that the blowing out of water is a symbol of emission. 'It is what men do.' It has been shown in *Rituals of Kinship* that the shades are driven out of the body in the sex act; that the shade and semen are identified; and that driving off the shade is a condition of health and sanity. The fact that blowing out water is *also* a symbol of confession—admission of anger, 'bringing out all that is within'—and supplication does not invalidate Mwasalemba's interpretation, for the same act is symbolized in many ways and the same symbol expresses events which are distinct, but associated. As in so many societies, abstinence is felt to be a necessary preparation for the celebration of a ritual, and the union, real or symbolic, of husband and wife the necessary conclusion.[1] All this is intelligible only in terms of the Nyakyusa ideas about procreation discussed in *Rituals of Kinship*. The shade is the vital force in men

[1] cf. I. Cunnison, 'Headmanship and Ritual of Luapula Villages', *Africa*, xxvi (1956), pp. 5-13; H. A. Junod, *The Life of a South African Tribe* (1927), vol. i, pp. 320-22; J. Roscoe, *The Baganda* (1911), pp. 48, 53, 55.

and women, it is procreative power, fertility. That power is constantly expelled from the belly but returns again and by that expulsion and return men live.

There was a great deal of criticism from the conservatives because no sacrifice had been made.

MWAMUNDA: Now people are talking much saying, 'We have abandoned that which they did formerly, we are doing something else.' People have many dreams (gesture head on hand as if heavy with anxiety), many say: 'I have dreamed of the dead, they told me to sacrifice a cow, to pray, we did not pray properly, that is useless, it will not effect anything.' So we have told the chief saying: 'Let us kill a cow at the grave of Mwakan'ata,' he has agreed, but the cow has not yet come.

Formerly, on the night following the day of the prayer we should have eaten the sacrificial cow, the chief would have killed two cows and the headmen from different villages would have come and eaten by night, and drunk beer provided by the chief, in the house of the senior wife of the chief. . . . They ate a little meat, raw, the rest they roasted. Then in the morning, when they had eaten and were satisfied, they would go to clear out the house, to throw out the ashes, and to pray, as we prayed now, and to make new fire by friction in the pasture land. The village headman made fire with medicine which the chief gave him, the name of the medicine is Mbamba, it's a tree. To throw out the ashes means to clear out all the filth, the filth which the witches and the shades have brought to us—the filth that is sickness. . . . Do not the witches eat meat at the fire? Human flesh? Some roast at your fires your bodies which they have seized, some go home with the human flesh to their own fires, hence comes the filth of the ashes. The village headmen eat the sacrificial meat at night with the shades, they celebrate for them with the blood which goes beneath. . . .

If the chief has done something wrong, then those above [i.e. the village headmen] pray to those beneath saying, 'Let us help one another to punish him who has strayed, but we do not wish that he should die, let him be ill; perhaps then he will seek something to nourish us.' Again the night before the throwing out of the ashes they confess their anger and say: 'You beneath, this our child (the chief) has remembered us, there is no accusation against him now, may sickness go away from the country, and children sleep, let us all sleep and the cows calve. We greet those beneath.' In my childhood I was repeatedly surprised at night when my father came in, he had a little parcel of meat. 'Where have you been?' I asked. 'We have been praying.' But since I grew up and became a village headman, and was recorded as such [by the administration] we have never seen sacrificial meat.

Mwandisi made a great deal of the fact that at the 'throwing out of the rubbish' the village headmen ate meat *raw*.

Formerly . . . we threw away the ashes and charred brands . . . that is to drive away the shades who warm themselves over the hearth in the house; they bring us sickness, let them warm themselves over there in the long grass! Also in the long grass there we killed meat, and the priests ate it *raw*: no one saw them doing that there in the long grass; we went by day with drums, people from all the home-steads, a moving multitude . . . then we came home . . . the priests remained with their wives, they threw away their bark-cloths, they cut off morsels of meat and ate them raw. Because the priests are witches it is they who ate raw meat before we chiefs came, the priests are witches. . . . The witches and shades gather and bring sickness together, we kill a cow in the grove, we drive them away. No, they do not eat raw meat in the grove, they cook it. But at the capital if the chief has killed a cow for men to eat the priests eat meat raw. We have seen them. I, Mwandisi, have seen Mwajole and Kalambo the senior village headmen eating raw meat at my place and my wives have seen them also.

'Yes', said one of his wives, 'we saw them and we ran away saying: "Well! Fancy doing it *openly*!" ' Mwandisi continued:

The senior village headmen are witches, children of those who ate raw food long ago. Some village headmen only rush to eat a cow we have killed, but some go to eat a person; those are the witches who eat raw meat!

The function of a chief is to feed his men on beef, and in doing so he placates the witches who are commoners and who, like their forefathers, prefer their meat raw. If they do not get beef then the witches eat men.[1]

(c) SMALLPOX

The prayer and 'clearing out of the rubbish', traditionally celebrated before an approaching epidemic, was described by an elderly Christian, Fibombe. It illustrates very clearly the com-bination of practical precaution—isolation—and magical pro-tection, and also the idea that sickness was brought into the country by witches.

When the chief had heard that smallpox was coming, or dysentery, he said, 'Let us pray'. Before my baptism I saw it, in the country of the

---

[1] cf. Monica Wilson, *Good Company*, pp. 92-4.

Penja chief, Mwalukasa. He called all his people because he heard that smallpox was coming and said: 'Let us pray.' And he called his fellow chiefs, those of the same lineage, and said: 'Let this illness not come, may it go to other chiefs. . . . Listen! I am the chief! We have heard that smallpox is approaching, who is here who rejoices at his approach? Who is here who wishes that it should kill us?'

THE CHIEFS: We, we do not rejoice that it is coming, we reject it, chief Mwalukasa, may it pass by this homestead.

THE COMMONERS: And we also reject it, may it pass by our homesteads.

MWALUKASA: And I, I reject it, may smallpox not come into our country. If there be one who has relatives in a chiefdom where there is smallpox and they come to call him to a funeral let them stay at a distance, and not sleep here, let him not go near until the illness has passed by, at the end of the year. If you witches go to fetch it, you will kill your fellows with whom you are chatting now. You will not enjoy my company or build with me, the chief, if you go and bring in smallpox and kill your fellows. We pray that it may pass. [For it is believed in this country that the witches go to bring in illness, or wild animals, from a distance.]

THE COMMONERS: Yes, indeed, may it pass by.

MWALUKASA: If you go to bury a brother in a country in which there is smallpox stand afar off, tie the cow you bring to a tree and call to them: 'Here is my cow for killing, come and take it.' Take your cow, but do not go into the homestead.

And the people did as he said. Then he told them to get ready for the ritual. He took his calabash cup and three other chiefs with calabash cups followed him. They blew water and prayed to Kyala and the shades. Then the people were gathered together; and the chiefs, led by Mwalukasa, ran round facing each group in turn and blowing out water towards them; the men held their shields in front of them and when the chiefs blew they shook their shields violently, as if fighting.

When all was finished then Mwalukasa said: 'When you go home, throw out the ashes and the fires; all make new fire with drills.' And they all did this.

Finally he had bamboos planted with medicine on the main roads between BuPenja and BuKukwe and BuPenja and BuNyiha. No one ill with smallpox, or who had lived in contact with smallpox, was allowed to pass, unless he had been ill and recovered. I saw the one bamboo clump on the boundary of Nyiha and Penja country. No one passed it, it was very fearsome (*lusisya fijo*).

As in cultivation there was a combination of ritual and science.

(d) THE WILD PIG

Another sort of cleansing, unorganized, but concerning groups of neighbours, not kinsmen, is the 'blessing one another' (*ukusajana*) which takes place if a pig-hunt fails and quarrelling between the hunters is suspected to be the cause. It was described by a Christian, who had called his pagan neighbours to help him in tracking down a pig, which he had wounded during the previous night in his maize garden. It eluded them, hour after hour, though they were close upon it.

The neighbours began to think that the pig was sent by the shades (*sili nemindu*)—they meant themselves. So they stopped hunting and gathered together to express their anger, and they said: 'Our fathers built together and drank beer together, why should this pig trouble us so? We don't suspect our friend who is a Christian for he has shown that he has no quarrel with us. Had he been angry he would not have called us to hunt with him. But if one of the rest of us has a quarrel with his fellow let him speak out, that we may all be free of anger (*tuje belu*) and seize the pig, for if we think hard thoughts about one another we shall not have strength to take the pig.' All said that they were in friendship with their fellows, so first one and then another took his spear and . . . laid it on the ground and said: 'I am without anger (*Une ndimwelu itolo*).' All of them did this. One spoke to his fellow and said: 'Perhaps you are angry over that quarrel we had over beer?' But he replied, 'No.' Then the first man took up his spear from the ground and said, 'Father help us to catch this pig, if there was a quarrel, forgive, do not think of that with which I caused you to be angry. We bless one another, we are without anger.' Then all the others did the same, and they set off again to hunt.

This account, and the commentary of Mwaikambo on it, made it plain that the true translation of *belu* in such a context is 'without anger'. The communal rituals in which a whole chiefdom, or a group of neighbours, participate all have this one end, the cleansing of the group of quarrels by their open expression and explicit rejection.

CHAPTER VIII

RAIN-MAKING AND 'SPRINKLING THE HOMESTEADS'

Two activities which are closely linked with sacrifice at the groves of chiefs, but which are distinguished from them because they consist in the manipulation of medicines, rather than prayers and oblations, are 'rain-making' and 'sprinkling the homesteads' to ensure fertility of the soil.

(a) RAIN MAGIC

Rain-makers (*abapelafula*) are men who use perforated instruments called 'rain' (*ifula*) to produce rain or sunshine. The heroes were believed to create rain by the virtue in their own bodies, but the Kyungu also had a much prized instrument of iron, perforated 'like a mouth organ', and several of the chiefs had perforated stones which were used to 'make rain'. In most cases the care of them was delegated to a junior kinsman, a commoner, or (in Ngonde) even a slave, but often the office became hereditary and rain-makers were men of considerable power. Such was Kasitile whose grandfather (44), a younger brother of the chief Mwamu-kinga (43), had been entrusted with his rain stones. The Kyungu was thought to control the rain in the whole of the Ngonde plain, the Lwembe in an area less clearly defined, but which included Selya, BuKinga, and parts of the Nyakyusa plain, Kyala in the eastern portion of the Nyakyusa plain, and parts of BuKinga and BuKisi. Chiefs were credited with making local rain, in their own countries.

The technique of 'making' rain was to seal the holes in the perforated instruments with ointment and immerse them in water.

The rain instrument that helped Kyungu was called Mulima. Its holes were its eyes. If they were empty it would be empty in the sky above also, there would be no clouds; if some were full then there would be a few clouds, if all were full then there would be many clouds and rain. If it were raining and he put it in a tree so that its eyes looked up, then the sun would shine. . . . If he opened its eyes that they might be empty and put it in a tree so that it looked up then the clouds dried up above, the sky also became empty.

The imagination of the Nyakyusa doctor who invented this magic was near enough to that of Shakespeare to be intelligible to an Englishman. The sun is an 'eye'. Clouds may close it. Holes in a rain instrument are also 'eyes' and if these are closed the 'eye of heaven' will also shut—with clouds.

The Kyungu seems to have kept Mulima (which was only 'the size of a spectacle case') on him, but the ordinary instruments—stones—were left in the chiefs' groves with potsherds in which they were immersed in water when required.

Kyungu Mwakabange had his rain-makers Mugoma and Komanga. Mugoma was a slave, Komanga a man of Ngonde. When the sky was hard he sent a message to them saying: 'Put them into water.' If there were too much rain he said: 'Take them out.' Each had two potsherds with two stones for each. To make rain they rubbed the stones with mutton fat and a medicine called *ilifugo* (fertility) and put them into the sherds and poured water over them.

Godfrey Wilson was taken by Kasitile to see his rain stones in the grove near his house in April 1935. Kasitile addressed his shades:[1]

My fathers, do not be angry, *Mwakalebela* (19) (he spat), *Mwanjala* (23), *Mwakisambwe* (30), *Mwakilima* (31), *Mwamapondele* (27), *Mwakihaba* (45), *Mwamukinga* (44), Mwalubange (58), Mwakagile (59), Mwandemele (?), Mwakanjoki (60), Mwaijonga (82), Mwafungo (83), Mwamwifu (84), Mwakabule (117), Mwaipopo (115), these are our friends (repeated urgently), you did not know them, you feared them, but now we do not fear them, they have come and met with us as friends.

There was a large broken pot and three stones, two of them with holes an inch or so in diameter. There used to be five stones —two had been stolen by the Ngoni when they raided this country. When he wishes to make rain, water drawn from a water-fall is brought by Kasitile's wife and left overnight in the grove. Then he pours it into the pot and puts in the stones . . . 'the water bubbles; it is cold, but it seems to boil and the *ifula* go whirling and knocking against the sides of the pot.' . . . The bubbling of the water is compared with rain. Kasitile did not know where his stones had come from. Mwakisambwe his great-grandfather had

---

[1] The names italicized are those G.W. actually heard in the grove; the whole list was given by Kasitile afterwards as names he had mentioned, but in fact he had not mentioned more than eight.

them first, then his grandfather, and father. Others told us that
rain stones always came from Kisi country, a very wet strip of
land on the north-east shore of the Lake where the clouds always
seem to gather when one looks south from the Nyakyusa valley
and plain, and a piece of perforated wood used in Ngonde for
making rain came from the hills of Misuku, also a very wet
country. Kasitile's stones were of two types, but no direct association of male and female was made. However, the Kukwe spoke
of a 'mother' stone having young. 'The rain-maker puts back the
stone in the potsherd without water (after rain has come) and
going later he finds that it has got young, perhaps seven, with the
mother there are eight.'

The rain-makers are subject to certain taboos: during the dry
season they may not wash lest they drive away the rain nor do they
shave for 'they compare hair and clouds saying, "Let it be black",
they compare a bald pate with sunshine.' And the rain-maker
may not eat roasted maize 'for as the maize crackles in the potsherd when it is roasted, so the thunder will crackle in the sky'.
He may not eat green maize (which is reaped during the rains)
until the dry weather begins 'because he creates rain, which
means he creates all the food which grows with the rain'. If he
begins eating too soon he may stop the growth. And when the
rain-maker is manipulating his instruments a sex taboo is observed.
'When I am making rain,' said Kasitile, 'I do not sleep with my
wives for two days, it's taboo. How would Kyala help us if I did?'

In theory the rain-maker always works under the direction of
the political authority—the Kyungu or a chief—but he is also
thought to wreak vengeance on those who anger him. Kasitile
was critical of his colleague in the hills above Isumba: 'He never
makes a nice gentle rain, it always destroys food. . . . He is always
demanding things from men, and, if they refuse, he brings his
rain to destroy things. . . . There is a very strong wind and heavy
rain which takes roofs off homes.' But when Kasitile himself was
angry, because his son was taken as a tax defaulter to work on the
roads, the weather grew bad.

People say I am angry, that this rain is because they came and beat
me because of tax. This time the tax collectors came to my place and
beat me and when I thought, 'It is not the custom with our forefathers
for the tax collectors to come at all to men like me', I grew angry and
prayed. . . . When I was in MuNgonde the country suffered from
hunger, all their children were in trouble. . . . Then I came up, and

began to prepare my rain, and made the country good. Food started to be plentiful. Why should I be treated thus? I asked. And the shades and Kyala heard me, so it rained *heavily* (too much). Do I grow angry by my own power? I do, and I put the rain stones in water, and when Kyala hears me then it rains too much, my anger has results; but if Kyala does not agree then, when I go the next day to the grove, I find there is no water in the potsherd. . . . I work by Kyala's power; when water is in the sherd I know it is he who has helped me. . . . We don't do it ourselves, it rains if the shades and Kyala help us. I cannot say that I do things alone without their help, it is they who give me breath (*imbepo*) and when they help I feel the power, the rain will fall very heavily. . . .

The way in which the weather was connected by the people of Selya with Kasitile is illustrated by the following entry in Godfrey Wilson's note-book:

Mwaipopo the chief had omitted to tell Kasitile formally that their kinsman, Mwaikyambe, had died. Kasitile had come to the funeral in the morning, and gone off in a huff saying, 'They did not tell me.' Mwaipopo then sent Ngulyo (the priest) after him with 1s. to pacify him. 'Yes, he paid because he had wronged his father.' Kasitile accepted the 1s. and came back. There had been rain during the night, but the early morning was fine. About 11 a.m. it began to rain, softly at first and then hard. I was in Mwaipopo's house drinking beer. They discussed the rain, hinting that it was caused by Kasitile. 'That Kasitile' was the most direct hint I heard. But they discussed the fact that 'this morning it was raining at Kasitile's,' i.e. that the rain began there and spread over the country. The rain was coming from that direction, it was true, but the morning at Kasitile's had been fine. Ngulyo said, 'When I got to Kasitile's place there was rain.' Suddenly there was a hush and someone whispered: 'Ssh! He is at the door, he is coming in', and Kasitile came in. Mwaipopo apologized again, through Ngulyo, for having omitted to call him: 'I had just got back from Tukuyu, I was surprised that no one had told you, Mwakisambwe (identifying Kasitile with his great-grandfather 30). You too, Ngulyo and Kissogota, are at fault, you should have told him. When I got to the funeral this morning and was told that Mwakisambwe had gone away again saying no one had told him then I sent you to tell him.' All this was said in a rather plaintive voice to Ngulyo, Kasitile being next Ngulyo. Kasitile said nothing. At noon, when we got up and went out, the rain had lessened, and it stopped almost at once. On my way back from the funeral later, I heard one of the young men, a son of Mwaipopo, who was with me, say to the other: 'Kasitile has forgiven, but only partially, the rain has spoilt the ritual.' About 1 p.m. the rain started again and it rained for an hour during the division of the meat; then again it lessened and stopped.

A showery and varied day was turned to account by Kasitile. The way he did it was to keep quite silent about the rain and about the insult, but let the others talk. No one directly connected the rain with him in his presence, but they talked about how heavy it was, now and again. If there is too much or too little rain, or Kasitile is known to be angry the weather is noticed and connected with him. The conclusion that Kasitile sometimes deliberately played up to the credulity of his neighbours is irresistible. But when there was a drought he grew very troubled. In January 1938 there was drought in Mwaipopo's country though in some of the neighbouring chiefdoms there had been heavy rain. We went with Kasitile to visit his fellow priest, Mwamakunda, in the bush country. There was discussion about the drought.

KASITILE: I have put in the rain stones, but nothing has happened, I tremble!
THE OTHERS: Kijaja went into a trance and said: 'Let a cow come from Mwakihaba (45), Mwakilima (31) has driven away his senior kinsmen and refused to send a cow, he has refused to return the cow which was given him by his senior brother. Let him return it, instead of saying: "Let the nasty old man (*ikangale*) celebrate there at his place." Then if it comes there will be much rain and food.' [i.e. Kijaja attributes the drought to the refusal of the junior line of chiefs to send the customary cow for the sacrifice at Mbyanga, *vide supra*, pp. 79-80].
KASITILE: Kijaja has gone into a trance and prophesied just recently. Kyala has brooded over him recently, he is a new prophet, but I, Kasitile, have not heard [i.e. have not been formally notified]. Had we been together with Kijaja I would have argued with him and silenced him. See! In Mwakihaba's country it has rained; it has rained heavily there, but not here. I would have said: 'Kijaja you are a new prophet. . . .' But I don't know about this rain. . . . Had I consulted an oracle the cause would have come to light.
MWAMAKUNDA (came and sat down): What about this rain? Have you put them in water?
KASITILE: Yes, I have put them in water and nothing happens, I put them in water and nothing happens. I have not consulted an oracle about this rain. . . . I tremble. . . .
MWAMAKUNDA: Yes, indeed! Consult an oracle. . . . Then you did put them in water. . .?
KASITILE: They have lain there two weeks, but the rain refuses to come.

10a. KASITILE THE PRIEST

10b. DIVINATION WITH PORRIDGE

11. RUNGWE CHURCH

. . . I put the stones into water, it is as if someone spilt it out, the sherd dries up. . . . Now Kyala has gone away, the shades have fled, formerly they clapped their hands (indicating satisfaction). . . . There is something about which the shade is angry, because in this homestead we were accustomed to pray frequently. . . . If I boast saying: 'It will rain tomorrow', will it rain?

MWAMAKUNDA THE YOUNGER (gravely, and with hesitation): No, not if Kyala does not wish.

WIFE OF MWAMAKUNDA: But formerly it agreed [i.e. the rain came].

A day or two later Kasitile came in, during the evening, with Mwalusanye, a young doctor, the son of doctors.

K.: This rain, do you not ask about it?

G.W.: Have you been to consult the oracle?

K.: Yes. I consulted it the day before yesterday.

G.W.: What did it say?

K.: It said: 'Your fathers are angry, and Kyala and the Holy Spirit (*NuMbepo Mwikemo*)!'

G.W.: What do they say we have done wrong?

K.: Since Mwaipopo received a Court what have the chiefs given us to say 'We did wrong?' Did they give me a cow? They did not. [Here Kasitile was referring to the insult to Lubaga, *vide supra*, pp. 35-8, and he identifies himself with the priests of Lubaga.] In MuNgonde I was a commoner, I ate meat, here I live hungry.

G.W.: And now who will speak out about this matter?

K.: You, you tell Mwaipopo 'Ask Pikumbaba (Kasitile 86) why this rain does not come, what has happened to it?'

G.W. refused and asked: Who should suggest this according to custom?

K.: Mwamakunda.

MWALUSANYE: Because according to custom, Mwaipaja (G.W.), if things were as they are with us now, if the rain refused, our fathers came to Kasitile (60), the father of this one, to ask him saying, 'Kasitile what has happened to the rain?' But now that our fathers are dead, we are bad, we do not ask.

And a few days later the chief said: We have thrown away our food, it's drying up in the ground . . . this drought! Kasitile says: 'It has defeated me . . . the shades (*imindu*) have caught hold of us.' Perhaps they claim a cow, perhaps it is because Mwaihojo (147) and his fellows paid here. . . . But those beneath are angry (pointing downwards and speaking with conviction), the owner is angry.

The rain-maker therefore is not conceived of as working independently; the goodwill of the shades of the chief is necessary, and perhaps also those of the rain-maker himself, though this is not quite clear. Nowadays, at least, Kyala is also invoked. In

I

drought, as in illness, a number of possible causes are discussed, and if one possible cause is dealt with and yet the drought persists, another will be put forward. A shrewd priest or doctor can turn this to account and find many reasons for the failure of his ritual, as the following case shows.

In the wet Nyakyusa valley rain-makers are not concerned only with drought, but also with flood, and, in the years 1935-8, with the rise in the level of the Lake which inundated many gardens.[1] On the Nyakyusa plain the rise was attributed to the action of a Kisi doctor, Mwatabi, who had first boasted that he could bring up the Lake and then been commissioned by the chief, Mwakalukwa (141), to do so, 'because there was much grass by the Lake and many mosquitoes, and it was dirty there'. He was told to 'take the Lake up a bit, but not too far' and given a sheep. Then, the following season, in April (a month of torrential rain), Mwakalukwa's son Mwakisisile (170, for Mwakalukwa himself had died) gave him a little bull saying,

Send the Lake back, it has come too far. Then the doctor went home thinking to himself, 'Why does he give me such a little bull?' and he met a headman of the neighbouring chief, Mwakabulufu (138), and said, 'Why should I send the Lake back, Mwakisisile has given me a bull only; had he given me a cow, I'd have done so, but now I am angry.' Then Mwakabulufu heard and sent a message to say he would provide a cow, since Mwakalukwa was dead. But the doctor refused: 'No, Mwakalukwa (the son, 170) is still alive, he must give it.' The following September, before the usual end of the dry season, there was rain on the plain. It is the Kisi's rain. Mwakisisile (170) refused to give him anything, he said he was a liar, but the commoners collected 30s. and a goat, and the Kisi performed a ritual just recently, and said: 'The Lake will go back, but my strength will bring the rain; it will rain during the dry season this month.' We laughed very much in Tukuyu to hear such a prophecy, but it is raining!

The following year—after the Lake had risen again—another reason was given. It was said that a rain-maker at Bojo in Kisi country had died, and just before he died he had thrown a rain stone into the Lake.

(b) MAGIC OF FERTILITY

We did not learn very much about 'sprinkling the homesteads';

---

[1] There is a periodic rise and fall in the level of the Lake. In 1937 the Lake steamer was anchoring in what had been the roof-tree of the District Commissioner's house at Karonga.

it was something done secretly, at night, and feared by everyone. Ambilikile related how, as a small boy growing up on the plain, he had been severely beaten by his mother when he called out one night, hearing a noise in the bananas, for it was made by the doctor 'sprinkling the homesteads'. The doctor heard and entered their hut angrily, and seized some of the calabashes. The medicine for sprinkling sometimes—probably always—contained human flesh, hence the anxiety of mothers not to draw the attention of the fearful doctor to their children. In Selya, after the sacrifice at Lubaga, the Kinga returned to Kasitile's homestead to sprinkle a medicine which contained the flesh of the child they had killed for the drum, and Mwamakunda (his assistant) went round by night pruning the bananas throughout Mwaipopo's country with a sacred knife, which was kept in Kasitile's homestead and Kasitile put porridge of banana flour, made from a stem of bananas provided by the chief's senior wife, in the grove called Kinyangwa ('the porridge of banana flour') near his house. Then fertility was said to spread from Kasitile's throughout the country. According to Kasitile himself, the medicine contained an ingredient he did not know . . .

My elder brother died without showing me the tree. . . . Mwamakunda does not know it either, he just got it from my father. We hope that it will appear in a dream, but it has not yet been revealed. . . . We dreamed of a cow, and of Mwaipaja (G.W.), but the medicine was not seen. I will seek another from a doctor . . . perhaps from Misuku.[1]

At this time also, in some—perhaps all—chiefdoms millet was taken from the sacred pot containing the 'power of growth', i.e. the hair and nails of the dead chiefs (*vide supra*, pp. 64-5) to mix with the millet seed about to be planted.

Besides this secret and fearsome 'sprinkling' on behalf of chiefdoms, there was a much more open use of medicines for fertility by village groups, when they burnt the rubbish heaps in which they planted millet,[2] and by private individuals in their own fields.

During the hot weather a chief sometimes sends to all the villages of his chiefdom a man, curiously dressed in a cap and jerkin of banana leaves, who forbids people to cut their bananas, or even leaves of banana stems that have not

---

[1] A district famous for its medicines.

[2] cf. Monica Wilson, *Good Company*, pp. 52-4.

yet fruited, and tells them to eat beans, sweet potatoes, and cow peas instead. The owner of a grove can cut a stem of bananas only with the permission of the man who proclaims the prohibition (*ugwa lusingo*), and those who trespass pay him a fine of a hen, a knife, a pot, or their sleeping mats. The avowed purpose is that 'bananas should ripen in all the homesteads and the country appear rich and productive', but there may be further implications which we did not discover.

CHAPTER IX

KASITILE THE PRIEST

WE turn now from the description of rituals to a personal docu-
ment, an account of the illness of Kasitile (86), the leading priest
of Selya, the causes suggested for it, and the rituals performed.
His case shows: (i) the power of village headmen over chiefs in
general, more particularly the power of the commoner priests
(village headmen of the previous generation) over hereditary
priests of the chief's lineage; (ii) the persistent linking of misfortune
with sin in both public and private life; (iii) the function of
divination in selecting between possible causes of disease; (iv)
the influences of Christian and Muslim teaching and Western
medical science on a conservative who goes so far as to invite a
Muslim to cut the throat of the sacrificial animal and speaks of
turning Christian in his old age; and (v) the very great importance
attached to 'speaking out' (*ukusosya*) and not leaving anger to
smoulder unconfessed. Beer is necessary for such a ritual 'speaking
out' and the participants are pressed to drink deep, for *in vino
veritas*.

The *dramatis personae* are:

KASITILE (86) of the chief's lineage, priest of Selya
JANE his senior and favourite wife
JANE'S YOUNGER SISTER and co-wife
KILULELE a third wife suspected of bewitching Kasitile
MWAIPOPO (116) the chief and senior kinsman of Kasitile
MWAKYONDE (148) the doctor who was treating Kasitile
KINGA *priests* (i.e. Kikungubeja Nsyanigwa, Kyamba Kitali,
vide pp. 24-34)
NGULUYO ⎤
NJOBOKOSA ⎬ Village headmen of Mwaijonga (82) and priests of
KISSOGOTA ⎦ his grove, *vide* pp. 74-7, 84-5
MWAMAKUNDA THE ELDER a hereditary priest, assistant to Kasitile
MWAMAKUNDA THE YOUNGER (Mwambagoje) son of the elder who
often acted in his place

NDEMBWE ⎫
NSOKI   ⎪
NSESA   ⎬ Diviners consulted by Kasitile
A SANGU ⎭
NDISA a kinsman of Kasitile

It will be remembered that, in accordance with the custom of delegating ritual functions to a junior line, Kasitile's grandfather (44) had been appointed rain-maker and priest responsible for receiving the Kinga when they came to sacrifice at Lubaga. Kasitile thus held an important public office. He was living on the plain (where he had inherited the estate of his father's younger brother) where his own elder brother (85) died and he came up into Selya to bury him and succeed to his position. But he failed to notify the Kinga priests of his brother's death and they were very angry, and told him he would die if he stayed in the homestead, so he fled back to the plain. There he fell ill, and he was carried back to Selya to be treated by the visiting Kinga priests, who told him he was sick 'because he went to the plain in a hurry and they had not given him medicine'. The idea here is that the heir to a chief or priest must cultivate the power that was in his father's body by drinking medicines: Kasitile was 'losing the *ifingila* of his father by not drinking medicines'. Now *ifingila* implies *both* the medicines of chieftainship and the power which they create in the body of a man.

So Kasitile was treated and we quote his own account of what happened:

The Kinga came to cook medicine by the tree where I pray—it is where the cattle byre of my elder brother was. They put some medicine for Jane [his senior wife] and me in beer ... and we drank together ... and they boiled medicines in a pot and told us both to wash with the infusion every day for two months. I found a goat and called the priests Ngulyo, Njobakosa, and Kissogota and ... they and the Kinga priests ate the meat together, and they told me to stay for two months and return to the plain again, and so I did. Then the Kinga sent for me to come back and I've come up to live. I found a cow, and called the priests and killed it at the sacred grove, Kinyangwa, and all the people ate the meat. Then the Kinga told me to move to my father's old homestead, and I did so this very year.

Before we arrived, therefore, Kasitile had been in conflict with his fellow priests, and he had been very ill, and attributed his illness to neglect of his duty to the Kinga. All the time we were in BuNyakyusa he was ailing—possibly he suffered from tuberculosis—and one wrongdoing after another was suggested as the cause of his illness.

His case is intelligible only in terms of the conception of 'the breath of men', that is, a power akin to witchcraft thought to be legitimately exercised by village headmen and others to punish wrongdoers, but which is referred to by the victims as 'witchcraft'. This has been discussed at length elsewhere.[1]

On 2nd July 1935, Kasitile had left his own house and was living with a friend in a neighbouring village. His doctor, Mwakyonde, said that he was being 'throttled by the witches' and had invited him to come and recollect himself (ukwipelekesya) in the tranquillity of a village of another chiefdom in which there were many people with spiritual power (abamanga) so that 'the witches' could not get at him. This is a common precaution in case of illness, for witches are thought not to have power ordinarily outside their own village and never beyond the chiefdom.[2]

The cause of the illness was explained as follows: Kasitile had quarrelled with Kissogota, the commoner priest, and others of the principal men of the country, because he had found them drinking the sacred beer (ubwikemo), brewed after the millet harvest (vide supra, pp. 84-5) without telling him, or sending him the pot which was his due. They invited him to drink, but he refused and they each sent him 1s. to beg pardon. Kasitile bought beer with one of the shillings and called the senior commoner priest, Ngulyo, and his fellows to drink saying, 'I was angry, friends, you "overstepped" me' (i.e. they had ignored his rights). He himself should have brewed when he confessed his anger, and slaughtered a calf or prepared food for them as well, but he had bought only one shilling's worth of beer and provided nothing himself. Then, when they had drunk, Kasitile fell ill. Hence it was said that the commoner priests were angry and 'ate' (i.e. bewitched) him. Kasitile's own comment was: 'The fault lies with the young priests (Ngulyo, a young man, had inherited his father's position), they are useless as priests . . . I was not told of that ritual beer, yet the medicine comes from me, from this home where I keep it. They should have come to me to get it and put it with the millet in the holy pot. They drank the beer without medicine. It is they who have brought cold and hunger on the country. I think the

---

[1] Monica Wilson, *Good Company*, pp. 91-121, 167-9.　　　[2] *op. cit.*, pp. 102-3.

trouble is that Mwaipopo (the chief 116) is getting old. . . .'
Here Kasitile suggested two different causes for the scarcity in the
country: (a) the negligence of the priests, and (b) the senility of the
chief. In the old days Mwaipopo would have been smothered, as
Angombwike explained (vide supra, p. 63).

On the 9th, Kasitile, much troubled by his cough at night,
expressed a great desire for the return of the missionary nurse to
Kabembe hospital. 'She is killing us by her absence, the black
people don't know anything about these things, only the Europeans. Why, I went there and the dresser just gave me an injection
without taking my temperature—no European ever does that.'

The following day he sent off his sons with 10 c. to inquire about
his case from a diviner. The diviner said: 'The wives at his home
are gossiping to other people about their husband. People want
the husband's body to be light. It is not Jane, because she is his
favourite, but the others.' Kasitile said:

I shan't do anything, I said 'Let's leave it.' I am still in Butola [the
village to which he moved for safety]. Mwakyonde is giving me medicine for my disease. It drives out the cold which is in my body. Yes, the
cold is the breath of the witches coming to throttle me—it's due to my
wives' gossip. But it started as a quarrel with other people [non-
relatives] first. One day I went to drink beer in Bujege and that night
I fell sick; that is how it began. Men are complaining because I, a
chief, a senior, do not cook food for them. They throttle me on that
account. They say: 'Let us see whether he is really a chief, a senior!'
But others say: 'He has done no wrong.' Yes, the sickness took me on
the way home from the beer. Perhaps Kyala asked: 'What has he
done?' and found I had done no wrong. If there had not been a Kyala
who saves us I would have been dead.

When I consulted a diviner he struck a spear and looked along it,
then he said: 'The disease now is from his wives—the earlier attack
was from men, but this one is from his wives. When they gather at the
hearth they say: "Come hither, we see him where he sleeps." '

'Are the wives witches?' we asked.
Kasitile replied:

Yes. They say: 'There is a favourite, we are not beloved.' If a man's
wives are good the witches can get into the house, but their cold breath
dissipates quickly; you are given medicine and recover quickly; but
if the wives are bad they gather together the medicine and press it
down, so that it is powerless. One of my wives is very bad, her lineage
is bad, it is she who calls to her aid the heavy ones, the witches. The

younger one[1] gossips with her fellow, she does not go to the witches herself, but just talks to the other wife who calls the witches to her aid. These two wives say: 'The favourite has borne many children to her husband; we are poor' [i.e. the favourite gets an unfair share of her husband's attentions].

Kasitile speaks of his wives as 'witches' which, according to Nyakyusa ideas, they were, if they injured him, but he was also in the wrong to have shown his preference for Jane so clearly. As was shown in *Rituals of Kinship*, the shades are thought to punish such favouritism.

Towards the end of August Kasitile went to consult Ndembwe, a diviner and doctor, living nearly a day's journey away in the hills, who used a 'stick in the ground' as a divining rod. On his return Kasitile reported:

Ndembwe says it's the 'breath of men', not the wives, but the dispute about the beer. I paid him 1s. and drank three preparations of medicine at his place. He is coming here—I have found some beer and I am sending to call him tomorrow. Then Kasitile added confidentially: About the source of the 'breath' I am uncertain. Ndembwe suggested testing my wives. He can see the heavy ones, for in Ndali country he has drunk much medicine to give him spiritual power (*amanga*). He told me to come home, not to go back to Mwakyonde's country, and he is coming to give me medicine to drink and also to sprinkle medicine in the house. He will sleep here and see who it is that comes—he will know if the wives are heavy, or if it is the people of the country.

Kasitile's uncertainty was apparent. The first diviner had stated clearly that the sickness came from the witchcraft of the wives, but Kasitile wanted a further test.

We were away from Selya for some time and did not hear of any further developments in Kasitile's illness until early in 1937. By then a new reason for his ill-health had been put forward, viz. his impiety in cutting all the branches off a tree growing at the entrance to a sacred grove which has sprung up over his father's grave. He cut the tree because it was encroaching on his homestead. Then he fell ill and he went to consult Ndembwe again.

He asked me: 'Have you done something wrong at home?' I replied: 'No, I have done nothing wrong.' 'But the oracle says you have done wrong at home.' I said: 'Perhaps it is because I cut a tree at the

---

[1] Sister of the favourite Jane. To accuse Jane's sister would cast a slur on Jane, for witchcraft is normally hereditary.

entrance to the grove?' Ndembwe told me, 'You will get no cattle', and indeed the cows are aborting. He told me: 'Brew beer and look for a sheep[1] and pray to your grandfather.'

Kasitile did not find an animal for sacrifice. He slaughtered a kid 'just for meat', killing it near the grove, but without praying or taking any of the meat into the grove, for it is not customary to offer goat's meat to the shades. His health improved a little, for a time, but again he got worse and went off to see another diviner, saying: 'Perhaps there is some other cause; perhaps Ndembwe is mistaken.' He decided to go to consult an oracle some distance away 'because the oracle near home does not convince us; those who live near know all our wrongdoings; those at a distance don't know the affairs of the homesteads here'. This time Godfrey Wilson was invited to accompany him 'since he was his friend'.

Record of G.W. 8/2/37
We left Isumba about 7 a.m. and walked for an hour over the hills through the bush. Kasitile had sent his wives, Jane and Kiluleli, on ahead to tell the diviner, Nsoki, that we were coming. . . . He came in from the fields to meet us and was taken aback by the presence of a European. Kasitile kept saying: 'Do not be startled, he is from home, he is our friend.' . . . Food was served, then Nsoki's wife brought out some cooked millet porridge for the divination. He broke off a large piece and began to roll it between his hands. He smeared ointment on his hands and added powdered medicine. . . . He rolled and rolled, sometimes throwing the ball up and catching it again, spitting on his hands meantime. He murmured as he rolled, then at last he said to Kasitile, 'Speak!' Kasitile called his two wives to come near, and he explained his symptoms and the circumstances, how the sickness had fallen on him just after he had cut the tree in the sacred grove.

Nsoki asked for other possibilities. Kasitile: 'Perhaps the country is angry—I am a senior there. If it is the fathers who are angry I admit having done wrong. Perhaps my wives have committed adultery in the long grass and they are the cause of the illness.' Nsoki rolled and rolled the ball of porridge speaking aloud: 'It is Kyala above?' (looking up). Kasitile interrupted him: 'Yes, indeed, Kyala, but Kyala stands where he stood at home, does he stand alone? He stands with the fathers.' Nsoki (as he rolled the porridge): 'Your fathers are angry about that grove?' Then the ball of porridge flattened out in his hands and he broke off . . . 'No, that is not the cause' (*vide* plate 10*b*).

Rolling it into a ball again he went on: 'Your wives have committed

---

[1] This was Kasitile's own account. Others told us that he had been advised to look for a *bull*.

adultery?' Again the ball flattened. 'It denies it.'[1] Then Kasitile, obviously dissatisfied, spoke: 'Nsoki, three cows have slipped their calves at my home, I sent to Ndembwe and he said: "Your fathers are angry, you cut a tree, Mwakisambwe (30) is angry; seek something", so I sought a kid and I recovered. Later I took my bill-hook and cut all round. Now the illness has begun again, and I thought perhaps it was because I did not go to BuKinga to buy a bull, because I sought only a kid?' Nsoki (no longer rolling the porridge): 'Perhaps my oracle is mistaken, it denies it, Kyala above has sent the breath (imbepo) to discipline you. I asked the oracle saying, "Perhaps it is the fathers?" but see, it denied it.' Kasitile: 'No, it is not mistaken.' Then he told all over again the story of his pruning the grove and of his illness and of his recovery after killing the kid, concluding 'then I cut again and fell sick.' Nsoki: 'But Kasitile, see! There is much illness about, Kyala has sent it all through the country, to discipline us.'

Shortly afterwards we left. I apologized to Kasitile for spoiling his divination for it was obvious, from his face, that it had gone wrong. He assured me that I had done no wrong but agreed that Nsoki had been afraid of me. . . . 'He feared your body, Mwaipaja [G.W.], you are impressive (nsisya), no one builds together with Europeans, he feared to speak. . . . Do you suppose that Kyala alone sent the fever? No! He stands with people, he stands with the shades.' I asked him what he thought. 'Ndembwe's oracle was not mistaken, the shades were indeed angry, but now Nsoki's oracle denies it. It really denied it, I saw the porridge with my own eyes, so I think the illness is from another source now. When he spoke of the "breath of Kyala" he meant "men".' Kasitile lowered his voice as he said this.

QUESTION: But what quarrel have they with you?

KASITILE: None! The oracle denied this. I have done no wrong . . . (later on) He spoke of the fathers, but he was afraid to speak out— they are angry; I should seek something.

QUESTION: To eat with whom?

KASITILE: With the village headman . . . (later on) See Mwaipaja, I cut the grove and at once I fell ill. If you come from doing something and fall ill, do you not begin to wonder? The shades are angry.

He was quite incoherent. First he said the 'breath of men', then the shades, then that the oracle denied the shades—'I saw it do so'—then that it denied witchcraft and that anyway he'd given no occasion for it. The one thing clear was that the divination could not be accepted as it stood. Kyala never acts alone in Nyakyusa thought, and Kasitile's conversation reflected the uncertainty of mind which he had gone to Nsoki to have resolved and which had not been resolved. His opinion

---

[1] He explained later that 'if the porridge becomes fluid and soft, that means it agrees to what has been said; if it does not change, it denies it'.

clearly inclined to the shades as it had before the divination, but as before the certain conviction was lacking.

Four days later (12/2/37) Kasitile went to Nsesa in Kituli village to consult the oracle again 'for that of Nsoki went wrong'. He told us afterwards 'This oracle supported the finding of Ndembwe's. It said: Your kinsman who is dead is angry; he says, "Why did you not celebrate the ritual? I am tired of the hair (*Ngatele nasyo inwili*). And what did you offer your father after cutting that tree?" ' Here yet another cause of Kasitile's illness is suggested—the neglect of the death ritual of a kinsman. The implication is that the chief mourners have not yet performed the concluding rite of shaving which makes it possible for the deceased to join his fathers. The hair which the mourners shave off is called 'the hair of the corpse'.

QUESTION: What are you going to do then?

KASITILE: I shall charge the young man, son of my dead kinsman, with neglect, and tell him to celebrate the ritual that the shades which have bound me may go out of my body.

QUESTION: And the bull?

KASITILE: If I can find one I shall kill it.

QUESTION: Who will be there?

KASITILE: The priests will be there, Ngulyo, Kissogota, Njobakosa, Mwalukuta and Mwakasukula,[1] and also Mwaipopo (116) himself. Were I a commoner I should kill alone with my younger brothers, but since I am a public personage (*ndi nkulumba*) the village headmen are there. (To Mwaikambo, the clerk.) It is good at your home in the hills; here things are bad.

QUESTION: But they also have shades?

KASITILE: But they are not important. Look you, I just cut a tree and they have seized me and dwell in my body. Are there sacred groves in the hills? Do men visit them? There in the hills rituals have died; the puberty ritual and the rituals of the groves are celebrated very little.

On 27th March Kasitile looked in to say that he was going to consult a visiting Sangu doctor 'from very far off' about his cough, but G.W. had better not come lest his presence spoil the divination. Kasitile came again after the consultation, full of excitement. 'What a doctor! That is a doctor indeed! That is a diviner! He took an axe and divined with it; he took coppers which I brought and threw them in a little pot, together with the axe, and ash, and he said: "You also take ash and throw it in" and I did so. Then he looked into the little pot and said: "You built on the plain!" He knew this without being told! I said: "Yes".'

SANGU: There was a quarrel there.

---

[1] The last two are priests of Mbyanga (*vide* p. 80) who did not in fact come. Mwamakunda, Kasitile's assistant, who did come is not mentioned.

KASITILE: Yes indeed.

SANGU: Now your body is sick, you are coughing.

KASITILE: Yes indeed, I am ill, and I am coughing a great deal.

SANGU: Yes, it is that quarrel down there. You came with the cough from the plain.

KASITILE: Yes, I came with it.

SANGU: You are a priest, you are a senior priest. (He knew this himself!)

KASITILE: Yes indeed.

SANGU: But the cough comes from the quarrel in the plain. If you were not a priest you would have died.

KASITILE: Indeed, we quarrelled over land, over the boundaries, on the plain. I hoed someone else's land—the land of a commoner there.

SANGU: They placed something to injure you.

Kasitile paused in his narrative and we asked how the 'something' operated.

KASITILE: In dreams, by means of their witchcraft.

The Sangu told me: 'It is this which causes you to cough continually, but there is something else also, you did not move to the plain from here without trouble.'

KASITILE: No, I moved with an accusation against me.

SANGU: Yes indeed, you did wrong and now your fathers are very angry.

KASITILE: Yes, I cut a tree.

SANGU: Mother! You cut a tree? The fathers and Kyala are brooding over you, Kyala is angry and broods over you. Pray, pray very much. It is you who are throttling the cattle of the country.

We expressed surprise and Kasitile continued: 'Yes, indeed. The Sangu said: "It is your wrongdoing (in cutting the tree) which is causing the cows to abort. I will clear out the thing which came with you from the plain. Bring 2s. tomorrow." He's a great doctor, Mwaipaja.'

The astonishing thing was that Kasitile, a man of considerable intelligence and inclined to query the truth of the revelations of some oracles, was so much impressed by the fact that the foreign doctor (staying in the country) knew that he was a priest and had sojourned in the plain, though to anyone knowing KiNyakyusa well his connexion with the plain was apparent in his speech, and his bearing indicated him as a personage.

Talking of the divination three days later, Kasitile told us the Sangu doctor had said: 'You have done wrong at home. This Kyala (pointing to the little pot into which he was looking) knows that Lwembe and the Kinga and your father are angry, your father is very important, he works with Kyala, he is with him.'

As a treatment for the cough the doctor put various ingredients with some live coals into a small calabash and held them against Kasitile's chest 'to clear out the blood of coughing'. To pacify the shades a pot of medicines in water was put on the fire; the doctor, Kasitile, and his 'senior wife' (actually her younger sister, as Jane was away) each held the pot with a crooked finger. Then Kasitile and all his wives and children were sprinkled with the hot medicines. And the doctor told Kasitile to sacrifice a bull.

During the following week preparations for the sacrifice went ahead. Kasitile walked for some hours through the forest to call Mwamakunda, his fellow priest who always assisted him in the celebrations at Lubaga and 'sprinkling the country'. Mwamakunda is a very old man, con-temporary of Kasitile's father, and he asked: 'Are you bringing your European to the sacrifice?'

KASITILE: Yes.

MWAMAKUNDA: But your father Mwakanjoki (60) did not know any Europeans, he feared them, he died without ever meeting one. After your father died, when your elder brother was alive, Europeans came —Germans—and cut down a tree, the *umwali* tree in the sacred grove near Kamesu; blood gushed out, it shouted so that it was heard in BuKinga.

Kasitile explained that the Germans had wanted timber. Afterwards Mwaipopo (the chief 116) sought a sheep and they tried to put the grove to rights ('close up') by sacrificing it. This was the tree beside which the sacred meat was always put when they sacrificed in the grove. Now one branch has grown up again from the roots.

Mwamakunda went on: 'But you did wrong at the beginning not to take the European to pray, and to tell Mwakanjoki (60) that he should not be afraid, the European has made himself our friend.' Kasitile, reporting the interview to us said: 'I concealed that we went together to the grove to pray (*vide supra*, p. 115) and Mwamakunda told me: "Let the European take something, let it stay overnight in the house, and go with him, and pray very much. . . . Mwakanjoki has gone off in a huff from your home, you have offended him yourself. Go with the European, take him to your father's home. Now your father has taken offence, he is shaking your body by night because you cut the tree; you have done wrong." ' i.e. two causes for the anger of the shades and Kasitile's consequent sickness were given: (i) the cutting of the tree by Mwakanjoki's grave and (ii) Godfrey Wilson's presence at rituals and at Kasitile's homestead. So before the sacrifice of expiation for pruning the grove was performed Godfrey Wilson went to be intro-duced to Kasitile's shades for the second time.

Record of G.W. 9/4/37

In the evening as the sun was setting, I went to Kasitile's house with a cloth and 2s. He put them in the house, took down the calabash which always hangs under the eaves and is only used for prayer, filled it with water and put into it a stone and a live coal from the fire. Then he took some roots from the roof (previously put there ready) and we went off to the same spot as before (*vide supra*, p. 115). Kasitile chewed the root, took water and blew it out, and began to pray:

'Do not be startled, come in your own persons, gather together, with Mwakanjoki (60). You made friends with him before, now he has entered, he has made himself our friend. Indeed I made a mistake, I have come to enter; I cut you on the head, I have done wrong. The sons of Kagile (i.e. 59 + his descendants) complain of me, saying, "It is he who has gone off with the millet, bananas, and maize; and children cry at night behind the huts; we are barren because he has cut Mwakanjoki." I have sought this cow which you wanted. Mwakanjoki (60), Lwembe (3?), Mwakalebela (19), Mwatonoka (29), Mwalubange (58), Mwakagile (59), Mwaijonga (82), Kyala (2), we have come to attend to you (pointing to the grave). Kikungubeja, Nsyanigwa Kyamba Kitali,[1] Lyambilo (12) come to your home if you are at Mwalubange's (58), come if you are at Mwaitende's (61), come Mwakanjoki (60) and the Kinga and Lwembe (3); Mwakalebela (19) come, give me cattle and millet, and the powerful medicine which you had. Since you are brooding over me go out from my body, go out! I pay my debt. We have come to take you to your home since you have gone off in a huff, come! I will never cut your branches again. I fear you and I will respect the branches. Come to your house, that of Mwamaloba (85), of Kanjoki (mother of 60), come. And he (G.W.) is innocent (*mwelu*), do not fear him. He is the owner of the ritual, he is Mwamaloba (85), he is my senior, I am the junior. Sometimes I wish to embrace him, sometimes I fear that he is going to imprison me.[2] May the bananas increase! I am left alone! It is I who am here! Move out of my body! And give us medicine! May the offering increase overnight, may the cattle increase and the maize, and in the morning let me tell Mwaipaja (G.W.) that the bananas and medicine have increased. If there is anything else you are a liar, if this chill begins again then I have gone, I am not here. Amen! (*sic*).'

Very early the following morning the sacrificial bull was killed. Kasitile had arranged that our Mohammedan cook should come to cut its throat.[3] Then, later in the morning, the crucial drinking and 'speaking out' began. Kasitile had provided two pots of beer.

[1] Three Kinga priests whose names are titles of office.

[2] In the earlier years of our acquaintance Kasitile had denied both the smothering of an ailing chief and human sacrifice for the drum. It is possible that he had co-operated in either one or both of these ritual acts. He himself reported that the Sangu diviner had told him: 'You have a European as a close friend. . . . You enjoy his company much, but there is something left . . .' (i.e. the friendship is not yet complete).

[3] Ostensibly so that he could partake of the meat, but the reason given seemed inadequate.

Record of G.W. 10/4/37

I was summoned two hours after sunrise and found at Kasitile's: Mwaipopo (the chief 116), Kissogota, Ngulyo, and Njobakosa the commoner priests; Mwamakunda the younger (his father is too weak to come himself), and a half-wit who has attached himself to Kasitile. Mwaipopo asked me: 'Did you escape the rain yesterday evening?' I said, 'No, I was caught by it, I'd come without a coat, and I thought it quite safe as I lived so near' (a quarter of a mile away). Mwaipopo replied: 'Ah, but you were at prayer. Do they not listen? Did you think you would escape the rain when you were at prayer?' and he laughed at me. During the afternoon it began to thunder close by. Kasitile glanced round and whispered to me out of the corner of his mouth: 'They are listening!'

Drinking continued all day, and all day, with intervals, they discussed the case (*ukujoba inongwa*) or spoke out (*ukusosya*) or prayed (*ukwiputa*). This half formal prayer (*ukwiputa*) over beer is an essential part of the ritual. They began by discussing the cutting of the tree by Kasitile. 'They are angry, Mwakanjoki (60) is angry, he is startled that Mwamaloba (i.e. Kasitile 86) cut him himself. Mwakanjoki says, 'Who is there?' [i.e. Kasitile did it without formally telling the shades about it]. They (*sic*) went off in a huff . . . we have come to fetch him (*sic*) back.'

Then Kastile told them about his prayer and how he had admitted his fault saying: 'Indeed, I, your wife, have done wrong, Mwakanjoki (60), indeed I come to enter, I Mwamaloba (86), I am a woman.' 'If you went to Mwalubange's (58) come, if you went to Mwaitende's (61) come.' 'Yes,' Kissogota broke in, 'you are a woman, and also you are a man, take the calabash cup and pray. It is you then (who are at fault).' 'Thank you,' said the others, 'thank you Mwakisambwe (Kasitile is identified with his great-grandfather, 30), thank you Mwakagile (Mwaipopo, 116), is identified with his grandfather, 59), for praying with water.' (Mwaipopo had also prayed at his place.)

So the discussion continued. 'We try everything, a sacred stem of bananas from Kalinga (senior widow of 115) is cut, it goes (to the shades), people milk their cows, they collect millet (*vide* pp. 84-5, 121), we try everything, we try everything.'

Then Mwamakunda started a new topic, the old *umwali* tree: 'But friends, do you say they have gone away now? They went away long ago. Did this *umwali* tree fall when Kasitile (60, father of the present one) was alive?' 'When he was dead,' they agreed. 'Well, then, where has your wisdom disappeared to?' 'Yes indeed,' broke in Kasitile, 'Indeed, but we attended to that. They said, "Mwaipopo seek a sheep." They attended to it again. And when I came from the plain, I killed a cow, the meat went there, we attended to it.'

All the time there was a constant refrain of questioning, especially from Mwamakunda (who as Kasitile's assistant acts as his mouthpiece to the others: 'But why has Mwakanjoki (60) gone off in a huff? Why?' There was a continuous effort to extract reasons.

The meat from the top of the foreleg (*ijammapa*) was cut up into little portions and some was put aside for the boys, sons of Kasitile. Then Kasitile led the way with a bill-hook and Mwamakunda and I followed. Mwamakunda carried the meat in a leaf. We went to the sacred grove, Kinyangwa. When we reached the edge Kasitile told us to wait and he cut a path into the middle with the bill-hook, then we followed.

Mwamakunda threw the meat slowly, piece by piece, into the rotting stump of an old *umwali* tree, from which a lusty growth had sprung, one shoot being 30 feet high. Kasitile prayed: 'Come Mwakanjoki (60), together with Lwembe (3?), Mwakalebela (19), and the Kinga, come, with—with—with—come. We pray of you millet, maize, bananas, all your food.' (Mwamakunda threw a piece of meat at each word.) 'We are still mourning you, we have tears. We finish now, that is all. Bring bananas, bring millet, maize, children, may the cows calve, stand by us Mwakanjoki (60), N—, N—, N— Lwembe (3?), Mwakale-bela (19), Nsyanigwe,[1] Kyamba Kitali,[1] Ngulube (9), N—, N—, N—. Don't come again Mwakanjoki, let us sleep well. This is Mwam-bagoje .[i.e. Mwamakunda the younger. It was his first visit to the sacred grove in place of his father]. I have brought him to you. Do not be startled at this Mwaipaja (G.W.), he is innocent, he is our friend. Move out of my body, let this chill go from my body! We have finished! Amen!'

Kasitile and Mwamakunda gave instructions and suggestions to each other in low voices from time to time during the prayer and throwing of the meat. We went out, Kasitile and Mwamakunda looking ahead, and Kasitile warned me: 'Do not look behind, Mwai-paja.' For the next two days Kasitile said he and Mwamakunda would wash with medicines, and refrain from intercourse with their wives 'because they entered the sacred grove'.

Then we rejoined Mwaipopo and the priests and the meat was cut up. Mwaipopo said: 'Indeed people gossip, where does the whispering go? To whom do the words go? Perhaps they went to you (the com-moner) priests?' Kasitile had something on his mind: 'When I returned from Lubaga who came to say: "Thank you, you have arrived back?"' [i.e. no one came to greet him formally on his return]. Njobakosa answered this saying that no offence was meant.

Then Njobakosa turned to Mwaipopo (116) and raised the question of his son, Mwaseba (152) who had seduced Mwaipopo's wife, Mpeta.

---

[1] The hereditary Kinga priests.

K

Why had Mwaipopo refused so long to enter into relationship with Mwaseba? Mwaipopo explained that the delay was on account of Mpeta. 'Let my wife come first,' he said, and told how, when the case first came to light, he had taken Mpeta to his kinsman Mwaiteteja, who took her to Mwaseba's village headman, Kakuju, and he to her people. She must come back the same way, and has not yet done so. Ngulyo said that at first he had been inclined to criticize Mwaipopo, but now saw that he was right. Kasitile spoke of the enormity of Mwaseba's offence, for Mpeta is a kinswoman of Mwaipopo's wife Kalobo, and on the death of her son Mwakalobo, Mwaseba was put in his place, so he has seduced a woman who, by legal fiction, is his mother, as well as the wife of his father. His act is *doubly* incestuous.

They then spoke of the separation of those who pray at Mbyanga (*vide supra*, p. 80) and blamed them for it. 'Have they millet though? Kyala judges them himself.' Then Kasitile reproved Mwaipopo (the chief) for another matter. 'But you, Mwakagile (116, identified with his grandfather 59) have little wisdom left. Why did you not give some of the beer which we drank recently at your house[1] to the people of Ipinda, the BaKalinga? The food from a distance you should divide.' And Mwaipopo agreed meekly [i.e. Mwaipopo has built with his young wives away from his inherited wife Kalinga (senior widow of 115) and is apt to neglect her; he must send some of the 'food from a distance'—ceremonial presents from affines—to his senior wives, not give it all to his friends and young wives.]

Then there were mutual compliments and self-depreciation between Kasitile and Kissogota (the commoner priest). Kissogota pointed to Mwaipopo and Kasitile, and said: 'You are impressive you, you are impressive, we are mere cannibals (*balyabandu*).' Kasitile replied: 'You are impressive yourself, if I look at you my body changes.'

Suddenly Kissogota got up and pretended to go: 'I am off, friends!' Ngulyo started to protest: 'We have not yet finished, we are speaking.' But Kissogota said, 'No, you told me to "be off"!' He went outside but returned admitting he had been only pretending. Mwaipopo: 'Yes, do you think we don't know you? Drink! Why do you not drink?'

The Mwamakunda began to ask angrily: 'Why do you shut up words in the heart? Why? Do you wish that Mwakisambwe (i.e. Kasitile, 86, identified with his great-grandfather, 30) should become a fool? Kissogota answered: 'We have not yet done so, Mwambagoje (Mwamakunda), we have not yet; do you think we are angry? Who went to fetch Kasitile from the plain? It was we, we went ourselves.'

Njobakosa took up the matter: 'We have power we have, if we please we can give the chief worms.' (This was said fiercely; Kasitile and Mwaipopo listened without comments. It was the crucial moment

---

[1] Sent as a present by Mwaipopo's affines.

to which all had led up.) Then Mwaipopo (116) spoke: 'We have taken home Mwakanjoki (60), we have taken home Mwakisambwe (30).' And the others agreed: 'We have taken him, we have taken him.' Mwaipopo went on to speak of the tree cutting: 'It was always a swept place, Mwakanjoki (60) built there, let it be a swept place again, let it be clear, let our prayers go beneath to enter the house here [i.e. no matter that the trees have been pruned], prayers go beneath in the swept place. See, we buried our father Mwaijonga (82) in the swept place, was it heavy? [i.e. a sacred grove] No, a tree grew later. So if I like I cut that it may be clear again.' To which Kasitile replied: 'Thank you, Mwakagile' (116, identified with his grandfather 59). Mwaipopo continued: 'Let no one whisper. Who whispered? Where do we all look? Here! It is our earth, here, it is our tree, here, it is our fertility of the soil (mboto), here. No one stirred up Mwakisambwe (30); he stirred up himself.'

So they prepared to go, saying, 'It's getting dark, it's getting dark.' But Kasitile stopped them. 'Wait, there is one thing left, tell Mwakagile (116, identified with his grandfather 59) that he should seek a cow, let us finish.' They took this up: 'Yes, since we have taken your grandfather to his home, let us go to your father, Mwaijonga (82), and to Mwakabule (117), let us finish them.'

Mwaipopo ignored this. 'It's getting dark, let us go.' And Kasitile softened it by addressing Njobakosa and his fellows: 'But Njobakosa have you cattle?' 'Yes!'

'And has Kissogota got some?'

'Yes.'

'Well, then, is it you who will seek this cow?'

'No!'

'Indeed, it hurts Mwakagile' (116, identified with his grandfather 59) [i.e. it hurts him to have to spend his cows].

'Do not "cut leaves at home" [i.e. summon a crowd and discuss the matter publicly], he will be startled, he will swear at us, speak with him privately.'

So they went off. Jane (wife of Kasitile, 86) took the breast of beef to Mwaipopo's (116) place. One leg went to the priests, Njobakosa, Ngulyo, and Kissogota, one to Mwamakunda and Ndisu (Kasitile's kinsman), and another kinsman who was not present, the hump and neck were sent to me; and two legs and the chine were kept for Kasitile himself and his female relatives.

A couple of weeks later, when Kasitile came to visit, he explained one or two points in the ritual. Asked about Mwamakunda's forceful words 'Why do you shut up words in the heart?' and the reply of Kissogota and Njobakosa, he said: 'That is very important. Mwamakunda is my man, he stands by me, he eats meat with me, he compelled them to speak out, because if they do not admit that it is they, then the ritual fails.'

QUESTION: What does that mean?

KASITILE: It is witchcraft!

QUESTION: Witchcraft? (in apparent surprise).

KASITILE: Yes, it is their witchcraft, the priests gathered with the shade, they bring a chill on my body.

QUESTION: Pythons? (still in surprise).

KASITILE: Yes, they fly in their witchcraft to come here, they speak with the shades, saying: 'Punish him! Let him find us something to eat!' They call the shades to help. Hence I sought something for them to eat that they should be satisfied.

QUESTION: But I thought witchcraft and the shades were quite separate? (still in apparent surprise).

KASITILE: No, they are together, look you, did not Kissogota boast? He said, 'Indeed we came, it is us, it is us. Why did you cut that branch? But now there is no accusation against you.' He boasted very much. He said: 'We have power, if we like we can give him worms.' [It is Njobakosa who was heard to say this, but Kasitile's personal quarrel was with Kissogota.] Did I not tell you that I had worms when I came up from the plain? I had them! I went to doctors and the diviners said: 'You are a chief, you were in the plain, why do you not kill a bull on your return?' Then when I killed a bull the worms disappeared! Where did they come from? They came from the priests, they called the shades to their aid. So I admitted to Kissogota, saying: 'Indeed I have done wrong, I your wife, I Maloba' (86, the feminine form of the name is used).

QUESTION: So, a white person (*umwelu, vide infra,* p. 141) cannot be a priest, but only a witch, a heavy one?

KASITILE: Yes, indeed, how can a white person take hold of the ritual? His fellows will drive him away. See! To a ritual do we call everyone?

No!

KASITILE: And is my home near to Kissogota's?

No, he lives at a distance.

KASITILE: Yes, indeed, it is the black ones (*batitu*) whom we call because it is they who punish us chiefs.

QUESTION: Well, then, is the anger of the shades always provoked by the witches? What about sores (*imindu*) on the mouth?[1] What about madness if a commoner does not perform the death ritual?

KASITILE: No, I do not lie, that is different. Sores on the mouth come from the shades, the witches are not there, and if a commoner fails to perform the ritual, madness also comes from the shades, it comes

[1] Cf. Monica Wilson, *Rituals of Kinship,* pp. 181, 219.

indeed from the whispering of men and the shades here, but people speak openly, saying: 'Why does he not celebrate the ritual?' The witches do not come into it.

QUESTION: Well, when the witches do throttle someone, do they always call shades, or not?

KASITILE: No, sometimes they throttle a man alone, and the shades are not there.

QUESTION: But your sickness?

KASITILE: Now the priests in their witchcraft gathered with the shades. The day after we had celebrated Njobakosa came to my place and said: 'We have finished then!' I replied: 'Yes, my body is better now, but the cough is separate, it is from Kyala.' And did you not hear what Mwaipopo asked in his cups—'How did the doctor (the Sangu) know that you are a priest? And that you had done wrong? Indeed they (Kissogota and his fellows) had told him!'

QUESTION: What did he mean by that?

KASITILE: That they had gone to the doctor in dreams to tell him.

Asked about Kissogota's words: 'You are impressive, we are cannibals, we are', Kasitile explained: 'It means, "You chiefs kill cattle for us, you are impressive, that is your impressiveness. Do we kill cattle? No! We eat men, we are witches." Because when we have killed cattle they receive blood, their witchcraft goes away, it stays in its house.'

QUESTION: And your reply, 'You are impressive, you are'?

KASITILE: I replied: 'You are impressive, you are, you are witches, if I were alone what would I do? It is you who brought the chilling breath on me and said I had done wrong. Even though I have not done wrong, you wish to eat meat. If I walk about among you, my body shrinks, it fears.'

Mwaipopo (the chief 116) had also prayed with water the night before the sacrifice, he helps me in prayer and if he prays at his house, I help him. We pray with water to bring out everything; if I do not pray with water then something is left within. I summon all the gods, all the fathers, and all the shades. (*Apa tukwiputa namesi ko kusyosya ilisyu loysa, lenga ndikwiputa namesi po lisyele limo nkati. Nikumpala kyala gwesa, tata gwesa, abasyuka bosa.*)

QUESTION:

KASITILE: Yes, when Kissogota and his fellows came in their witchcraft to call my shades to their aid, I saw them in dreams, I saw them! And if they correct Mwaipopo like this in witchcraft, together with the shades, he sees them; he complies immediately, he seeks a cow. And if they just come to throttle me I see them. It is the village headmen of the country who come to throttle me, the shades are not there, no, only Kissogota and his fellows, they stand with the shades, not the others they come and suck my blood and they go away again. I do not speak, but I see them. It's taboo to speak. They must seek blood and they go off; we fear them!

QUESTION: Why do you chiefs never speak out if you are throttled?

KASITILE: If I speak how many would there be to name? Very many! For us it's taboo to accuse a man of witchcraft, but the commoners accuse one another. Look you, do few people keep you company?

Many!

Like us chiefs, everyone comes. It's taboo for us to speak out, we fear. Look you, when Mwambene (Mwaipopo 116) and I were alone we feared to throw out the beer, we said: 'If we throw it out will they leave?' But when Kissogota came, he said: 'All right, I will throw it out myself.' We fear the fierce great priests, the terrible witches, they are angry.[1] We shrink when they appear.

The village headmen of the country call on the priests for help against us, they whisper by the fire, the priests come in their witchcraft, they call on my shades saying, 'Let us punish him', also they eat, together with the shades. Our shades never initiate anything, never; they look to the priests. But with a commoner the shade may initiate matters himself. Yes, people whisper indeed, but is that witchcraft? No! They whisper openly and ask, 'Why did you not perform the ritual?' But even although people are silent, still the shade comes saying, 'Why did you not perform the ritual? I am on the road.' He initiates the thing himself.

QUESTION: But don't people eat meat at the ritual of a commoner?

KASITILE: Yes, and if he does not celebrate it they accuse him, but they accuse him openly.

QUESTION: If the heir buries him with a few cattle?

KASITILE: If a rich commoner dies and the heir buries him with only one cow, the shades are angry and the people also; their chilling breath comes on his body, perhaps he falls ill himself, perhaps his child falls ill, but the people and witches do not meet together, people are angry here, and the shades there; all of them and the shades too, because he has celebrated with one cow only. People are angry because they wish to eat the meat. But the oracle says, 'The shades are angry.' It does not speak of people, it knows that people also are angry, but it speaks of the shades. And at the celebration he prays in the evening, the next day he calls people and kills a cow, and throws the sacred meat in the banana grove, saying, 'Here is your meat, father.' People say, 'Indeed he did wrong, his father was angry', but they do not confess saying, 'It was we', no, they say 'the shades' . . .

We chiefs have bodies which are different, the commoners arrived first in the country, they ate raw food, we fear them saying, 'They eat raw food.' It is we who followed and brought fire. To us they confess

---

[1] *Iminyago indosi mikalala.* The noun class implies size, ferocity, and dislike.

(their witchcraft); to each other they say: 'It is your father.' Because if they confess to a fellow commoner saying, 'It is we', he says, 'You are "eating" me, drink the ordeal'. The witch is driven out. But to us they admit saying, 'It was we who were angry.' They do not fear us. Commoners are the seniors in the country; they arrived first.

It will be remembered that the commoners are spoken of as 'black people' (abatitu) and that the first chiefs were 'pale' (mwelu) but these words also have moral implications. 'It is said that a person "has a black heart" or "has black blood", or "is black in his face towards us" when he is thought to be a witch, eating his fellows, or when he is a thief, or a liar, or an adulterer, or dirty. Even though his body is light coloured (mwelu) the word "black" (ntitu) is used of him metaphorically.' And mwelu implies innocent, pure, as well as light in colour. The comparable symbolism of 'nigger' and 'white man' is all too familiar in Johannesburg or Charleston.

That Kasitile himself was much afraid of the commoner chiefs and was relieved by the 'speaking out' was clear, and the people of the country as a whole were glad that the ritual had been celebrated, for they expected an increase in fertility. Some days later Mwakyonde (148), came in and said, laughing, but half serious: 'Congratulations, Mwaipaja (G.W.). You have celebrated the ritual, we rejoice greatly, you give us fertility of the soil, you are a great priest.'

In some moods Kasitile was inclined to become a Christian, but he felt an obligation to the country as priest, and believed too strongly in the efficacy of the traditional rituals to abandon them. He said to G.W. one day, over a pot of beer: 'If it were not for the ritual I would get you to speak to the Europeans of the mission, and I would go with my wife Jane, and be baptized. If my son was old enough and had agreed to carry on the ritual I would do it; perhaps I will when I am old. . . . It is good to have one's heart washed clean, we are dirty inside. The Christians say to us: "You with your four wives each, you are all dirty, you love one and squabble with the rest." Well, it is so with me, I love Jane only; I would like to go and be baptized with her. But I fear for the ritual, I fear hunger, the hunger of the people. For I am the food of the country, I am the maker of food.'

We left Selya shortly after this and were not able to observe the effect of the ritual on political relationships in Selya. Kasitile lived another seventeen years, duly performing his functions, and in 1954 he was succeeded by his brother's son, James.

CHAPTER X

MEDICINES

THE Nyakyusa regard medicines as an ultimate source of power —given the right ingredients and the 'know how' a man may achieve anything. This conception is integral to their view of reality, moreover the distinctions made regarding the just use of them throw light on the Nyakyusa moral system, and must be examined. But a full analysis of Nyakyusa medicines (*imikota*) would require a book in itself together with an expert knowledge of botany and of the properties of plants. Here we are concerned only with those aspects of the belief and practice in medicines which touch directly on social relationships or which illuminate the Nyakyusa conception of reality and morality, and their use of symbols.

Already many references have been made to medicines for they are an adjunct of most rituals, but their use is not confined to these; often a private individual is treated alone, and such a treatment is not classed by the Nyakyusa as a ritual (*ubunyago*), so we must stray, for a little time, beyond the limits of our title.

(a) TYPES OF MEDICINES

A classification in terms of purpose shows a close conformity with the use of medicines by other peoples in Africa. The use of medicines for protection and cure; for fertility; for success in any chancy undertaking from hunting and fishing to love-making, theft, a court case, or securing a job; for exacting vengeance; and for oracles, is familiar enough. What emerges from a detailed analysis is that the intractability of *persons* is felt to be at least as great a problem as the intractability of *things*, and many treatments are directed towards transforming personalities and developing moral qualities. The medicine given to a bride at puberty is to make her 'patient and polite' as well as fertile; the medicines given to chiefs and village headmen are to make them dignified and wise. A thief is often treated with medicines by his relatives to cure him of his thieving habits; and the famous *gwambemula* medicine is used to control the anger of a husband, a chief, an employer, or a superior officer. (It is said to be much in demand among police and soldiers as well as wives.) Then there are medicines used by men and women to make themselves more attractive and persuasive as lovers, litigants, leaders, clients, servants, salesmen, and so on.

Certain Nyakyusa medicines are based on observation of cause and effect. Their pharmacopia includes purges and poisons— for example, castor oil has long been cultivated and used both for making ointment and as an aperient—and some of the drugs administered, and the poulticing with hot leaves, may well be therapeutic; we have no systematic knowledge of the plants used and cannot assess them. But the scientific element is demonstrably limited, for a great many medicines are based on the principle of association, a feeling of likeness between things, and things *felt* to be alike are believed to react on one another, like producing like, or like things being antagonistic.

No distinction is made by the Nyakyusa themselves between those medicines which one trained in western science would say are based on observation of cause and effect (e.g. a purge or a poison), and those which are based on association—indeed our friends constantly cited supposed observations of cause and effect as evidence of the efficacy of all sorts of medicines and taboos. Mwakyonde used charcoal, mixed with iron from a forge, as a medicine for protection against lightning, burying a little, and powdering a little, and sprinkling it about a homestead, 'because at the forge they blow the bellows and it says, "*Muli, muli, muli*" (i.e. boom, boom, boom) and the lightning *jikumuleka* (booms). When we blow the bellows at a forge it makes a noise like thunder.' There was no hint that he was aware that electricity might be attracted by iron, but he insisted that where he had buried the charcoal and iron the lightning *never* struck again, and he regarded this as cause and effect. Therefore the distinction we have made between observation and association is ours, not theirs.

That the symbolic element is at least as important as the practical was apparent from Lyandileko's treatment for sterility, which was famous for its success. She had three patients one morning, all women wanting to bear children. In front of her she ranged seventeen banana petals and mixed four different medicines in them. Then she chose three young banana shoots and bored a hole in each, inserting into it a length of the mid-rib of a banana leaf, slightly hollowed to form a runnel. She told an onlooker to bring the first petal full of medicine and poured it into the runnel.

The patient knelt and received the medicine in cupped hands, guiding it into her mouth. Lyandileko hung a little medicine horn on the runnel before pouring. The patient kept the medicine in her mouth until the runnel was removed and she spat through the hole. Then the hole was filled up with the petal off which the medicine had been poured. Lyandileko smeared the patient on the belly with medicine from a horn, and pushed the horn down under her bark-cloth to the genitals, in front, and on to the buttocks behind. As she did this she said, 'If you are barren the banana will rot, if you are fertile I give you medicine to bear a child.' This was done for each patient in turn. Then the banana suckers were planted and the medicine from the remaining petals poured into bottles (two made of banana leaves, one a Vermouth bottle) for the patients to take home. They were to take a dose each day for a week. As the treatment was proceeding Lyandileko talked of her successes: 'So-and-so drank twice and her belly sprouted. . . . So-and-so drank and she came back to me pregnant. . . .'

After a week the women came back to see whether their banana suckers had sprouted. Lyandileko explained: 'The banana sucker is the child, it sprouts quickly, it is the belly which sprouts quickly. If it dies they consult an oracle—the woman does not conceive.' And her son added, 'If a woman's sucker dies Lyandileko tells her: "Don't say I have not worked for you, don't you see your banana? You are rotten in yourself, indeed they must have allowed your cord to fall between your mother's legs."[1] They rejoice very much if it has grown.' Each petal represents a child; Lyandeliko used male and female symbols (plantain and sweet banana petals) alternately for boys and girls. One mother who had no child had asked for ten, another with two already for eight, another with three already for six. Lyandileko's arithmetic had gone wrong for there were only seventeen petals altogether. The horn is the horn of protection (*ulupembe lwa ipingo*) and it means here, 'May the "iron" stay nicely within, may it not come out in front or behind, may it stay inside.' (Iron is a symbol for the reproductive capacity of women.) Neither Lyandileko nor her son (who were both forthright in their discussion of ritual) seemed to be conscious of any symbolic enactment of coition, though a knowledge of the symbolism of the death and puberty rituals suggests that.

[1] Cf. Monica Wilson, *Rituals of Kinship*, p. 145.

(*b*) MEDICINES AND MORALITY

Doctors classify most of their medicines in terms of the supposed mystical causes of disease, and the determining factor in diagnosis is what quarrels have occurred in the patient's circle of kinsmen and friends, or what wrongdoing he has on his conscience. The medicines mentioned to us by various doctors were for treatment of sickness caused by 'the breath of men', by sorcery, by vengeance magic, by the protective medicine put on wives, by the anger of the shades or living senior relatives, by incest, by spearing or binding with ropes,[1] or abnormal birth. Only a few of the medicines listed were for the treatment of observable symptoms such as fever, too frequent periods, or swelling after snake-bite, rather than the supposed mystical cause.

The emphasis on discovering the mystical cause and counteracting it was shown very clearly when Godfrey Wilson accompanied Mwakyonde, the doctor, to the home of a patient, a young man so weak that he could not lift a limb. Mwakyonde spent two minutes examining him, and provided leaves with which he was poulticed, and a medicine which was rubbed into cuts made all over his body, but the greater part of the day was devoted to discussing the quarrel between kinsmen, from which his illness was thought to have arisen, to persuading the kinsmen to 'speak out', and to preparing and administering a medicine which would cause the death of any one of them who was working sorcery against another.

Medicine for the treatment of a disease is held to be ineffective —at the best a temporary palliative—unless the underlying cause is discovered and dealt with. For example, doctors spoke of possessing a medicine against *ilyepa*, the disease caused by a kinsman to whom a debt in cattle is due, but it is not effective alone. 'The wrongdoer drinks medicine and pays his kinsman. He must pay, for though the medicine may cure him temporarily the disease will come again if he does not pay his debt.'

The ultimate cause of disease is believed to be friction in social relationships—a breach in moral law—and so the study of medicines takes us directly to problems of morality. There is a deep-rooted conviction that medicines will not be effective if there is quarrelling in the family which uses them. This applies not only to medicines used in sickness, but also to those for protection

[1] *op. cit.*, pp. 172-9.

and achievement. An account of the treatment of a field for protection against wild pig emphasizes this.

If people wish to protect a crop from wild pig they go to a doctor to ask for medicine. When he gives it to them he tells them that there must be no quarrelling in the home after they have barricaded the field. Four women go to the field with the husband of the one who cultivates it. They go after sunset. One women is shaved; her head is a symbol of the garden devastated by pig. A second woman, who keeps her hair, has a head-pad on her head and carries bananas with medicine. She enters the field and eats the bananas. The husband climbs a hill at a little distance, and two of the women go into the long grass close to the field. The bald pate twists a head-pad and the one with hair smears it with medicine and as they do so they look towards their husband and abuse him saying, 'You lay with your mother', and he swears at them saying, 'The leather aprons of your fathers' . . . and many other insults. Then the women walk round the edge of the field, sprinkling medicines, and they go out the way they came in. The circular pad is a symbol of the barricade placed round the field. When they return home they do not eat but go to sleep hungry (though the clever ones eat beforehand). If they quarrel, the pig finishes the food. It is as if quarrelling destroyed the fierceness, the power, of the protective medicine; you must put aside all quarrelling that the medicine may be powerful. If the pigs come it is as if there were a quarrel, so the woman and her husband quarrel in the field mimicking the pig. The husband on the hill is like the pig approaching the field, his wives in the long grass also represent pigs. . . . The husband and his wives quarrel only in the field. If, when the maize is ripe, the husband beats one of his wives for any cause she does not go to pick the maize herself, a friend picks it for her. If she goes in her anger she finds the maize finished, nothing but earth is left.

Here the link between medicines and morality is made plain. Quarrelling weakens medicines of all sorts and renders them ineffective. But a mimic quarrel between husband and wives in the fields renders the medicine effective. It represents the battle between the pig and the medicines. There is a suggestion elsewhere (pp. 69, 113) that pigs are *sent* by the shades when kinsmen or neighbours quarrel, but in the account just quoted it is implied that quarrelling in the home directly injures the medicine.

In themselves, many medicines are neutral. They may be put to good or evil ends, but because they are mysterious and powerful, they are feared, in the same sort of way as atomic energy is feared in contemporary society. Men use medicines themselves 'for purely peaceful purposes', but they are shocked at the prospect of their enemies using them. The notion that medicines are a weapon which may be used rightly or wrongly is very clearly brought out in the attitude towards 'making' animals. If a private individual 'makes' lion, or leopard, or crocodile which kill men that is sorcery—there is no question about it—and we heard of at least one man who had been driven from his home because he was reputed to have made leopards which killed children and cattle,[1] but when Mwakyonde 'made' lions which drove off pig and did not attack men, that was a public service (*vide* p. 69). And when one chief uses lions in his conflict with another the action is felt to be comparable with war, rather than murder. In February 1937, four lions were hunting in a piece of bush country near the salt lick, which two chiefs claimed. Mwansumbwe, a chief from the hills, had sent some of his men to clear fields in the bush, but Mwakagile (50, or his heir), the neighbouring chief, objected saying, 'This is my land.' There was a long case and finally the District Officer gave judgement in favour of Mwakagile and refused Mwansumbwe any compensation for his work in clearing the bush. 'You got a crop for your labour,' he said. Mwansumbwe was incensed by the judgement and grew even more angry when his men elected to remain on the land they had cleared and became men of Mwakagile. So, everyone said, Mwansumbwe had sought medicines and created these lions. They killed seven cattle in a few days, attacking even by daylight. 'Yes,' we were told, 'there are always lion in the bush, but they do not ordinarily kill cattle as they have done now.'

Another chief who tried the same sort of thing was not so successful. 'Some time ago the chief Mwakila made elephants, he turned his wives into elephants and they ate the bananas of Malapula, but Malapula said, "Let's try", and he created much rain which poured down on to the elephants and those wives died. Then Mwakila was defeated. How about you Europeans? Have you this custom? Do you turn a wife into an animal?'

'No!'

'We have it, if I choose I give my wife *isigita* and she becomes a lion which roars, it roars and eats people.'[2]

---

[1] cf. Monica Wilson, *Good Company*, p. 124.

[2] This, and the tale of a young man fleeing from justice who obtained a medicine to turn himself into a lion, were the only accounts of lycanthropy we heard—usually the medicines themselves (such as those of a chief) turn into animals, or the young of ordinary lion, leopard, or crocodile 'smell the medicines' and become attached to the 'owner' who feeds and commands them.

A second class of medicines is not neutral at all, but itself selects between right and wrong. The most famous is the *mwafi* ordeal which is used to reveal the truth. The *mwafi* poison was formerly administered by a doctor,[1] before witnesses, and the innocent were believed to vomit almost immediately, while the guilty did not vomit at all, or were slow to do so, and fell ill, some even dying. Nowadays *mwafi* is administered only in the greatest secrecy, but various minor methods of divination, all of which turn on the correct use of medicines, are in common use. The 'divination with porridge' has been described (*vide supra*, p. 128). The medicine added to it is spoken of as 'a kind of *mwafi*'. Another method is to rub an inverted wooden cup on a smooth board. Questions are posed, as to the porridge. When the answer is 'no' the cup slips; when the answer is 'yes' the cup sticks. Sometimes a stick of *musika* wood is rubbed on the ground in place of the cup on the board, and there are half a dozen other methods using bells, horns, segments of bamboo, a pipe, or boiling water. In each case virtue lies in the medicines added to the porridge or rubbed on to the cup or stick, and into scarifications in the diviner's hands. An ordinary man who has not been treated cannot use the instruments, and porridge without '*mwafi*' is useless.

Certain medicines used for protection and to wreak vengeance, are also thought to be selective, and to injure only the guilty. These are horns, owned by doctors. Mwanjesi (who came of a family of doctors) told us:

My father had a water-buck horn filled with medicines and ointment, as a protection against witches. He used it, like other doctors, for burning the grass, for burning the rubbish heaps before planting millet, and for protecting a child. When the millet crops are poor, people say the witches have eaten it, and the next year the chief sends for the doctor and his protective horn. . . . He comes and makes fire and treats the tinder with ointment from his horn, and each pile of weeds is lit from that fire. . . . He sends some to the chief to fire the grass for fresh grazing. Then there is much milk, the cows that eat that grass give much milk for the witches stay away and neither eat the millet nor throttle the cows. So with a child, if a man has lost many children and has one left, he calls the doctor to come with his protective medicine (*ilipingo*) and treat the child with medicines from his horn as a protection against witches. My father used the same horn for all these things.

[1] For a description of the procedure, cf. Monica Wilson, *Good Company*, pp. 115-16, 241-6.

If a man has quarrelled with a kinsman, or is conscious of having bitter enemies, or hears that someone with whom he has had a dispute has 'gone to the doctors', he is likely to go to a horn doctor for protective medicine, even though he is perfectly well.

'The horn' is believed to discover and punish the guilty whether they are known to the injured or not, but if someone uses it without just cause the medicine will recoil on himself. The seven cases of using the horn reported to us[1] were all used in revenge: two for theft, two for seduction, and three for withholding cattle due. And it is revenge that was emphasized in one account of the treatment:

If someone has stolen my cow I go to a doctor and pay him a bull. Then he prepares the medicine (the horn) and stands facing it, with a spear over his shoulder, pointing towards it, and he speaks aloud saying: 'So-and-so, if you have not taken the cow you will recover, if you have eaten it you will die.' Then the breath (imbepo) goes to the man named and if he has really stolen the cow he dies. . . .

But another informant, listing the contents of a 'horn', stressed the protective element. It contains 'the bile of a crocodile, the skin of a python, and inyifwila medicine (vide p. 58) which has been used to kill men' . . .

If a witch comes to throttle and kill you then the bile of the crocodile throttles and strikes him [the witch], and the inyifwila does the same, it is to kill the witches, it spears those who come to throttle you. The skin of the python means that if people come to throttle you they find you have changed yourself into a python.

Another type of vengeance magic, ilyepa, is thought to work only between blood relatives.

If your father-in-law is angry it is your children he kills, not yourself. If the diviner says the disease comes from the woman's side of the family the protective medicine is given only to her, not to the man; if from his side only he is protected, not the wife. The relative who is angry drinks a medicine; he puts a barbed spear into the fire and when it is red hot he slashes a banana sucker with it and speaks the name, then the kinsman who is mentioned dies.

A third type is that used to secure property (ukusinga) and snare thieves or adulterers; for the exclusive rights of a husband over his wife are treated as property rights. Often a medicated stick is placed in a field to ward off thieves, and some husbands

[1] cf. Monica Wilson, Good Company, pp. 212-56.

are said to give their wives a medicine (without their knowledge) which will cause any man who lies with them to fall ill
of gonorrhoea or some other venereal disease. Many Christians
believe in this medicine and some inquired whether Europeans
did not use it also. One family of doctors are specialists in it:

> The sons of Manyafu are very famous, they are great doctors.
> People fear them very much. No one can steal anything belonging to
> them or run off with their wives. If a man runs off with a wife of theirs,
> he will return their wife and pay. . . . Because when he has slept with
> the woman by night they stink in each other's nostrils, the woman
> stinks in the face of the man and he likewise in hers. And if rain falls
> by night the roof comes off the hut in which they sleep and the rain
> enters. Perhaps the man quarrels with the woman, perhaps frogs and
> snakes are numerous, perhaps gourds sprout in the house—sometimes
> they sprout bringing evil. So it is also if a man has run off with the
> wife of another and the husband goes to the sons of Manyafu. They
> agree to work, but he must pay them.

Lyandileko, whose husband's family have owned a 'horn'
for generations, was very insistent that vengeance magic maintained law and order for it could injure only the guilty. 'A thief
feared to steal lest he be caught by my father-in-law (Mwaisyelage). He feared the horn if he used sorcery. He feared to
seize another's cow thinking, "They will go to Mwaisyelage".'
And protective medicines which cause an adulterer to fall ill of
gonorrhoea, or a thief to die, are considered perfectly legitimate;
the misfortune would not have befallen the man unless he had
done wrong.

The prohibition by the government of the *mwafi* oracle has
puzzled people. Medicines are admittedly dangerous, but it is
held that Europeans 'encourage' witches and sorcerers by for-
bidding the use of the one effective weapon against them, and
doctors with vengeance magic or other strong medicines 'fear the
fate of the *mwafi* doctors'. There is an inescapable contradiction
here, the Nyakyusa relying on *mwafi* and vengeance magic as
a means of discovering criminals, and the Europeans punishing
any doctor found administering poison, or intimidating people by
threats. Furthermore, it is widely believed that Europeans themselves use strong medicines made up with blood. Any Europeans
without an obvious occupation are suspect of being *abanyambuta*,
who go around killing people and taking their blood for the
Government to use for medicines. One of our European friends,

a missionary, was warned by her servants before Godfrey Wilson's arrival in her neighbourhood 'not to go out at night as there were *abanyambuta* about, sent by the Government to kill people and take their blood', and women going for firewood made a long detour to avoid his camp. One was overheard asking when she caught sight of him: 'Is that the man who kills people?' Angombwike explained that, since all really strong Nyakyusa medicines contained human blood, it was argued that European medicines, which were so powerful, must contain it also. 'They follow their own customs.'

It seems obvious to the Nyakyusa that Europeans must have strong medicines because their confidence and success are so great. Moreover, it is held (in theory) that they are immune to attacks from witchcraft. X, who had been a clerk and lost his job, and was bitter, expanded on this:

People say that Europeans have *inyifwila* (*vide* p. 58), see they are brave, they do not fear, if someone seizes a spear they do not fear, they just come to him, they are very brave. And also the witches say that they are unable to choke Europeans. When we hear people boasting of their mystical power (*amanga*) we always say to them: 'But if that is so, go and choke a European, show us!' Then they always say, 'Oh no, we can't do that, when we go to a European house at night we find it all lighted up and flaming, we can't get near them.' I think this is the power of the Holy Spirit which you Europeans have.

He came of a well-known family of doctors and perhaps spoke from first-hand knowledge. He just laughed at the suggestion that the light might come from lamps. But the fact that Europeans were held to be immune did not prevent our servants and friends attributing our recurring attacks of malaria to witchcraft.

(c) DOCTORS

Among the Nyakyusa, as perhaps in every society, the doctors with the greatest reputation are those at a distance, and a high proportion of the practitioners in the country are of foreign lineages, their fathers, or grandfathers, or great-grandfathers having come in, bringing medicines with them, and begun to practise. In fact, we were assured that there were *no* Nyakyusa doctors who were famous, they were all Sangu, or Kinga, or Kisi, or from Ngonde or Misuku in Nyasaland, but detailed investigation proved this to be false. The trade in medicines from a distance is a very old one and continues today. As we have seen,

L

inyifwila comes from west of Ngonde, or east of the Kinga; *mwafi* came from 'Nyasaland'; medicine for fertility of the fields from Misuku which is rich in food; war medicine from the Sangu and Kinga. Whether neighbouring people get medicines from Bu-Nyakyusa we do not know—no one ever suggested it, but it is likely that they do.

Since foreign doctors and medicines have the highest reputation new treatments are welcomed. This is where the practice of medicines differs radically from the rituals directed to the shades in which the charter is tradition, and any deviation must be justified. But the willingness to accept something new did not lead to any systematic experiment, or any regard for experiment as such.

Anyone who chooses, and can pay the fees, can become a doctor by apprenticing himself to a practitioner of repute, but it is very noticeable that the majority of well-known doctors come from families of doctors, the medicines being passed down from one generation to the next and sometimes taught to wives as well. Lyandileko, who has often been quoted, was taught certain medicines by her husband, and had a large practice. The diviners we knew were all men, but many women know a number of medicines. Once in practice, a doctor may add to his knowledge by buying a medicine from a fellow practitioner or exchanging medicines with him. One doctor we knew had paid two bulls for the secret of his protective medicine (*umkota gwa ipingo*). The teaching includes what plants or other ingredients to collect and how to 'cook' them, i.e. what to mix together and what quantities to use. As elsewhere in Africa, it is the material substance, usually vegetable, which is held to be important in any treatment. The spell—the words addressed to the medicine—is of little significance except that when vengeance magic is prepared the man on whose behalf it is done may say the name of his enemy (if he knows his identity) and state his own innocence in a phrase like the following: 'Return this medicine, thou Kyala, I have done no wrong whatsoever to cause me to be killed; if he says he will kill me let him die.'

The doctor (*inganga*) who 'knows medicines' is distinguished from the priest or officiant (*unyago*) who knows how to conduct a ritual directed to the shades or heroes. The *unyago* uses medicines in celebrating rituals, and he or she may be able to collect and prepare plants himself, but he sometimes has to apply to a doctor for an appropriate medicine, and his main function is organizing the observances.

(d) SYMBOLISM

In the field of medicine imagination runs riot, and associations are unpredictable. The ingredients of most medicines are professional secrets and unknown to the user who takes the concoction on trust from his doctor, and inquires no further. Therefore the study of medicine is not linked to the study of social relationships in the same manner as is the study of ritual, for the symbolism of medicines is individual and free, whereas the symbolism of ritual is common and obligatory.

Nevertheless, the imagination of doctors works within the general symbolic system, and such knowledge as we have indicates that many of the associations made are similar to those used in ritual. In medicine, as in the rituals of kinship, one type of banana stands for a male, another for a female, a banana sucker represents a kinsman, a sprouting shoot conception. Smithing and coition are felt to be alike, and the molten iron that trickles out of a forge is linked with menstrual blood. Hair stands for growth, and a bald pate a devastated field. A ring, or circumambulation, implies a protecting fence. Pythons, crocodiles, leopards, and lions stand for power and majesty, spears and thorns for attack; vomiting and emptiness for innocence, spitting for forgiveness. There is colour symbolism in medicines (though we know little of it save that the *ikipiki* which stands for the blood of the lineage is red, or reddish brown), and auditory symbolism, the rumble of thunder and the groaning of a bellows being identified. Men mime that which they wish to avoid, as well as that which they desire; like things are antagonistic as well as sympathetic. No doubt a laborious study of prescriptions would reveal further general principles of association, as well as the range of individual imagination, but such a task has yet to be undertaken.

CHAPTER XI

NYAKYUSA COSMOLOGY

WE can now piece together, from myth and ritual, the traditional Nyakyusa view of their universe. They have no elaborated system of ideas and the synthesis which follows is more systematic than any uneducated Nyakyusa would formulate.

The origin of men was a 'dark house', located high on the Livingstone plateau, and from here the Nyakyusa themselves, and people familiar to them, are thought to have sprung, but there is a hint of the first of the heroes having come 'from the north', and there is also the contradictory notion that the heroes were creators. 'It was Kyala who made us in the beginning with iron ore'; 'Kyala is the smith who forges us'; 'Mbasi is the smith who forges us'; 'Lwembe made Mumfu out of clay to be the father of commoners'. But all are agreed that Lwembe (or Mbasi) was the ancestor of the chiefs and no clear distinction is made between creator and progenitor.

Crops and animals and fire were distributed by the heroes. Of their first creation or invention there is no tale for, though Lwembe created animals, he was already a herd-boy when he did so. Moreover, the 'owners of the soil' in the Nyakyusa valley had some crops before Lwembe came bringing them others, together with cattle and fire; but which were the indigenous crops of the valley and which the new is not discussed. If contradictions between the various myths are pointed out they are explained, like divergences in ritual, in terms of differing origin: 'It is the Lambya people to the west who say that cattle came out of an anthill, and the Nyakyusa proper who say they were brought by Lwembe', and so on. Differentiation is epitomized and accounted for by the separation of lineages.

The heroes had a creative force in their own persons, which is inherited by their descendants, the divine kings, and, in a lesser degree, the chiefs; as in Egypt 'the King's potency is felt in the very body and person of each of his subjects'.[1] That potency is partly innate in the royal line, but it is nourished by the use of medicines of which the greatest are reserved to rulers. Vigour is

[1] H. Frankfort, *Kingship and the Gods*, p. 60.

thought to be embedded in the visibly growing parts of the body of a chief, and the horrifying practice of plucking out the hair and nails of a dying man is an assertion of the value of vitality, energy, force of personality in a leader.

The separate origin of chiefs and people, and the reciprocity between them, are constantly emphasized. Among many primitive peoples a myth of common origin is the charter for unity, and foreign lineages are linked by some fiction to the dominant line; but among the Nyakyusa it is the *reciprocity* between cultivators and cattle-owners, between 'owners of the soil' who ate their food raw and immigrants who brought with them cattle and fire, which is the basis of unity. The chiefs (like the descendants of the Pilgrim Fathers or the Voortrekkers) speak of themselves as having brought civilization to a savage land, but they acknowledge the contribution of the previous 'owners of the soil' in a way in which the white Americans and South Africans do not. Characteristically, the dichotomy of chiefs and commoners is couched in terms of descent, but in fact this is a fiction, for the younger sons of chiefs join the ranks of the commoners, and the mother of a chief is often of commoner origin.

The complementary character of the economies of chiefs and commoners is matched, in belief, by a balance in mystical power. The divine kings have an innate creative power while the commoners have pythons in their bellies with which to destroy their enemies. It sounds like a myth of good and evil put about by the chiefs, but we never heard it expressed in that way even by Kasitile, who so feared and hated the commoner priests. The destructive power of the commoners can be used morally, to maintain the established order, as well as irresponsibly by witches. The constitution was a balance between chiefs and commoners, not a dictatorship. Chiefs maintain their position by feasting their men on beef, and this, the Nyakyusa think, prevents the witches from attacking; sated with meat their pythons 'lie quiet'.

Ultimate power is symbolized by the python, for though the chiefs—like English kings—are commonly associated with lions and leopards, the terror of the grove of Lubaga, and the source of the *ifingila* medicine upon which the potency of divine kings and chiefs depends is a python, like that which lies in the belly of a witch. The most fearful thing of the tropical forest (and the forests on the Livingstone escarpment and Rungwe mountain are but the remains of much greater ones) is a natural symbol for power.

There is no single supreme power; it lies in the several heroes, in medicines, in witches, and with the shades. Kyala is a hero, a forefather, to whom sacrifices are made, and he is comparable to Lwembe and Kyungu, though he left no direct descendants. The evidence suggests that the names Kyala, Lwembe or Mbasi, Kyungu, and Ngulube were used in the same way in different areas, Kyala being the hero of the north-east shore of the Lake, Kyungu of the north-west, Lwembe of the central Nyakyusa valley, and Ngulube of the scarp edge of the Livingstones. Some-times informants used Lwembe and Kyala alternatively saying they meant the same thing, although, as we have noted, Lwembe (or Mbasi) was specially associated with cattle, whereas Kyala, who was killed and rose again, only controlled crops, and may perhaps be taken as personifying vegetation. The distinction is in no sense clear-cut, but there is a hint of a cultivating people having been defeated by cattle-keepers with iron weapons, since Kyala was finally killed with a 'razor' (*ubwembe*), and The Razor himself —Lwembe—could not be killed though men tried.

In their creative aspect the heroes and shades are closely identified: 'Kyala creates desire'; 'the shade rouses up in the belly when a woman conceives'; 'Kyala and the shades stand together'. Kasitile said:

Lwembe . . . makes a child. I lie with a woman; Lwembe is there, he works. Sometimes, if he is angry he works badly and a leg is missing, or the woman has a miscarriage. Sometimes he works well. Lwembe goes about looking upon the mothers; he is in my bellows (i.e. in my wife). It is he who came from BuKinga . . . and wished first to build at Nsamba's (i.e. where Nsamba 90 now lives). He failed there and went to Kasambala's and failed there and he seized Lubaga. All is his. A child is his and a cow, and the iron which the Kinga make is his, and food is his. . . . He is in a bull and a man. Where do you get the 'blood' (to beget a child)? Are you alone? . . . No, the Kukwe do not know Lwembe, but the people of the plain do, they are one with us.
QUESTION: And Kyala?
KASITILE: He is there, Kyala and Lwembe are together among us and the people of the plain. It is Lwembe who creates twins. You do not. Who has made your body? Who has created you? Who has given you strength and breath so that you are born, and live, and grow up, and marry? It is Lwembe and Kyala together.[1]

---

[1] cf. J. Busse, 'Die Zwillingsgeburt bei den Nyakyusa', *Zeitschrift für Ethnologie*, 73. Jahrgang, pp. 194ff.; 'Aus dem Leben von Asyukile Malango', *Zeitschrift für Eingeborenen-Sprachen*, Band xxxv (1950), p. 210.

The shade is the principle of life represented by seed, or the root of a banana, or a tree growing by a grave;[1] the hero embodied a vital force which caused grain to sprout and clay cattle to breathe. The line between a hero, the shade of one of his successors, and the shade of a chief is a very faint one. They all have power over people other than their descendants and are approached by hereditary priests. As some elderly men of Ngonde put it: 'The nobles, not the living Kyungu, go to the groves of the Kyungus to pray; they go because the Kyungus who have died are shades to us all (*bo basyuka betu twesa*).'

The heroes had miraculous power but it differed in degree, rather than in kind, from that possessed by their descendants. Like that of the divine kings and chiefs it lay both in their own bodies and in medicines, especially the *ifingila* which is still used by chiefs.

Kyala and Lwembe dwell 'beneath' (*pasi*) with the shades, as opposed to 'above' (*kumwanya*), which implied traditionally 'on earth' not 'in the sky'. There is no hint of a sky god in the traditional system, and the distinction between black and white offerings, which the early missionaries took to be a distinction between offerings to the shades and to a sky god,[2] was unequivocally interpreted by the priests in another fashion. The white (*mwelu*) offering to Kyala or Ngulube is a symbol not of purity, but of an unclouded sky, and the numinous quality of the heroes is conceived of as contamination, not holiness. Like the shades, the heroes must be 'driven off' lest men go mad, and it is when they have driven them away that men are *belu*—white, innocent, free of anger. Men should be *belu* but this is never cited as an attribute of the pagan Kyala. It is the terribleness, not the goodness or purity of God of which the Nyakyusa are aware. This is underlined by the fact that a madman who, 'when he comes home rushes off', and 'does not see that his fellows are human beings,' and who 'has a loose heart' (i.e. is passionate and quarrelsome), or 'whose heart curls up like a leaf in the sun, or turns upside down', is called 'Mbasi' or is said to have been 'caught hold of by Kyala'.

Kyala is one hero among others but, as has been shown, the name is *also* used in the sense of 'the lord'. Kyala as 'the lord' of a commoner or junior kinsman is distinct from Kyala the hero with his own place in a genealogy and his own shrine. The difference

---

[1] Monica Wilson, *Rituals of Kinship*, pp. 205-7, 211 *et passim*.

[2] F. Fülleborn, *Das Deutsche Njassa- und Ruwuma-Gebiet*, pp. 321-2.

is illustrated in the references made by priests to the python which appears in Lwembe's grove as *kyala* (*vide supra*, pp. 29, 33). This python is 'the lord', Lwembe.

Nowadays Kyala is spoken of as a first cause—the origin of death, and of social institutions, as well as the creator of life. The current version of the myth of the origin of death begins: 'When Kyala created the country and the people at the beginning there was no death. Then he thought there should be death and life. He asked people to choose between life and death, and they chose life.' And when men are asked the reason for a custom or ritual they may answer 'Kyala made us so', 'Kyala made us black people like that'.

Since Kyala is nowadays regarded as the creator of the natural order he is often blamed for the intractability of things—the log that splits, the lorry that skids. Once a vendor of very small potatoes said, when the buyer complained of the size, 'Kyala gave them to us like this', only to be jeered at by the onlookers who admonished him: 'Had you cultivated better they would have been larger.'

Much of the material quoted is susceptible of the interpretation that Kyala is an overriding power to which the shades, witches, and medicines are subject. 'The medicine will be effective if Kyala wills'; 'rain will fall when the rain-maker soaks his stones if Kyala wills'; 'when the doctor treats the tails they "vomit" (froth over), then if Kyala has helped us the cattle give much milk'. Even in 1935 conservatives like Kasitile sometimes expressed such beliefs, but they did not do so consistently. Their preoccupation was with other forces and acknowledgment of Kyala seemed to be tacked on almost as an afterthought. This came out very clearly in Kasitile's session with the diviner who, fearing the presence of a European, gave 'Kyala' as the cause of Kasitile's disease, and Kasitile rejected the verdict saying: 'Kyala never stands alone.' The influence of Christian teaching on pagan thought was already considerable in 1935—Kasitile added 'Jesus' and 'the Holy Spirit' to the shades invoked—and we believe the mention of Kyala in many of the pagan prayers at that date to have been due to Christian influence. The idea of a supreme power is accepted very readily *as an addition* to the belief in the shades, the witches, and medicines, though it does not easily replace them altogether. By 1955 the shift in emphasis was clear. Besides Kyala 'the lord' of a commoner or junior, and Kyala the hero who is worshipped at his cave and who, though a creator, is equalled by other heroes and dwells in the bowels of the earth, there was Kyala an ultimate power and first cause, unique and omnipotent, who dwelt in heaven 'above'. The implications of *kumwanya* (above) have changed along with the implications of *Kyala*.

The new balance between the different elements in pagan thought was reflected in everyday speech. In the 1930's men spoke constantly of the shades (*abasyuka*), the witches (*abalosi*), and 'the breath of men' (*imbepo sya bandu*); Kyala did not figure much in the conversation of pagans. But in 1955, from the moment when the bus I arrived in skidded off the road and the passengers began assuring each other that *Kyala alimo* (God is present), because no one had been injured, I heard the name constantly. Such a change is hard to prove, but the impression of a marked shift in emphasis was strong.

The conception of the hero Mbasi has also radically altered. During the years before 1914 a man, with two boys in attendance, posed as Mbasi and went round Selya by night, growling in a gruff voice that he was Mbasi, and seizing cattle and fowls and food. He was eventually taken by night, by some Christians, and died after seven months' imprisonment in Tukuyu. Today the Christians never use 'Mbasi' for God, but sometimes identify him with 'Satan', and the pagans use 'Lwembe' rather than 'Mbasi'.

The range of relationships in space was narrow in the traditional Nyakyusa society, and the range of relationship in time was correspondingly so. Only a limited number of chiefdoms cooperated in sacrifice to a hero (and often they seem to have acted separately, rather than in concert), and all historical time was contained in the genealogies depicted. There was a dawn when men ate food raw and lived without fire, or cattle, or chiefs, but history began when the heroes descended from the mountains, ten or twelve generations ago. Time was telescoped when all the known world lay within 100 miles.

A social revolution occurred once, with the coming of the chiefs, but then time stood still, and ever since the heroic age has remained the pattern of right behaviour. Departure from the rituals laid down spells madness and death, for 'Kyala created us so'. Part of primeval reality is the conflict of generations expressed in the myth of the seduction of a young wife by her husband's father, in the rules of avoidance, and in the ritual of the 'coming out'. There is no convention of fighting on this last occasion (as among some other peoples with a corresponding ritual), but the young men seize cattle belonging to the older generation, thus asserting their authority. The opposition of generations is taken for granted and given expression in constitutional form: the ritual is a celebration not of 'rebellion' but of growth. For all their reluctance to hand over power the fathers 'rejoice and are glad because their sons have grown up'. Change in the structure of society after the revolution of the heroic age, is not celebrated, and is scarcely admitted, but the process of growth, of death and procreation, is expressed in every ritual. Indeed, the ritual cycle is like a fugue with the theme of death and rebirth constantly recurring.

The pagan universe is just and orderly. There is a nemesis attached to spilling blood or binding a man with ropes. The anger of men,[1] or of the shades who are roused by men, is what brings most misfortune, and often, the Nyakyusa think, such anger is justified. Even medicines may be selective, injuring only the guilty. The good man who celebrates the proper rituals, fulfils his kinship obligations, and keeps on good terms with his neighbours, is protected, while the evil-doer falls ill. But some evil men, witches and sorcerers, attack the innocent out of jealousy and spite. Evil to the Nyakyusa, lies primarily within men: it is 'anger in the heart' which materializes as pythons that throttle others. Because they are aware of angry impulses in themselves the Nyakyusa find it difficult to believe that any society without witchcraft can exist; to say that there is no *ubulosi* is like suggesting that there is no ill will or anger in a community. And since anger brings misfortune there is an obligation on those whose anger might have caused sickness or ill luck to express goodwill by spitting or blowing out water, and saying, 'May the patient recover' or 'I am without anger'. Among commoners the man required to show goodwill is usually a senior relative, rather than a suspected witch (as among the Azande). But a neighbour or friend who might be a witch or sorcerer should also express goodwill when he visits the sick, and fellow hunters who have ill luck may stop to declare their goodwill to one another, as we have seen. If a chief or priest-chief is sick the village headmen and priests must wish him well and confess any anger they have felt towards him. The blowing out of water is a symbol of confession, 'bringing

[1] For a full account of the belief in witchcraft and the 'breath of men', cf. Monica Wilson, *Good Company*, pp. 91-121, 198-261.

out all the anger that is within', 'admitting that I have done wrong', begging pardon (*ukupelesya*) and *also* a symbol of emission and so of driving off the shades (*vide supra*, pp. 104, 108-110; 139). Good health depends upon good social relationships, and of one who is ailing it is commonly said: 'It seems as if they (unspecified) had hated her.' Further, the proper working of the natural order is held to depend upon the proper working of the social order. Drought, or 'cold', or pestilence falls on a chiefdom if there is quarrelling between chief and priests, and the anger of the Lwembe with his 'sons' will shrivel the crops of Selya. The heroes, the shades, many of the men of power (*abamanga*), and many medicines help to maintain an orderly universe; only the witches and sorcerers work against it. In short, order and right living are an integral part of Nyakyusa religion as they are of Christianity.

The ultimate good is the power of fertility, of generation, which lies in the heroes and shades; the punishment for evil-doing is ill-health of body or mind and sterility. And towards the heroes and shades, who are both life-givers and avengers, the attitude of men is clearly ambivalent: the shades are driven away—'let them warm themselves over there in the long grass', men say when they throw out the ashes (*vide supra*, pp. 109-11) but they bring them home again to 'warm themselves by the hearth'.

In analysing the rituals of the Nyakyusa, I have been driven to the conclusion that they are, in fact, dogged by a sense of guilt,[1] for this is the only hypothesis on which the linking of misfortune and sin, the preoccupation with 'filth', and the recurring acts of purification can be explained. One of the sources of this sense of guilt is, I suggest, awareness of anger within, for it is believed that such anger injures others. An act of confession is essential to many rituals, and what must be confessed are anger, hard thoughts, ill will against others. The anger is acknowledged to come primarily from men—it is the angry parent who rouses the shades to action by muttering over the fire—but the guilt, the filth, is projected on to the shade or the hero. It is when they 'brood on' men that men are contaminated. A shade or a man that is *ngolofu*—good, righteous—is one without a grudge, without anger against anyone, free of witchcraft, and free of sex transgression—'there is no accusation against him'.

[1] I doubted this earlier, cf. 'Nyakyusa Ritual and Symbolism', *American Anthropologist*, v, 56 (1954), pp. 237-8.

Sacrifice is offered that a particular shade, or all the shades of the lineage, may be 'satisfied, assuaged'. The word used is *ukuhoboka* which is also used of a man who has been hungry and has eaten well of fine food, of a man who has married a bride who pleases him, and of a living father or father-in-law who has been angry but is now pacified. In its applicative form, *ukuhobokela*, means to forgive. And the act of sacrifice is an offering, a gift, to the shade strictly comparable to the gift a young man makes to his father when 'begging pardon' for some offence. A son who has committed the most heinous offence of all, seducing one of his father's wives, can 'beg pardon' only by offering a cow; but many smaller offerings are made by juniors to seniors to beg forgiveness for lesser offences.[1] When a cuckolded father receives his son he kills the cow brought to him and eats with his neighbours. It is held to be essential that the living who are insulted (and a man's neighbours are insulted with him) should share in the meat and express satisfaction.[2]

Other conceptions also are, however, manifest in sacrifices. At the offering to a recently dead chief the sacred cut of the meat is divided between the shade, whose portion is placed on the earth near his grave (ideally beside the stone set up at his marriage), and his young grandsons, who are identified with him. The conclusion that this is a communion between the living and the dead is inescapable. At a sacrifice to Lwembe it is certain of the hereditary priests, and they alone, who may share the sacred cut. At the sacrifices made by private persons the communion between shades and grandchildren is explicit when an offering of fish is made.[3] It is less clear in the sacrifice at a funeral, but is made plain in the eating of grain or bananas with the *ikipiki* medicine which symbolizes the lineage. Then the shade is told 'all the food we have eaten you have eaten . . . farewell.' The communion of sacrifice is indeed but one manifestation of the identification of the participants in a ritual with the shades for, as has been shown in a previous book, the essential character of all the rituals of kinship is a death and rebirth, a death in which the participants—the kinsmen chiefly concerned—are made one with the shades and born anew,[4] and this theme is repeated in the ritual of the 'coming out'.

One paradox remains to be clarified. The shades must be

[1] *Rituals of Kinship*, pp. 181-6.   [2] *Good Company*, pp. 107, 240.
[3] *Rituals of Kinship*, p. 185.   [4] *ibid.*, pp. 203-5.

assuaged and men should be *mwelu*, pure, innocent, without anger in their hearts. But, as has been shown, this quality of purity is the very *opposite* of spiritual power (*amanga* or *ubusisya*). It is attributed neither to Kyala and the other heroes nor to the priests; according to Kasitile (p. 138) a pure person cannot be a commoner priest and the chiefs themselves, though *mwelu*—pale—by comparison with the black commoners who are witches, are also 'heavy' (*nsito*) with the medicines they have drunk. Men become *mwelu* by confession; 'speaking out' is a condition of efficacy in sacrifice and the officiant blows out water as a symbol of bringing up all the anger that was in his heart. The parents of twins and the priests of Lubaga, having celebrated their awful rituals emerge, crying, '*Tuli belu*'—we are pure. The very quality which rituals produce in men is the *opposite* of that which characterizes their heroes, their priests, and their rulers. Galahad whose 'strength was as the strength of ten because his heart was pure' is wholly foreign to Nyakyusa thought.

Truthfulness was never mentioned as a characteristic of the righteous or the pure, nor is it a quality of the heroes or priests. Men censure one another for *ubutungulu* which is commonly translated as 'lying', but means rather 'speaking indiscreetly'. In one Nyakyusa text the child who is told certain ritual secrets by his father and reveals them when he should not is *ntungulu*, and this is an accepted use of the word. No burning concern with truth or falsehood is apparent in the Nyakyusa tradition though they are passionately interested in what they conceive to be right and wrong.

The conception of witchcraft and sorcery implies a freedom, a choice of good or evil, for the individual. Much is determined. In Nyakyusa thought, the sins of the fathers are visited on the children, and a child may fall ill because his great-grandfather shed blood or was bound with ropes, and was not adequately cleansed, or because his father has neglected a ward; moreover, kinsmen are 'members one of another', and a ritual neglected by one may bring suffering to others; but there is *also* the notion of individual responsibility. A witch or sorcerer acts consciously and voluntarily—our informants scouted the idea of a witch being unaware of his actions—and he may repent and desist. There are now, periodically in Africa, 'revivalist' movements in which a pagan doctor or diviner urges men to throw away their evil medicines and repent from their witchcraft. One such movement swept through BuNyakyusa in the early 1930's; perhaps other similar movements preceded it—we do not know. What is clear is that traditionally there was continuous public pressure to overcome hatred within the village and the kinship group; to rid oneself of it by confession and an expression of goodwill. In pagan thought Utopia is a society without witches or sorcerers and, though it was never achieved, everyone is convinced that formerly these evil-doers were fewer than now, because they were restrained by law, whereas 'witches' now go scot-free.

The interests of the Nyakyusa are personal and practical. Health, fertility, and amity between kinsmen and neighbours are what they seek. It is with rain and drought, with the rise of the Lake or the striking of lightning which destroys property; with stock, crops, and the wild animals which prey upon them that the myths are concerned. We could trace no tales of the sun, moon, and stars, and no rituals are directed to them. Reference is made to volcanic disturbance in the myths of the heroes— 'the ground rumbled' when Nkekete and Kyala walked, and there are stories of small lakes disappearing and reappearing elsewhere— but the concern shown is surprisingly little if an eruption indeed destroyed villages last century as Mr. Harkin's single informant suggests (*vide supra*, p. 16).

Reality is thought to be revealed to men in dreams, by prophets who 'go down thinking like the roots of a tree' to the world of the shades, and by oracles. What men seek to know are the causes of misfortune—public and private—and the identity of witches. Occasionally, it is said, a prophet has looked into the future and foretold drought, or flood, or the coming of Europeans—'white things on the Lake'—against whom it would be foolish to fight, but for the most part they are concerned with the misfortunes that exist, and urging men to pray in the groves. The contemplative is not honoured in Nyakyusa tradition; the man of spiritual power is a detective—a discoverer of evil-doers—or an administrator whose awfulness adds to his authority.

Men are preoccupied with their relationships to other living men—their kinsmen, neighbours, and fellow office-holders— and with their dead fathers. They are not concerned with their relationship to Kyala. The rituals celebrated by kinsmen are directed to the shades not to any supreme God, and it is quarrelling between kinsmen that angers the shades and makes the celebration of certain rituals necessary. The communal rituals are

directed towards heroes who are also forefathers, and it is quarrelling between chiefs and priests or village headmen that disturbs the
natural order and causes disease and failure of crops. Kasitile was
a famous priest, a man of perception, more than usually aware of
the deeper implications of the rituals, but he never spoke of any
personal relationship with Kyala, and he brushed aside the
diviner's suggestion that his sickness was due to Kyala. He was
dogged by a sense of guilt which, in pagan terms, could be re-
deemed only by sacrifice to his father and persuading his fellow
priests to 'speak out' and admit their anger against him. Only
when he was referring explicitly to Christian doctrine did he hint
at redemption by Kyala (*vide supra*, pp. 128-9, 141). The genius
of Nyakyusa religion is an awareness of the corrupting power of
'anger in the heart' and the necessity of confession and reconciliation if men are to be healthy in mind and body; they have no
developed conception of God comparable to that of the Nuer.
To them it is not 'the first and greatest commandment' which is
familiar but 'the second which is like unto it'.

CHAPTER XII

PAGAN AND CHRISTIAN

(a) THE GROWTH OF A CHRISTIAN COMMUNITY

WITH the arrival of European missionaries at the end of the nineteenth century[1] a new set of religious ideas was introduced and a new form of social grouping established. The early missionaries settled on land which they bought from various chiefs and gathered round them workers and refugees—the survivors of slave-raids in neighbouring areas—many of whom gradually became converts. In BuNyakyusa a new type of village, a Christian village, was established on mission land and the converts who occupied it were largely withdrawn from the authority of the chief, looking instead to the missionary as their leader. In Ngonde the development was rather different. The converts were not gathered on mission land but stayed in their own villages, where they were expected to spread the gospel among their neighbours. The difference was partly due to a difference in policy between the Scottish mission operating[2] in Ngonde, and the Moravian and Lutheran[3] missions operating in BuNyakyusa, but it was emphasized by differences in the history of the two areas. In Ngonde the missionaries became the allies of the Ngonde against the Arab slavers, whereas in BuNyakyusa there was no such alliance. The Scottish mission deliberately sought to convert and train the traditional leaders, and so gain the whole community, whereas the Moravians and Lutherans preferred to withdraw their converts from the surrounding pagan community.[4]

The number of converts increased much more rapidly in Ngonde than in BuNyakyusa, but after forty years of missionary activity the structural pattern was growing similar. More and more

[1] For an account of the first contacts of the Nyakyusa and Ngonde with Europeans, and bibliography on it, cf. Monica Wilson, *Good Company*, pp. 81-1, 275-6.

[2] The Livingstonia Mission of the Free Church of Scotland which later united with the Church of Scotland. It is still referred to in Ngonde as 'Free Church'.

[3] The Berlin Society (Berlin I).

[4] For an admirable account of the development of mission policy in East Africa, see Roland Oliver, *The Missionary Factor in East Africa* (1952). Dr. Oliver describes the withdrawal of converts on to mission stations as typical of the *first* phase of mission activity and this is true for the Moravian and Lutheran missions, but Christians in Ngonde were never so withdrawn.

12*b*. NYASURU, LEADER OF THE AFRICAN
NATIONAL CHURCH

12*a*. NGEMELA, FOUNDER OF A SEPARATIST
CHURCH

13. MARIA, A CHRISTIAN ELDER

of the Nyakyusa converts chose to live, not in Christian villages on mission land, but in Christian sections of pagan villages—often grouped round a school—and after the establishment of Indirect Rule in 1926 the independence of Nyakyusa living on mission land from the authority of chiefs was no longer recognized officially, though in practice they were not regarded as chiefs' men in quite the same way as other people when it came to calling up conscripts for labour service. One of the signs of the difference between pagan and Christian in relation to the chief is that Christians are not punctilious about sending to the chiefs the customary cut (the breast) of every animal killed, as are pagans, and even the most conservative do not fear the 'breath' of their neighbours if they neglect the tribute.

After the war of 1914-18 three new missions were established in the Nyakyusa valley: the White Fathers, the Benedictines, and the Pentecostal Holiness Association. Two churches of purely African origin emerged: the Last Church of God and His Christ, commonly called the BaNgemela after its leader, and the African National Church led by Paddy Nyasuru, which flourished in Ngonde and had a few members across the Songwe in Bu-Nyakyusa. And there was a small group of Watch Tower[1] with Nyakyusa leaders, but acknowledging a vague affiliation with a Watch Tower mission in Northern Rhodesia, and corresponding with the Watch Tower offices in Cape Town, from which they obtained literature. As the publications sent were in English or Nyanja, neither of which the local Watch Tower members could read,[2] and the correspondence was also in English, the link was a tenuous one, but Rutherford's apocalyptic pamphlets, prophesying a speedy judgement on 'the goat class', were carried about reverently.

Therefore, by 1935 there were a number of different religious associations, more or less closely connected. The Moravians, Lutherans, and Church of Scotland worked in different areas and co-operated closely; but between them and the Roman Catholics and Pentecostal and the purely African or 'independent' Churches there was little co-operation and sometimes tension. The great bulk of the Christians (74 per cent) belong to the three long-established missions—Moravian, Lutheran, and Church of

[1] Jehovah's Witnesses. For an account of the tenets and international organization of this denomination, see Horton Davies, *Christian Deviations*, O.U.P. (1954), pp. 63 ff.

[2] We ourselves were called upon as scribes and translators.

Scotland—and it is with their organization that we are primarily concerned.

Each denomination is divided into congregations, local groups living in villages surrounding a central Church which usually has its own pastor or minister—European or African—in charge, though the shortage of men and funds after 1914 meant that one minister was sometimes in charge of two congregations. For the fifteen congregations of the three Churches mentioned there were eleven ministers in 1937, three of them Africans, and the congregations varied in size from just over 600 to 3,000 members. They included communicant members—that is, adults who had been baptized, and the children of Christians who, after having been baptized in infancy, were confirmed during adolescence—children of Christians who had been baptized but not yet confirmed; 'hearers' and catechumens who were undergoing a two or three years' period of instruction before baptism, and members under discipline who, because of some serious breach of Church law were not, for the time being, admitted to communion. Women members outnumbered the men by more than three to one in the congregations in Ngonde (where many men were away as labour migrants) and by three to two in the Moravian congregations in BuNyakyusa.

The functions of the congregation are worship, evangelization, religious instruction, and sometimes, general education and welfare. Each congregation chooses elders from among its members and they, together with the minister, form the 'Session' or Church Court which deals with matters of discipline and administration within its area, as well as discussing matters of Church policy which may later be brought up before a higher court or council.

Both men and women are eligible for office as elders, but their duties are somewhat different. Each male elder is in charge of the Christians in a given area, usually those living in one age-village. He organizes services in the village, often taking them himself, and choosing suitable people from among the residents to help him. He instructs candidates for baptism, holding the weekly classes for 'hearers' and catechumens; he visits the sick; above all he must try and compose quarrels among his people. It is customary among pagans for a husband and wife who quarrel to take their dispute to a senior kinsman or to a neighbour; among Christians such disputes are usually taken to the elder, since the Church is immediately concerned in maintaining the marriage bond. The elder watches over the morals of his flock and it is his duty to report to the Session any breaches of Church law among his people. Through him the cards entitling members to attend communion are distributed, and cards are withheld from those whom the Session has agreed must be suspended from membership. Each man has, on the average, 125 people to care for. The women elders organize the women's weekly meetings, and take parties of women on preaching tours in pagan villages. They are the leaders in any charitable activities of the congregation and in the instruction of a Christian girl at her marriage. A woman elder settles disputes between two women, and in family quarrels she is often asked by the elder in charge of the village to help him to reconcile the couple. She is also a supervisor of morals and reports to the local elder if she 'hears any woman speaking like a pagan'. Deacons are elected like elders and are primarily responsible for the collection of Church dues and the administration of Church funds, but in a village in which there is no elder a deacon will carry out some of his duties.

In practice, then, each local group—a Christian village or village section—has its chosen leader, a male elder or deacon who conducts daily prayers in the local school house or his own home, and also fulfils many of the functions of an assistant village headman, arbitrating in disputes and acting as the spokesman of his village section. The traditional organization of the age-villages, in which an individual had some choice as to the village he should join, and was not bound by kinship connexions, makes an adaptation to villages in which those of the same faith live together easy. It is noticeable that the Pentecostal and Watch Tower converts build their own village sections apart from Moravians or Lutherans. And since the traditional village leaders are chosen, not hereditary, it is very easy for a leading Christian to become an assistant headman, more or less formally recognized by the village headman named at the 'coming out'.

At first the teachers were more directly under the supervision of the missionary than of the congregation, being selected by him and paid by the mission, but in the middle thirties, when funds from Germany ceased coming to the Moravian and Lutheran missions, the payment of village school teachers fell on the congregations of these denominations. Each village wanting a school had to provide a building, and in this pagans and Christians often co-operated, for many pagans also wanted their children to learn to read and write. In BuNyakyusa none of these village teachers was qualified and none received Government grants; they taught only the three R's in the vernacular and gave religious instruction. In Ngonde, however, some of them were qualified. Besides the village schools there were by 1935 central schools at mission stations, organized by the missions, and some of them drawing Government grants, which took children up to Standard IV; and at Rungwe and Kondowe (Livingstonia) just south of Ngonde, there were mission boarding schools, giving further education and (at Kondowe) training teachers, evangelists, and ministers. The policy of different missions regarding education varied; the Church of Scotland missionaries believed in it whole-heartedly and achieved a relatively high standard in their village schools; but the Lutherans were doubtful how far it was the function of a Church to give anything except religious instruction, and in their village schools children barely learnt to read. Opinion among the Moravians was divided. But despite these differences, all the missions have, in fact, played a great part in education. The first step—the reduction of the language to writing—was the work of the missionaries alone, and village schools have been very closely linked with congregations because, whatever their views on education in general, Protestant missionaries were agreed that to read the Gospels is the making of a Christian, and so literacy is usually required of candidates for baptism. Hence, the same man is often both teacher and elder, and the German missionaries who questioned the value of education laid the foundation of Nyakyusa literature with an admirable translation of the New Testament.

The missions have also been concerned with medical work. From before 1914 there has been a hospital run by the Lutheran mission at Itete, and one run by the Church of Scotland at Kondowe and, for a period, a large leper-settlement was run by the White Fathers at Mwakete. Medical activities are not directly the concern of congregations but Christian women are often drawn in as voluntary helpers in one way or another. In Kabembe the women deacons drew water for the sick and prepared food for a newly confined mother; at Karonga the women's association of the Church made clothes to be distributed through the babies' clinic, and so forth.

The congregations are not wholly self-supporting—the European missionaries are all paid from overseas and, until the middle thirties, funds for paying village teachers and evangelists were largely drawn from overseas also, but a consistent attempt was made to teach members to contribute to their Church. In 1935 2s. a year was expected from a man, 1s. a year from a woman, i.e. four to six days' unskilled labour for a man, or a pot of beer for a woman, at the rates then ruling. Ten cents (1d.) a term was charged for each child in the village schools. Members of the congregation also provided labour for Church building.

The organization of Church government varies somewhat with the denomination. The congregations of the Scottish mission have joined with those of some other denominations to form the 'Church of Central Africa' and, following the mother Churches, they are grouped in presbyteries, composed of the minister[1] and three elders of each congregation in a particular area. The various presbyteries of the Church of Central Africa in Nyasaland and Northern Rhodesia are united in a synod which meets every four years and is the final authority in the Church. The organization of the Moravian congregations is similar; but until 1938 the Lutheran congregations were directly under the European Superintendent who was responsible to the Mission Board in Germany.

In the mission churches the universal aspect of the Church is stressed, and there is an awareness of unity with members of the same denomination outside the local area, with mother Churches in Europe, and with certain other denominations, even among the less sophisticated. In sermons in village churches the fact that their congregations were praying together with congregations of other tribes and denominations was repeatedly mentioned by African preachers. By contrast, the two 'independent' African Churches are local Churches without connexions beyond the north Nyasa area, though they do include members from different tribes.

The African National Church began in 1927, the initial impetus coming from a Nyasa, Gordon Nsumba, who had been for some time in South Africa; another of the pastors was Robert Sambo who had worked with Clement Kadalie (himself a Lakeside Tonga) in the Industrial and Commercial Workers' Union in South Africa;[2] but the organizer and leader was a Henga, Paddy Nyasuru, who had never travelled far. He was an ex-teacher and elder of the Church of Scotland Mission and had been a clerk in

[1] European ministers are assessors only, not full members.
[2] cf. Monica Hunter, *Reaction to Conquest*, O.U.P. (1936), p. 567.

Government service for a number of years. Most of the members of the Church, and all the office-bearers, were Henga, some of them living, like Nyasuru himself, in the Kyungu's country, but there were also a few Ngonde and Nyakyusa.

Silwani Ngemela, the leader of 'The Last Church of God and His Christ', was also an ex-teacher and elder of the Church of Scotland Mission. He was of Ngonde lineage, the son of a minor chief, and had been a member of the Watch Tower, but had broken away from it and formed his own Church in 1925—retaining the practice of baptism by immersion 'in Jordan' which he had learnt from the Watch Tower. He, too, had been closely connected with a man, Jordan Msumba, who had worked in South Africa; indeed some said that Msumba, who had been for many years in Cape Town, was the real founder of the Church. Most of Ngemela's members were Nyakyusa or Ngonde.

Nyasuru and Ngemela each emphasized the independence of his Church from any other and each was somewhat jealous of his position as a leader. As Ngemela put it, 'The Governor corresponds with me alone'. In his Church all monies go direct to him, and there had already been a quarrel with one 'pastor' who had split off because he said that the Church funds should be lodged in the Boma and used to build a school. The BaNgemela had no schools and none of their pastors was paid. Nyasuru made a point of the fact that his deacons collected the Church funds and banked them in the name of the Church, and the African National Church did in fact run several schools (one of them within the Ngonde area) and pay the teachers.

Though the membership of the 'independent' African Churches was not very large (in the Nyakyusa-Ngonde area a total membership of 8,577 was claimed in 1938, but some of these probably lived outside this area), yet these Churches are symptomatic of a movement that has been important elsewhere. Nearly a fifth of the Africans who are professing Christians in the Union of South Africa belong to 'independent' Churches,[1] and a substantial number in Kenya. These Churches are a structural expression of the conflict between European and African, and of the desire of Africans to be independent leaders, but yet recognized as

[1] *Official Year Book of the Union of South Africa, 1952-3*, pp. 251, 497. But the proportion had declined from 16·5 per cent to 9·6 per cent of the total Bantu population between 1911 and 1946. *Official Summary of the Report of the Commission for the Socio-Economic Development of the Bantu Areas within the Union of South Africa* (U.G. 61/1955), p. 21.

Christians. A revealing phrase was used of Ngemela by one of his followers: 'He is our European.'

Two sets of rituals are celebrated in BuNyakyusa, but there are not two communities. Nearly all the Christians have pagan kinsfolk with whom they co-operate in practical affairs, many of the Christians live in pagan villages, though usually in separate sections of them. In the early years of the missions there was clearly some friction—there were accusations of witchcraft against those who learnt to read and write for if they were not witches how could they have learnt? And there was talk of people 'hiding their witchcraft in Christianity'. Pagans averred that in the land of the shades Christians ate frogs—a symbol of difference and dislike oddly familiar to Englishmen. But by 1935 it had become almost conventional for a boy who went to school to become Christian, and if later he became betrothed to a pagan girl, she was expected to join a catechumen's class and be baptized also. The opposition from pagan kinsfolk was small except in the case of an heir to wealth or office. Then there was bitter objection. For if a young man became Christian he could neither inherit his father's wives nor increase the influence of the lineage in the approved fashion by marrying several wives himself, and much of the family wealth would pass to a junior line. If a convert were heir to a chiefdom, or likely to succeed his father as village headman, it was felt that he would not be able to maintain his position with only one wife, and succession to a pagan priesthood was totally impossible.

The Christians, for their part, press their pagan relatives to join them in the Church, and a considerable proportion of conversions occur in this way. It is common for a mother to join her son, or a younger brother his elder brother of the same house. For a father, to whom baptism would mean sending away all his wives save one, the step is a much more difficult one and indeed not pressed by some missionaries, who are aware of the difficulties of elderly women so divorced. But whether kinsfolk worship together or not, there can still be amity and friendship.

Thus, in addition to the traditional system of chiefdoms and villages with groups of chiefs co-operating to perform sacrifices to common ancestors and certain more distant heroes, there are Christian Churches whose members are organized in local congregations, and presbytery or diocese. The traditional religion expresses the unity of lineages and chiefdoms: the new religion expresses the unity of groups of believers who associate in Churches. But the two systems are not wholly exclusive: the Christian still belongs to a lineage and a chiefdom, though he does not worship as a member of either, and thereby impairs their solidarity.

(b) THE CHRISTIAN WITHDRAWAL

What is the attitude of Christian converts to the rituals performed by their pagan kinsmen and neighbours and what replaces the traditional pagan rituals in the Christian community? These questions have already been touched upon in the accounts of pagan rituals, but we must now consider them more fully.

Christians withdraw very largely from the pagan rituals of kinship which, as was shown in a previous book, are directed to the shades. They attend the funerals of pagan kinsmen to weep and comfort the mourners, and they often undertake the work of grave-digging so fearful to pagans, but they take no part in the 'farewell to the dead' nor do the stricter among them eat of the funeral meat, since the cattle killed are an offering to the shades. Christians do not participate in the twin ritual which brings together such a large number of pagan kinsmen, nor do they share in the puberty ritual, and they forbid their daughters to keep a pagan bride company during her seclusion. For the most part their withdrawal is accepted tolerantly by their pagan kin who carry on without them, a pagan father even performing the 'farewell to the dead' for a Christian son who has died, lest his lineage shades be angered by the omission, but occasionally the non-participation of Christians leads to strained relations, as when pagans refuse to visit or eat with a bride or a remarried widow who has not celebrated with them after her union with her husband, and sometimes a Church member, under pressure from pagan relatives or driven by his own fears, celebrates the ritual for a pagan father. The dropping of the elaborate twin ritual creates surprisingly little difficulty considering how much the pagans fear sickness from twins. Their birth is interpreted by Christians as a special blessing —a bounteous increase—rather than 'an illness' as the pagans call it. A Christian woman, asked if a mother of twins was not fearful when the ritual was omitted, gave a classic reply: 'What she thinks in her heart I can't see; what I think in my heart you can't see; but we *do* see that no one avoids her when they meet her face to face.'

The negative rituals—the taboos which surround the pro-creative functions—disappear rather slowly, but a Christian father will enter his wife's hut to greet her after she has given birth to a child, and will eat food cooked by her a week or two later, which the pagans think extremely rash. An atmosphere of scepticism and experiment begins to develop; a few Christians spoke of breaking even the deeply-entrenched taboos surrounding menstruation 'to see what happened'. But that many Christians, especially women, feared the old taboos was apparent when one watched the behaviour of Christian daughters-in-law towards their fathers-in-law. In theory Christians disregarded the rules of avoidance if their fathers-in-law are Christian, or avoid 'only a little', but in practice a Christian woman is usually embarrassed and fearful if, by mischance, she meets her father-in-law face to face.[1]

Christians withdraw from the pagan communal rituals even more completely than they do from the rituals of kinship. No Christian takes any part in the sacrifices to the heroes, or at the groves of chiefs, or in cleansing the country, or in rain-making, or sprinkling the homesteads. As for the ritual of chieftainship, from that also Christians withdraw. At the time we were first in BuNyakyusa only two chiefs were professing Christians, one of whom was already baptized before his installation. The 'coming out' performed for him was much curtailed since he refused to use the traditional medicines and, because of the difficulty over medicines, Christians were not acceptable as village headmen. In Ngonde, where the proportion of Christians was much greater, there were Christian headmen and chiefs, but the ritual of 'coming out' had disappeared altogether, and the Kyungu had delegated the celebration of all pagan rituals to one of his councillors who still believed in them, he himself being a sceptic.

There are tales of the early missionaries visiting the groves to challenge pagan belief. The pagans believe that they were confounded and some of the more conservative Christians also think that the terror of the grove drove the Reverend — Jauer from Lubaga (*vide supra*, p. 29) and that *because* the Reverend — Kleus summoned the teachers and school children to a feast in the grove of Mbyanga, and killed 'a black cow' for them there, a season of plenty followed. 'Many people said: "He seems to have been advised by someone, why did he go to Mbyanga and sing

[1] For an account of such a meeting, cf. Monica Wilson, *Good Company*, pp. 84-5.

there?" And after he went there was much food.' In fact, it appears that he took the teachers and schoolchildren to the grove that they might no longer be afraid of it: the girls gathered fire-wood there, and everyone entered and made a noise, thus breaking great taboos. But all this happened long ago (the visit to Mbyanga was in 1913 or 1914) and, as was indicated earlier, the common view among Christians is that pagan rituals *used* to be necessary and efficacious, but are so no longer. We were assured by Christ-ians who themselves took no part in twin rituals that 'formerly people fell ill if they did not celebrate'. 'Yes, of course, they were very sick indeed in the old days, the whole body would swell.' Some even maintained that it was still necessary for pagans to celebrate though not for Christians. A Christian chief explained:

The sacred grove of Mwakihaba is just here in my country; . . . in the old days they used to take a little fresh milk and an unripe stem of bananas, and put them in the grove. . . . The next day the calabash was full of milk and the stem was ripe. This was really so in the old days, Kyala heard men and agreed to their requests in this way. We went to ask for rain and food in the groves; the chief would kill a cow and Kyala agreed, food and rain came. Now that the Gospel has spread, since the Europeans have opened the Gospel to us Kyala refuses to agree, he says: 'Since they are proud and refuse to hear the Gospel I will discipline them', and he refuses to agree to the old ways.
QUESTION: What about witchcraft?
Perhaps there were people who were witches in the old days; at any rate I know that when milk ran short and a man was accused to the chief of bewitching the cattle, the chief used to take his cattle and drive him out of the country, and then milk was plentiful again. Of that I am sure.
QUESTION: And now?
No, it is not like that now.

Many pagans attribute the decline in fertility which is taking place, and the decrease in the yield of milk, to the decay of the old communal rituals and the unhampered activities of witches.

Nevertheless, as the number of Christians in an area increases, the pagans tend to curtail their rituals more and more. The direct parallel between pagan confession, sacrifice, and com-munion with the shades, and the Holy Communion of the Christian Church is recognized by many, and one is felt to replace the other. Regarding the rituals of kinship we were repeatedly told: 'We see that the Christians, who say the only rituals are the

Christian ones, do not celebrate and nothing happens to them, so we no longer fear ourselves.' By 1937 the pagan rituals of kinship had been largely dropped in Ngonde, and around Rungwe mission they were disappearing, though in Selya no pagan dared neglect them. They were taken more seriously by the women than by the men, and many of the young men were openly scornful. The young men are eclectic in their beliefs, jeering at the twin ritual when they may be fearful of any neglect of the ritual of death; doubting the power of rain-makers, but terrified of a neighbour's sorcery.

(c) CHRISTIAN RITUAL AND DOGMA

And what are the alternatives to the traditional rituals? Celebrations at death, marriage, and birth continue—probably some sort of ritual on these occasions is universal in human societies. There is no celebration of a girl's puberty, as among the pagans, but the ritual of confirmation is, in one sense, parallel, for it is an acknowledgment of maturity by the acceptance of an individual into the full fellowship of the Church; but maturity in the Church, and the symbolic death and rebirth, are not necessarily linked with physiological development, as they are in the pagan ritual of *ubusungu*.[1]

All the Christian rituals are *communal* in the sense that they are centred in the Church—the Christian community; none is primarily a ritual of kinship. This is most pointed at a christening, when a child is received into the fellowship of the Church, whereas in the pagan birth ritual it is acknowledged as a member of the father's lineage by being given *ikipiki* medicine (which is 'the blood of the lineage') by its paternal grandmother. Sometimes both rituals are celebrated by Christians who interpret the *ikipiki* as an acknowledgment of legitimacy, and a medicine necessary to the child's health, but this is frowned upon by the more orthodox. A dying man is comforted by the priest or elders of the Church, and in some communions he receives the sacrament, the symbol of his salvation through Christ and his membership of the community of believers. At a funeral the members of the local Christian congregation take the leading part, comforting the mourners with prayers and hymns, digging the grave, and burying the dead. The contrast with a pagan funeral, in which cattle are

[1] The pagan rituals referred to in this section are described in *Rituals of Kinship among the Nyakyusa*.

killed that the dead man may be received by the shades of his lineage, and his immediate kin eat *ikipiki* medicines with him for the last time, is marked.

Marriages and funerals, and in a lesser degree births, are occasions for gatherings of kinsmen in Western society—such a penetrating study of kinship as *The Forsyte Saga* bears adequate witness to this—but the gathering of kinsfolk is a ceremonial rather than a ritual.[1] The attendance of the Forsyte men at Aunt Ann's burial service is in no way essential to the service, though it is felt to be a mark of respect and 'proper feeling' on their part to come. So also at Nyakyusa Christian funerals, the attendance of relatives and fellow villagers is conventional—people are shocked if they do not come—but the peace of the departed is not thought to depend upon his kinsmen killing cows at his grave and celebrating the 'farewell'; the ritual element is the concern of his fellow Christians, led by the priest or elder, irrespective of kinship connexions. The conventions are binding, however. Though a kinsman or village neighbour is not accused of having killed his fellow if he fails to come to the funeral, nevertheless it would cause offence if he did not come, being free to do so, and should he go to work in the fields on the day of the funeral of a grown man, a neighbour, his position would be intolerable.

At a Christian funeral the emphasis all through is on resurrection and life. The hymns sung to comfort the mourners and the prayers and words of the burial service stress resurrection: 'This corruption has put on incorruption, this mortality immortality' ... 'the body of the flesh is buried, but the body of the spirit rises.' ... 'Our friend is not dead but liveth.' . . . 'Oh death where is thy sting, oh grave (*busyuka*) where is thy victory?' And the weeping, though extravagant to English ears, is much more restrained than among pagans. Again and again we were told by Christians: 'We do not fear death as the pagans do', and certainly fear is not played up as in the pagan ritual. As one Christian put it: 'No Christian smears himself with mud; only the pagans fear very much at a death, they are desolate, but we do not fear, we say: "Indeed I shall die, but I shall rise again", so we do not smear ourselves with mud and grieve very much. . . . We say: "Why mud? We shall meet with him above." ' And there is no later shaving or other purification, for the mourners are not identified with the corpse.

[1] For a discussion of this distinction, cf. *op. cit.*, p. 9.

The corpse is buried in a coffin, if the kinsmen can afford one, but it is still placed in a niche dug in the wall of the grave, which is usually in the homestead, for though cemeteries have been marked out in the Christian villages most families prefer to bury their dead at home. The Lutherans kill cattle, some distance from the grave, to feed the mourners but the Moravians and Presbyterians do not, on the grounds that the pagans believe that funeral cattle go with the dead and if Christians kill they seem to support the belief. Relatives, especially sons-in-law, are expected to bring white cloths in place of cattle to show their sympathy and these are used as a shroud, or to bind the chief mourners' bellies, to support them. And the family provide as much fine food—rice, chicken, groundnuts—as they can, for the mourners. But the crowd is smaller than at a pagan funeral for a man of equal standing, because the pagans crowd to funerals to enjoy the feasting and dancing. The Christians sing, and their hymns change from mournful to cheerful ones after the burial, and on the second or third day the young people may dance a little, but without the wild exuberance that succeeds the pagan passion of grief. Often, however, the funeral is a mixed one. Most Christians have pagan relatives and family obligations are not obliterated by differences in faith. So we sometimes heard drumming alternating with Christian hymns, or saw a war dance succeed the burial service, or a pagan woman honouring her Christian sister by dancing with her grain basket, and providing for her future comfort by burying her cooking-pot and cosmetics in the grave. All this the Christian elders present take with tolerance: 'It makes no difference if they choose to do it.'

The wedding celebrations of Nyakyusa Christians are in two parts: there is the solemnization of the marriage in Church and registration by a priest or minister who is a marriage officer, or the blessing of the union by an elder of the Church; and there is the handing over of the marriage cattle accompanied by feasting and dancing and certain other elements of the traditional ritual. The Moravian missionaries are reluctant to celebrate a marriage unless they are very certain of the characters of the bride and bridegroom because of the difficulties and expense of securing a legal divorce if the wife is later deserted by her husband. They prefer that a customary marriage should be blessed by an elder who is not a marriage officer, then, if one partner deserts, a legal divorce is easy.

The festivities and display are most often linked, not to the Church ritual, but to the handing over of marriage cattle. Since the feasts of the puberty ritual are not celebrated, the Christians concentrate their energies on the *ukukwa*, when quantities of food are provided by the bride's family, and a crowd gathers to sing and dance. Then, some time after the cattle have been handed over, the bride is taken to her husband by a party of 'mothers' and friends, and a feast is provided by the groom. The pattern is very similar to that of the pagan handing over of marriage cattle (*ukukwa*) and bringing home the bride (*ukubeka*), but new songs and dances replace the somewhat bawdy pagan ones, and the Christian youths, unlike the pagans, dance without spears. Often at a Christian wedding pagans also attend, and there are rival groups of dancers, pagans, and Christians, between whom quarrels readily flare up. And when the new songs and dances of the Christians are copied by the pagans, as they sometimes are, then the Christians drop them, for they wish to be different.

The traditional examination of the bride by the 'mothers' and the giving of a bull if she goes to her husband a virgin, are maintained in the Christian community. The bull is usually killed as a feast for the mothers 'to say thank you for nourishing her', but there is, of course, no offering of the sacred meat to the ancestors, and sometimes the bull is not killed at all, or the groom brings shillings instead. As so often happens, a former ritual survives as ceremonial, an observance felt to be specially appropriate to the occasion, but no longer regarded as a condition of health or salvation.

When she is taken to her husband the bride is exhorted by her 'mothers' on her duties as a married woman. The traditional emphasis on separation from her mother is still there: 'You have left your mother, your husband is your mother, we have separated. . . .' And she is exhorted to be chaste, to obey her husband and answer him submissively, to be clean and diligent in her work, to be hospitable, and above all, as a Christian, to feed 'those from a distance'. Here the contrast between pagan and Christian ethics is emphasized: a pagan wife is only obliged to cook for kinsmen and neighbours, not strangers, but for a Christian to let a stranger starve is spoken of as a mortal sin.

The annual festivals of the Church are not so closely parallel to pagan communal rituals, for they were developed in a northern and temperate climate with a rhythm very different from the succession of 'sun', 'rain' and 'cold' into which the Nyakyusa year is divided; but there are parallels in the traditional prayers for rain, and at seedtime and harvest, which the Christians are quick to point out. What is totally new to the Nyakyusa is the division of a year into weeks, each with a day of rest and worship; but the conception once introduced has been accepted very quickly, and it is common to find pagans as well as Christians refraining from work in their fields on a Sunday. This is partly the effect of experience in European employment when Sunday is a day off, but partly, perhaps, it is because the idea of taboo is deeply embedded in pagan thought, and the teaching of some missionaries and converts has been in terms of taboo—of prohibitions connected with 'the Sabbath'.

In the Christian villages and village-sections, some at least of the converts gather for morning and evening prayer and on Sundays in their little mud Church or school-house, and once a month or once a quarter they gather in the main Church of the district. Besides this, those seeking baptism or preparing for confirmation gather for regular weekly instruction over a period of two or three years. There is thus regular common worship and instruction, and a strong sense of community between fellow Christians, particularly when they are in a small minority in an area.

But though the Christian is a member of a Church and worships in community, the emphasis (at least in the Protestant Churches in BuNyakyusa) tends to be on the individual, and some pagans spoke as if turning Christian implied an abandoning of public duties. Kasitile's remark that if it were not for his responsibility for the ritual he would be baptized, has already been quoted (p. 141), and the young priest of PaliKyala said the same. Whether these two were serious in wishing to become Christian is irrelevant here; they both believed that they had duties to their community which could not be fulfilled if they were Christians. The 'individualism' of young Christians is a matter of concern to many missionaries who are struggling to create among Christians that very sense of mystical union which pagan kinsmen exhibit.

The idea of the corporate nature of the worshipping group, with all that implies in mutual responsibility, is but one example of the profound similarity between the underlying ideas of pagan and Christian ritual that will be apparent to most readers. In the pagan tradition confession, oblation, and communion are as essential to the sacrifices at the groves as they are to the Christian eucharist;

marriage is a sacrament, a mystical union of husband and wife who wash together in the 'blood' of the husband's lineage; and at death kinsmen share a communion with the 'faithful departed'.

We have already touched on the changing conception of *Kyala*. The idea of a supreme power, or creator, distinct from the shades and heroes, is clear enough to Christians and is becoming more and more familiar to pagans, a young priest even insisting that his father and Kasitile could bring rain only 'if God wills' (*vide supra*, p. 119). Christians believe that 'God alone sends rain', and they are profoundly sceptical of the pagan rain-maker.

The Christians also speak of Satan (*Satano*) whom some identify with 'Mbasi' (Lwembe) and to whom the more orthodox attribute evil dreams of snakes and lions and fighting, which the pagans attribute to witchcraft. To the pagan the snake *is* the witch come to attack him; to the Christian it is Satan come to tempt him. The orthodox, following the teaching of missionaries, deny the existence of witchcraft, but most admit to a lively fear of sorcery which is rationalized as 'poisoning', though when the conception is examined it can be shown to include much beside poison put in food or drink. Some of our closest Christian friends admitted their fears. X, the Christian wife of a pagan chief, said one day when we were discussing witchcraft: 'You dissemble like all Europeans, you do not wish to admit belief in witchcraft, you are just pretending.' 'You really think we believe in it?' 'Yes, we all know that Europeans just hide their belief.'

Another chief's wife, Y, also a professing Christian, said: 'We all believe in witchcraft, it really exists.' Then she went on to tell how someone had come to 'choke' her one night recently when she was visiting her own people:

I woke out of a heavy sleep with a pain in the back of my neck and my head. It was as if someone was stamping on my head. I woke up feeling heavy, I was very heavy. I said: 'If I die, you also will die. Who is outside? Who is choking me? Do they not fear God (Kyala)?' Then someone kicked the door and I shouted, 'Mother, mother!' and I heard footsteps going away.

When asked whether she believed that village headmen protected their people from witchcraft she went on:

They fight the witches by night, they protect their people, they see the witches and drive them away.
QUESTION: How do you know that witches really exist, do they admit themselves to be witches?

Yes, indeed, they boast, they say threateningly (she put her arms akimbo, and imitated a menacing voice) 'Don't speak to me like that!'

All through this discussion Y was excited and spoke with vehemence. Next day she came in looking worried and said:

About that choking of which I was telling you, what do *you* think it is when you wake up with pains like that? I'll tell you how it was. I went to see my sister, and found her very ill. She had had a miscarriage and her in-laws had not looked after her properly; they had not sent her to hospital, and when she was lying ill her mother-in-law even refused to come and cook for her. And so I was very, very angry with them. And that night I woke up feeling as if someone were stamping on my head, and I heard the knocking on the door and the footsteps I told you about. What do you make of such things when you dream someone strikes you or is throttling you?

The conception that misfortune is the result of sin, which dominates pagan thought, is reinterpreted in terms of the changing conception of God and the changing social structure. We found that many Christians believed that misfortune had been brought on certain wrong-doers by the 'curse' (*ikigune*) of a priest or elder, or the anger of their Christian neighbours. A missionary or elder rebuking a man was repeatedly thought to have 'cursed' him,[1] so that he lost his job, or fell ill, or was eaten by a crocodile, and in one case a young couple who had not had a child were said to have been cursed by their Christian neighbours because the young man had provided no feast at his wedding. The Christians who believe in such a 'curse' explain that the power comes from God who 'hears people who murmur'—a direct parallel to the pagan belief in the power of senior relatives and neighbours to bring misfortune on wrong-doers—and it is the *words uttered*—the rebuke of one in authority or the murmuring of neighbours—which are held to be dangerous.

How the reproving words of a missionary may be interpreted as a curse is shown in the following case.

The wife of Z was a thief. She stole things from the loft of her mother-in-law's hut. She herself began to say: 'I am tired of my husband', and she began making love to other men. When her husband asked her to do anything she refused. She complained to neighbours, saying: 'My husband is a hard man. He watches me when I am preparing food to

---

[1] Thirteen cases of this type are recorded in *Good Company*, p. 109. cf. Monica Hunter, 'An African Christian Morality', *Africa*, x (1937), pp. 265-9.

N

cook. I want to leave him.' She said to her husband: 'I want to leave you; I should like to be married to another man. I am not old; I shall not fail to get a husband.' The case went to the Church Session. The husband was called. He said: 'I am astonished. This woman is just making trouble. I have not harmed her. But she is a thief. She steals my mother's things.' She said: '*He* is mean. He watches me when I am cooking—either ordinary food or meat. He is a wicked man so I am leaving him.' The Session said: 'Go home and think first.' She came again and said: 'I will leave him.' They said: 'Go and think again.' They sent her home three times. After the third time she came, saying: 'I will leave him.' Then the missionary said: 'We do not find any cause for divorcing your husband. It is astonishing that you, a Christian, wish to go to another man. We find many faults on your side and none on your husband's side. I tell you that the trouble which made you quarrel with your husband will always stay in you. Wherever you go it will follow you.' So she has now become a wanderer, just going about from place to place. People say that this is due to the words of the missionary.

This story shows very clearly how a missionary's insight into a woman's character was interpreted as an external cause of her subsequent misfortunes. The idea that character is a direct cause of misfortune is foreign to the pagan community, and has not been assimilated by many Christians.

On one occasion two Christian teachers and a Christian clerk, who had related several stories in which loss of a job was attributed to a curse, asked our opinion of them. When we explained that we thought that the people mentioned had lost their jobs because they were unsatisfactory servants or teachers our friends expressed surprise. 'I had not thought of that,' said the clerk.[1]

Most of the Nyakyusa Christians we talked to believed in a curse exercised by those in authority in the Church: only a few among the better educated of the leaders scouted the idea. And there were lively arguments about the morality of cursing. Many held it was perfectly justified. Others argued that a Christian should only rebuke his fellow 'openly, to his face', and not curse him but leave the punishment of sinners to God; but, as has just been shown, an open rebuke is often interpreted as a curse.

Often a judgement is thought to be delayed. One young man who committed adultery in particularly offensive circumstances was eaten, seven years later, by a crocodile, and the two facts

[1] Quoted with amendments from 'An African Christian Morality', *Africa*, x (1937), pp. 273-4.

were connected. And if the expected judgement does not fall when a son has wronged his father it is said: 'The father loves the child so much that he only complains half-heartedly.'

It is admitted (when the point is pressed) that misfortunes *may* fall on good men as well as evil, and then they are interpreted as a discipline, a testing, from God, but this is 'a hard saying', scarcely to be believed. The *inequalities* in the fortunes of men demand explanations and Christians, as well as pagans, find it very difficult to believe that they are 'natural'. They always suspect some human intervention; they believe that men manipulate mystical power to buy fortune for themselves. The reality of pythons in the belly may be doubted by the better educated, but belief in 'medicines' has scarcely diminished, and new medicines are constantly coming in from outside, among them costly patent medicines guaranteed to cure any and every disease, or to make the user popular and successful. Some sort of distinction between medicines which it is permissible for a Christian to use and those, like love-potions and defence against witchcraft, which are not permissible, is attempted, but the line is an arbitrary one. And often there is a conflict in the individual's own mind: as one elderly woman of a chief's family (who would normally have taken the first-fruits medicines) put it: 'It's taboo to use these medicines; even if we do fall ill we say: "No, I will not take it, I look towards God (pointing upwards)." '

Most Christians have pagan kinsfolk who are quick to interpret misfortunes in pagan terms, and the sort of conflict of ideas that arises is illustrated in the case of a young woman who died in childbirth. She and her father were Moravians; her husband had joined the Pentecostal Church which rejects all Nyakyusa medicines. Her first child was still-born, the second died shortly after its birth, and her father insisted that she should have been taking a medicine which it was customary for women in his lineage (he was a Penja) to drink during pregnancy; the girl herself wished to be treated, for she did not accept the teaching of the Pentecostal Church on this point, but her husband refused. During her third pregnancy she was ill and finally, with her husband's consent, she was carried to a Nyakyusa doctor of her father's choosing; nevertheless she died. Her father and her husband had been on bad terms, the father demanding, rather arbitrarily, the balance of the marriage cattle; and there was a great deal of gossip, some neighbours hinting that her own father had killed her by his anger, others that the husband was to blame for rejecting medical treatment earlier on. The girl herself was reported to have said to her mother-in-law, when she was lying ill at the doctor's house: 'Are you angry with me and has your anger caused the trouble? Perhaps I did not help you in collecting firewood?' But her mother-in-law replied: 'No, I am not angry with you at all.' And the girl continued: 'I know that my father is angry. Someone might go and ask him to pray for me.' There was also tension with the husband's pagan father who had protested that his son was praying for the death of his own children when he prayed with his Pentecostal friends that God's will be done. 'The Pentecostal people say: "I like to die. I don't take any medicine . . . if someone dies or not it is all the same thing." '

Nevertheless, it is true to say that the field in which natural causation is accepted is much wider among Christians than among pagans. It expands very slowly, but the change is evident. Even two cases of 'madness' (*ukubopa ikigili*), invariably the symptom of the wrath of the gods in pagan thought, were interpreted to us by a Christian teacher in terms of grief and shock. The first was of a young man whose wife and grandmother (who lived with him) both died very suddenly, and whose only cow was taken by other relatives and killed for the funeral feast. The loss of the cow following the loss of his wife and grandmother was held to have shattered him finally—'the lineage was finished'. The other case was of a mother, devoted to her daughter, who was distraught when the daughter went off to a distance, accompanying her husband to his place of work. For a daughter to marry beyond easy visiting distance was traditionally inconceivable.

The vagaries of the weather, attributed by the pagans to the neglect of sacrifices or quarrels between chiefs and priests, are explained in scientific terms by some Christians. Heavy rain fell around Rungwe in October 1937 and prevented people burning their rubbish heaps to fertilize their millet gardens. The pagans insisted that such early rain was unheard of and kept asking each other what could have caused it. A Christian elder assured us that the early rain was *not* very unusual in the hill country; he had seen other seasons like it. And in January of the same year the people of Mwaipopo's country were 'astonished' because no heavy rain had fallen and young maize and millet were shrivelling in the ground. They said: 'It has rained all round' and 'it seems as if we had offended Kyala'. Kasitile went to divine (*vide supra*, p. 119).

We remarked to a Christian friend, a deacon, that the rains were late. He replied: 'Well, it is not so very unusual. Sometimes rains begin in one part of the country and not in another. Sometimes we do not get heavy rain down here until the end of January.' In short, the more educated Christians are beginning to think in more general terms: they do not as yet define probabilities statistically in terms of rainfall averages, but they are tending in that direction.

And what of the positive content of Christianity? The supreme attraction, mentioned again and again as the reason for conversion, is: 'There is life' (*ubumi bulipo*), and it is life in a world to come rather than 'more abundant life' here and now that is spoken of. The contrast is between heaven above and the shadowy world 'beneath' of pagan thought, or a fearful fiery hell in which most Christians believe and to which, some think, all pagans are condemned. Constantly in sermons by Nyakyusa preachers there was stress on life, resurrection, and on the rewards and punishments of the future life, and this theme recurs again and again in the dreams of Christians.

There is a gulf also between the pagan conception of 'driving off' the shades and the heroes lest by 'brooding over' a man they bring madness and death, and the Christian ideal of union with God. Sermons stress the goodness and love of God, characteristics quite foreign to the traditional picture of Kyala.

Something of the quality of Christian thought and feeling may be grasped by an examination of the names taken at baptism—the convert from paganism always chooses a new name for himself and the meaning is more immediately obvious to everyone than it is with modern English Christian names derived, as they mostly are, from languages no longer familiar. Many of the Nyakyusa names express a very direct personal relationship with God, the Redeemer: 'He has looked upon me', 'He has roused me', 'He has waited hoping for me', 'He has died for me', 'He gives me courage', 'He has changed me', 'He has chosen me out', 'He has comforted me', and a score more of the same type. Some refer to the Gospels: 'Word of Truth', 'The Word has taken hold of me'. A few speak of purification: 'Make me white', 'He has washed me'. Some express that union with God which the pagans so greatly fear: 'We are with him', 'He has come near', 'He has brooded over me', 'Let us approach', and some thanksgiving: 'Let us sing to Him', 'We praise Him', 'We have rejoiced', and some life: 'He is risen',

'I have entered into life'; a few express the Christian virtues: 'Love', 'Joy', 'Peace', 'Hope'.

These, then, are the things that the ordinary Nyakyusa emphasize. As will have been obvious to the reader, we are not concerned to outline the orthodox teaching of the mission Churches: that can be readily found in creeds and catechisms; but it is not so easy to discover how these are interpreted by converts just emerging from a pagan society. Our Nyakyusa friends are unanimous in asserting that dogma is never a hindrance to conversion: the only dogmatic conflict that arises is over the Christian denial of traditional pagan belief in the power of the shades and witches. What hinders people from joining the Church is the difficulty of keeping the rules of life, such as monogamy and chastity. This, we were assured, is the reason why there are more women Church members than men, though most conversions come through the schools and more boys go to school than girls. Many men leave the Church because they marry or inherit a second wife and few middle-aged or elderly men come to be baptized because most of them are polygynists, but the first wife of a polygynist (and in the Moravian and Lutheran congregations all the wives) may be Church members and many women are baptized during middle life and old age.

Most of the early converts in BuNyakyusa were already living and working at the mission stations before their baptism. They came either from groups of refugees from slaving caravans who were rescued by the German Administration and settled at the newly founded mission stations, or from the poorer Nyakyusa who found at the mission an opportunity to earn cloth and cattle which presented itself nowhere else. Again and again we were told by elderly converts: 'We came to work at the mission and we listened to the preaching and then the word of God took hold of our hearts.' In the early days those who worked at the mission stations and received some instruction there were the only men in the district with any knowledge of western techniques and manner of life. Later, most of the converts came through the schools, and Christianity, education, and the expectation of skilled employment have gone together. There was a strong feeling among Christians in the 1930's that they could expect something better than work as unskilled labourers. In Ngonde the first Christians were not refugees, but there was the same alliance between Christianity and education. At the request of one of the early missionaries the sons of leading men had been sent to Kondowe to be educated and their influence had been important in gaining the support of the Kyungu and chiefs for the mission.

In the second generation of Christians not nearly all those baptized in infancy come to be confirmed or 'blessed'—an elder in Ngonde put it at about half. There is, therefore, a large group of people who have been Church members and have been struck off the Church register because they have married a second wife or committed adultery or become drunkards, and show no sign of repentance, and of those who have grown up as Christians, but have not maintained any connexion with a Church in later life.

So far we have talked of Christian rituals and dogma in terms of the three mission Churches whose converts form the great bulk of Christians: differences between them are negligible. The doctrinal differences between Protestant and Roman Catholic do not bulk large to the Nyakyusa, and since the Roman Catholic Church had not been operating for any long period among them and had a membership of under 1,000, many of whom were Ngoni from Songea or Kisi, who had settled in Tukuyu district, it was not possible to make any adequate comparison of the differences between Protestant and Catholic groups.

Two small Churches, the Pentecostal Holiness and the Watch Tower, had certain peculiarities. The Pentecostal Holiness Church holds highly emotional services at which members are expected to 'speak with tongues'; during prayers the whole congregation begins to jabber, each man usually being unintelligible to his neighbour, though words of other languages can be distinguished. Our informants maintained that the attraction of the Church was that its members seemed to 'have more of the Holy Ghost', as demonstrated by the 'speaking with tongues', though the more cynical of outsiders mentioned also 'the loaves and fishes'—cheaper Bibles, and the fact that the European leader was the largest employer of labour in the district and those who belonged to his Church got on best with him. Many of the members had formerly been Moravians. Its rules were strict: members were not permitted to smoke or drink, or use any Nyakyusa medicines.

The Watch Tower members emphasized that their Church, through its leader, Judge Rutherford, interpreted prophecy in a way in which no other Church could do. They practised baptism by immersion and were strict about not eating the flesh of animals without a cloven hoof, and avoiding beer, but made a point of not being sabbatarian and working in their fields on Sundays— these were the things they emphasized to us. They were also pacifist and would not join the Police or King's African Rifles, since Rutherford taught that all Government was evil.

(d) 'INDEPENDENT' AFRICAN CHURCHES

There is a great cleavage between the mission Churches and the 'independent' African Churches, which also claim to be Christian, read the Gospels at their services, and recite the Apostles' creed, but whose rules of life are avowedly based on the Old Testament rather than the New (*vide* p. 191). Both the 'independent' Churches operating in BuNyakyusa approve polygyny; the bulk of their members are middle-aged polygynists and they have at least as many men as women among them. Nyasuru's statement on polygyny was interesting:

When we young men went to join the mission we found that many of our fathers were attracted by it. They said to us: 'If only the Europeans would let us come in with all our wives we would come.' . . . Sometimes it would happen that the son of an old man's second wife would join the mission and become a preacher and he would preach even to his father, saying: 'You pagans do wrong, you marry many women, you must repent, your ways are evil.' Then his father would say to him: 'On the contrary, it is not I who do wrong, if I had married only one wife you would never have been born, and you young men take one wife only and then what happens? You steal other men's wives, continually, in secret, and the country is full of lawsuits about women. It is our custom which is good.' . . . And so we, now, we have our Church and our fathers come in with us. It is our aim to take the old people with us, not ourselves to go forward alone. All the other matters which the missionaries brought to us we think are good, only this European custom of marriage is difficult.

Nyasuru and Ngemela had both been suspended from the Church of Scotland Mission for marrying second wives, and Nyasuru, a man of fifty-three, had four wives when we knew him. He kindly provided us with a copy of a statement on the beliefs and constitution of the African National Church, which is worth quoting in full:

The African National Church

Belief

1. We believe religion is an essential component of man's growth and that man should live according to his religion and not merely be a nominal member of a Church whose rules he cannot carry out. Like all other countries Africa is in need of a Church which would correspond with her God-given customs and manners.

2. We believe the commission of the Christian Church to Africa was to impart Christ and education in such a way as to fit in with manners and customs of the people and not that it should impose on the African the unnecessary and impracticable methods of European countries, such as having one wife, etc., which have no biblical authority.

3. We believe the immoralities now prevailing among us are the direct result of the unnatural position into which the African has been driven, coupled by the false and misleading theory that outside one's own Church beliefs others can do no good.

4. We believe in the fatherhood of God and the brotherhood of man regardless of colour and creed, and that the African religion with its traditions, laws, and customs was instituted by Him so that the Africans may realize Him by their own observance.

Constitution

1. The name of this Church shall be called the *African National Church*.

2. This Church shall not be antagonistic towards other organized Churches but shall acknowledge and recognize them in their own spheres whether Christian, Jewish, Mohammedan, or Buddhist; and all African religions serving God through their ancestral spirits because all are trying to uplift man towards the love of God, our opinion being that all were given by Him for the guidance of man.

3. As the African National Church is a new movement having no previous form in Nyasaland, and the first to affect the educated Natives who are outside the other organized Churches by suspension or otherwise, its ministers and other office-bearers shall be elected and ordained by the vote of the whole congregation.

4. The governance of this Church shall be according to European methods, that is to say, it shall have buildings for worship, hold conference and counsels, and keep proper records of its proceedings, funds, etc.

5. Members of the Church shall be people of good character according to the Native traditions, laws, and customs, as contained in the *First Five Books of the Christian Bible*, whether polygamists or not.

6. The Rules of faith shall be based on the said *Five Books of the Christian Bible*, and members shall be suspended only when they break such, our guidance for discipline being the *Ten Commandments*.

Aim

The aim of this Church is the uplifting of the African *en masse* taking in its rise the old people who are at present being left out by religions of the North and its civilization, as well as winning those who are considered bad because of polygamy and drink, and are refused any latent qualities for doing good any more, to try and restore an atmosphere of a deeply, naturally religious life as prevailed in the days of long ago which was manifest in words as well as deeds.

Regarding the organization of the Church, it was stated:

Every district requiring a Pastor shall submit its application to the annual General Conference for its approval.

Any novice Pastor elected and ordained by the minister shall not be entitled at his early appointment or nomination to administer the ministerial duties, but shall sit with his Presiding Pastor for at least six months for his qualification as a minister.

If any Church, elders, preachers, deacons or group of Churches shall be found ordaining a Pastor or Pastors without the approval of the Annual General Conference, leaders of such offending Churches shall be brought before the Annual General Conference for trial and if found guilty be suspended or expelled from the organization.

The office bearers of our organization shall be as follows:

(a) The Secretary who is the sole head of the organization.
(b) The Presiding Pastors.
(c) Pastors.
(d) Preachers.
(e) Elders.
(f) Deacons and Deaconesses.

The Society shall be divided into districts over which one Presiding Pastor shall be stationed to supervise a Pastor or Pastors under him in that area.

It shall be the duty of every Pastor to feed his flock and to sit as Chairman of his Kirk Session, to enforce the discipline of the Church and to forward his monthly report to his Presiding Pastor.

It shall be the duty or duties of the Presiding Pastor to visit his Pastor or Pastors showing or teaching them good governance of the Church and to send to the Secretary his quarterly reports of his district activities.

If any of the Presiding Pastors or Pastors shall fail to comply with the rules of this constitution they shall upon conviction thereof by the Annual General Conference, be suspended or expelled from the Church.

It shall be the duties of the Elders to look after their Church members going about visiting them in their homes and leading them in a Christian life and to report to his Session all the offending members.

It shall be the duties of a Preacher to go about preaching the Gospel to beginners as well as helping Pastors to encourage members at the Church on Sundays. He should keep records of his itinerary and report the same to his district Pastor.

It shall be the duties of every Deacon whether male or female, to see that all members pay their monthly contribution which is one penny per month and to bring monies or foodstuffs to his or her Pastor at the end of every month, and to bring to the Session those who neglect to pay.

Pastors through the Presiding Pastor are empowered to administer Sacraments—to Baptize and dispense Holy Communion and to ordain or remove any Elder, Preacher or Deacon who neglects his or her duties, and to report their activities to their Presiding Pastor.

To clear away suspicions among the people, Christians or non-Christians, Pastor or Pastors in the district if found guilty of misconduct or any case of adultery shall be brought to their Session to be tried, and if found guilty shall be suspended from the ministerial duties until his case is referred to the Annual General Conference by his District Pastor.

Any Presiding Pastor or Pastors found intentionally violating these rules as constituted and approved by the Annual General Conference shall, at the discretion of the said General Conference, be suspended or expelled from the Church.

All monies of the Church shall within three months' time be forwarded to the Secretary of Religion who shall Bank same in the Savings Bank.

The term of service for Elders and Deacons or Deaconesses shall be for two years only, but an office-bearer may also be suspended before the end of his or her term if:

He or she has committed misconduct.
He or she neglects to fulfil his or her duties.
He or she does not attend Church worship.
He or she is a drunkard.
He or she is unruly.
He or she marries unlawfully against Native law which binds African marriages.

No office-bearer of any rank shall be found preaching when he is drunk, but shall hand the Service over to someone else.

Every member of the African National Church shall kneel down when praying. One who is preaching can kneel or stand.

Every member of the African National Church shall cease to drink during worshipping hours, but shall reserve same until evening when worshipping is over.

Any member found contravening these rules shall be dealt with by the Session and if found guilty shall be suspended or expelled from the Church.

The term of Chairman for the Annual Conference shall be two years, but he shall be elected again if required.

The Annual General Conference shall be composed of a body of men chosen from each division, viz. Pastors, Elders, Deacons, and other notable men.

A general confession with words and music composed by one of the Pastors of the African National Church, Robert Sambo, is used as an alternative to the Ten Commandments. Nyasuru translated it for us from the original Tumbuka.

Jehovah God we have come before Thee to worship and to confess our sins which we have done during the week.

Response: May they all go away (*fyosa fibukege*).[1]

We have sinned before Thee in speaking to people, we have offended Thy creatures, we have spoken bad words, we have grieved their hearts, Father.

May they all go away.

We have sinned against Thee in thoughts coveting the wives and husbands of others; we have broken the Ten Commandments, Father. We have done wrong in our village, Father. Witchcraft, adultery, and hatred, all these are in our village. We pray forgive all, Father.

May they all go away.

Our chiefs do not love one another in their hearts. Take such hearts from them and give them one heart.

May they all go away.

A new commandment you have given unto us all to love one another as in Heaven, where there is no quarrelling. Teach us all to keep Thy Word, Father.

May they all go away.

That our chiefs may be one in loving and ruling their country and their people, and lead us all well. This we pray, father, grant us.

May they all go away.

The old worship is broken down; we have come as wild animals which are without God. Call us again to worship, Father.

May they all go away.

Africa is the land of our forefathers. We have damaged her with our new ways, by leaving all the ways of our forefathers, ways which gave peace to the country, Father.

---

[1] The phrase used in the pagan ritual for cleansing the country, cf. p. 105.

May they all go away.

Our Church is calling everyone to come in so that the house of marriage may be filled. It is Thy work to give them[1] all new dresses.

May they all go away.

We are taking beer as wild animals; we forget worship which is our life. Teach us to drink beer moderately, Father.

May they all go away.

We have forgotten all the laws You gave to our forefathers. We have married women by snatching. Turn us to a life of new marriages according to the ways of our forefathers, Father.

May they all go away.

Father, Son and Holy Ghost, One God, ever and ever. Do unto us according to what we have said. Amen, amen, amen.

In spite of the assertion in the constitution that the rules of faith are based on the first five books of the Bible, a sermon we heard was based on New Testament parables; candidates at baptism must give their assent to Apostles' creed; and the doctrine of the resurrection is preached at funerals, John xi. 25-6, and Job xix. 25-7, being read.

The African National Church has five schools at which half the fees charged in corresponding classes in mission schools are levied, but not all of them succeed in keeping their pupils. In 1937 there was a 'strike' by African National Church parents against sending their children to one school because 'the children of the leaders in this area are attending the Livingstonia schools and none goes to their own National Schools'.

The members of Ngemela's Church were less sophisticated than those of the African National Church and we heard of no written constitution. The services were also simpler. The only sermon we heard was on repentance.

Repent and repent soon; do not delay! Repent in your hearts! There is no virtue in baptism; it is just water; but let your hearts be washed clean. The world is full of things which excite wonder and envy. Many when they see the riches of their fellow say to themselves: 'I will go and steal his things', but we must not do that. Many go and commit adultery in the long grass, but we must not do that. God has sent us the Gospel. These are the words of Christ and none other are his words (holding up the New Testament). Our Fathers had never heard of it, but we have, and Christ calls us to repent. In the old days when a

[1] Referring, Nyasuru said, to the wives of polygynists. Many women in Ngonde objected to polygyny on the ground that where there were several wives they were not properly clothed.

stranger came through the country our fathers lay in wait for him and killed him, but we are learning and have to learn to give him food and a night's shelter. Repent and let your hearts be washed!

We differ from other Christians because we baptize in Jordan, and they baptize in a dish in the church. They say we are wrong, but we say we do what Christ told us to do. They also say we are wrong to marry more than one wife. The words we say are just the same as the creed of those at Kabembe (i.e. Lutherans) with two differences, that of baptism and that of having more than one wife.

Communion services are celebrated half-yearly at each of several different centres by the leaders of the 'independent' Churches, and since they are unable to obtain wine, sweet tea or a light beer are used instead.

The members of Ngemela's Church contribute to buy a bull and rice and beer, and share a feast together after a communion service, and it is alleged by outsiders, though stoutly denied by members, that these are 'love feasts' at which members exchange wives,[1] to show that they are 'one body'. The African National Church also holds feasts after services and some outsiders say these too are 'love feasts', but outside opinion on the African National Church's feasts was much less unanimous than about Ngemela's feasts. It is certain that in Ngemela's church men and women drink sitting together in a manner not conventional among the Nya-kyusa. Members of the mission Churches spoke of members of the independent Churches as living 'just like pagans' and averred that, despite their polygyny, their members ran off with other men's wives and were scarcely disciplined for doing so.

It is also clear that the would-be members are baptized almost immediately, with no period of testing and instruction such as is insisted upon by the mission Churches; that very many of them are members who have been suspended by other Churches; and that the 'pastors' have no special training for their task.

Nyasuru's church attracted more educated people than did Ngemela's and, in terms of Dr. Sundkler's classification,[2] his was a typical Ethiopian Church with its emphasis on African national-ism. Ngemela, the son of a minor chief, behaved much like a chief and attracted the less educated. He emphasized 'washing' —baptism by immersion—and repentance, and he was peripatetic

[1] This is also alleged of the Watch Tower in Northern Rhodesia. cf. Ian Cunnison, 'A Watch Tower Assembly in Central Africa', *International Review of Missions*, xl (1951), p. 467.

[2] B. G. M. Sundkler, *Bantu Prophets*, Lutterworth Press (1948), pp. 53-9.

like most of the leaders of Zionist Churches in the south.[1]

It is noticeable that the two 'independent' Churches have a more elaborate form of service than the Church from which their leaders have sprung, and Ngemela habitually wears conspicuous vestments. There is, of course, great variation between different denominations in the emphasis placed on ritual, some Protestants abjuring it and turning their very insistence on starkness and simplicity into a ritual in itself—a taboo. There seems to be a clear tendency in Southern Africa for 'independent' Churches to express themselves more and more in ritual and less in dogma. In this way they reduce the gap between themselves and the pagans, for the pagan religion is expressed almostly exclusively in ritual, whereas Christianity is expressed in creeds and confessions as well as in the rituals of the Church.

(e) THE CONTRAST BETWEEN PAGAN AND CHRISTIAN

There are certain common elements in the rituals celebrated by pagans and Christians: some of the occasions are the same, and in the conceptions of sacrifice, of death and rebirth, of confession and cleansing, there are similarities; but there are also profound differences. The conception of life, immortality, replaces the pre-occupation with fertility, for though most Nyakyusa Christians, like the pagans, regard celibacy as evidence of physical abnormality, and the conventional desire of a woman is to have six children—a quiverful in Nyakyusa eyes—yet fertility is no longer the end of all being, sought in every ritual. There are profound differences, too, in the values expressed in the rituals regarding sex relations, the range of moral obligations, and social change. In pagan thought polygyny is good—a man should have many children. Child marriage is defended on the ground that a girl 'gets accustomed to her husband' if she goes to him early, and homosexual relations between youths and young men are tolerated since they have no wives and *cannot* marry if the older men are polygynists. What is upheld is the chastity of women, and a total separation of the sex activities of members of successive generations, expressed in the taboos limiting familiarity between mother and son, father and nubile daughter, father-in-law and daughter-law. In Christian thought it is the 'pure in heart' who 'see God' and this is interpreted by the mission Churches to imply monogamy. Only in the 'independent' African Churches is it asserted

[1] The emphasis on healing, so common in the south, is absent.

that polygyny is compatible with Christianity, and indeed sanctioned by the example of many of the heroes of the Old Testament. It is here that the cleavage between pagan and Christian ways of life is felt to be greatest: the desire to marry or inherit a second wife is the main reason for many men leaving the mission Churches. The traditional way for the well-to-do man to expend his capital and maintain his position was to marry again and the wealth of the lineage was concentrated in the senior line through the rule of inheritance of widows.

Again and again in sermons Nyakyusa preachers came back to the problem of polygyny. 'Let not those who know not the law deceive you saying, "You, Christian, what is one poor little wife? (*ikikikulu kimo kyene*) See, do not your children also die (like those of pagans) and constantly fall ill? Take a second wife." Perhaps the BaNgemela tell you that God also favours that. If you agree you are uprooted. What, after all, is a second wife? In Jesus there is life.' (2 Peter iii. 17.)

Young men are also caught in a contradiction of values when their fathers have betrothed them while still quite young.

It is very difficult for a man to refuse a girl whom his father has engaged for him. To a pagan man it does not matter very much because, provided he has cattle, he can always marry a girl of his own choice as well, but a Christian cannot. Such was the case of a friend of ours, A, a Christian teacher. When he was a child, before he was baptized, his father, a senior village headman and a powerful and wealthy man, engaged for him B, a little girl who could barely walk. A got on well at school and when he was growing up the missionary said to him: 'When you marry choose a girl of some education, because it is good for an educated man to marry an educated girl.' A fell in love with C, a Christian, who had learnt to read and write, and sew and launder, and who consequently was one of the best-educated girls in the district. They came to an understanding together, our informant being the 'go-between'. A went to the elders of the congregation and told them he wished to marry C. They replied: 'We, on our part agree; go and ask your father.' Then A's father said: 'Well, no, B is your wife (though she was still a child and the marriage had not been consummated), but you are my eldest son, I have many cattle, I agree to arrange marriages with them both for you at once.' So A thought and thought and went back to the elders and told them saying: 'My father refuses, he won't hear of it unless I marry

them both, but I don't want to leave the Church.' Then the
elders supported his father saying, 'We don't like sons to be dis-
obedient and the girl will make a good wife for you.' 'But,' argued
A, 'my wife is a child and C is grown up.' The missionary supported him saying: 'We are going to send him to a distance (to
train as a teacher), it is better that he go married.' But the elders
supported his father, following the Nyakyusa custom. Then a
message came to A saying that B had 'grown-up'. He said to us,
his friends: 'What can I say now? I can no longer argue that my
wife is a child.' And to the missionaries and elders he said:
'Send me away for my training. I must think, I am not at peace.'

While A was still away D (who was a close friend of A's)
came back from school, and he too fell in love with C. But before
he spoke to her he wrote to A asking him: 'Have you broken
with her, or are you still agreed to marry? Can I make love to her
or not?' Then A wrote back: 'Yes, I have broken with her, it is
true that I love her, but I cannot square marrying her with
Christianity. Go ahead.' So then D came to our informant to ask
him to be the go-between again, and to take him to the girl. So
they went and showed her A's letter, and asked her if she could
love D. Then she was very sorrowful and would give no answer
until she had written to A herself. 'Is it true that you have left
me?' And A replied: 'Indeed, my dear, I have left you. I love you
truly, but what can we do? Perhaps the powers do not wish that
we should marry. My father refuses. He says he will arrange a
marriage with you, for me, as my second wife, but what of our
Christianity? Are we both to leave the Church?' So then she
agreed to marry D.

All this time the elders had supported A's father in his refusal
saying: 'B also is a proper woman. We are surprised at the
young man.' And A's father said to him: 'I betrothed this girl for
you when she was quite tiny. *Kyala* has already given you this
woman.' But the marriage of A and B proved a failure—they were
constantly quarrelling—and later they were divorced.

The 'go-between' of this story was more fortunate in his own
marriage. Like A he was the son of a wealthy pagan and two wives
had been betrothed for him before he became a Christian. When
he decided to be baptized he flatly refused to marry either of
them. His father was very angry. 'For a time he treated me as if I
were not his son, saying: "Since you refuse these girls I will not
give you any cows to marry at all." So I said: "All right," and

o

went away to work again and in time I earned four cows which I hid with friends far from home. My father knew nothing about them. Then I wrote to my father from Mwasebe [about twenty miles from where his father lived] where I was working, saying that I had found a girl there, the daughter of a Christian, and please could I have the cows with which to marry her? My father said: "No, she lives too far away." ' Then later he found a Christian girl of whom his father approved and a satisfactory marriage was arranged.

A common topic of discussion among Christian women was whether parents should choose mates for their children, or leave them free to choose for themselves, for though traditionally a girl had to signify her consent to marriage, she was betrothed very young and her freedom of choice was small. The growing insistence on personal freedom in marriage is symptomatic of a radical change in the attitude towards persons.

The pagan rituals were the main occasions of recreation. It has been shown, in *Rituals of Kinship*, how pagan funerals and marriages are the occasion for feasting and dancing and display, and how the seclusion hut of a nubile girl is the gathering place for the young men and girls of the neighbourhood. Even a twin ritual is a festival with beer for the older men and some meat for everyone. The sacrifices at the groves were feasts for the leading men of the country, and the 'coming out' was the occasion of the greatest feast of the generation, and dances were practised for months ahead. Partly because of a change in sex morality, and partly because the meat and beer at pagan feasts are offered to the shades, Christians are largely excluded from these festivals. They may not participate in pagan dances, or join in the lewd songs, or attend the initiation hut of a girl, and they are partly debarred from the feasts of the pagans: certain of the Churches (notably the Church of Scotland and, for a time, the Moravians) forbid Christians to drink beer at all.

And the Christian rituals, though some of them are 'festivals of the Church', are scarcely celebrated as such. There has been a separation between ritual and recreation which has left a gap in the Christian community. It is true that the Christian young men and girls sing and dance at funerals and marriages, but the elders, for the most part, look on with dubious eyes, saying that dancing leads to adultery, and several of the dances introduced by

Christians in Ngonde (e.g. *amapenenga*) have been banned by the Kirk Sessions. The European-style dances, such as are sometimes organized by the educated men in centres like Karonga or Tukuyu, are not attended by these men's wives: respectable women avoid them. While we lived near Rungwe mission there was much discussion among the villagers over what recreations were permissible, and hot arguments between those who wished to permit beer drinking and dancing to Christians and those who wished to ban both. It is the Nyakyusa elders who are most puritan in their views—much more so than many of the missionaries who are very conscious of the need for recreation; indeed, the Livingstonia Presbytery once instructed all its Sessions to look into the matter. The chief outlet for young Christians is in ballads. A good singer is much admired and the composer may even sell his songs, with words and music written out. One of the former missionaries is honoured as the man who first taught the Nyakyusa to read music as well as to sing by ear.

In pagan thought moral obligations are limited to kinsmen and neighbours: they do not extend beyond the chiefdom except to those relatives who may live beyond its bounds. As we have shown, the common moral sanctions are the anger of senior relatives, and 'the breath of men', and these operate only within the lineage and age-village. But Christians have read the parable of the Good Samaritan and taken it to heart. Sermons stress this: 'If a Kinga comes and asks for a place to sleep the night and you refuse you are among the goats.' 'If a traveller from the coast asks for a place to sleep and you refuse, do you show love?' 'We tell a bride she should be hospitable to her neighbours if she can, but she *must* cook for those from a distance.' It is one of the points on which the Christians are most conscious of a difference between themselves and the pagans. And the exclusiveness of Europeans is one of the reasons why they are distinguished from Christians in the song on the title page of *Rituals of Kinship*. 'If all Europeans made friends with us (*ukwangala*) like X and Y', we were told, 'the whole country would have been Christian long ago.'

Linked with the concern for strangers is the obligation to preach the Gospel to others—something constantly stressed in sermons, and finding expression both in preaching in the surrounding villages and in tours of more remote areas, often areas of another language. Such tours implied hardship in travelling and a leap in sympathy; as one of our friends explained, she found it hard to accept food from the neighbouring Safwa who were 'so dirty in their cooking'.

Both pagans and Christians pin their faith to resurrection, but the interpretations differ radically. To the pagan the shade is resurrected 'in the body of his child', it scarcely has any separate existence. To Christians the personality, the individual soul, is something indestructible and continuing. This theological difference is but one facet of a deep cleavage between the pagan view of a man and his relations with his group, and the Christian view.

Because the traditional religion is a cult of the shades, piety consists in doing just as father did. It is neglect of traditional rituals, departure from traditional ways, that is held to bring madness, sterility, or death. But Christianity is revolutionary; it is the yeast working in society to transform it. That is often forgotten in communities with a Christian tradition, but where the Gospel has been preached only for a generation and confessing Christians are but one in six, it is in men's minds all the time. The Nyakyusa could not be unaware that the Gospel implied changing their society.

In the pagan tradition the meticulous performance of the rituals is stressed: the right medicines; the right persons; the right order of events are all important. The attitude of mind of the participants matters also—if they are on bad terms the ritual will be ineffective —but goodwill and forgiveness alone are useless without the performance of the proper ritual. In the Christian tradition, as interpreted to us by Nyakyusa converts, it is the inward and spiritual attitude of the participants that is stressed.

Finally, all the pagan rituals are directed to driving off the shades or the heroes, whereas the Christian rituals are the 'means of grace', of coming near to God. Christians pray that the Holy Spirit should take up his abode within them; they seek to emulate the saints who 'walked with God'. Our Christian friends were quite clear about the contrast here between the pagan and Christian tradition: it is crystallized in the attitude to dreams: if a pagan dreams of converse (*ukwangala*) with shades, he fears death; 'if a Christian dreams of converse with God he rejoices greatly because it means he is gaining strength in Christianity.'

CHAPTER XIII

TWENTY YEARS' CHANGE

How does Christianity interact with other revolutionary forces in the community? It has been possible to observe the changes that have taken place among the Nyakyusa after a lapse of twenty years, and a summary of them is necessary before we proceed to a discussion of the links between religious and secular change.

The first thing that strikes a visitor returning to Nyakyusa country after many years, is that the isolation, which was so typical of the valley, has greatly diminished. Buses, filled with Nyakyusa passengers, cross twice daily the high pass that leads out of the valley, and where once travellers died of exposure and starvation there is a hard road fringed with homesteads and fields. The belt of unoccupied country that even twenty years ago separated the Nyakyusa from their neighbours has disappeared, for they themselves have spilled out of the valley to the north and west, and their Kinga neighbours have come down the Livingstone escarpment to the east and cultivate the mountain slopes, for 'they no longer fear that people (i.e. the Nyakyusa) will seize their property'. Men travel abroad to find work and they go much farther and stay away longer than before. In the remotest village there is some man who has visited Burma or Malaya as a soldier, and a dozen lads who will argue the relative merits of the Orange Free State gold mines and the Copper-belt as centres of employment. Many women now accompany their husbands to Rhodesia, or other parts of Tanganyika, and some travel to visit daughters or sisters. The older women enlarge on their journeys and joke about how fearful they used to be.

Travel implies learning another language, most often Swahili, but also Bemba and English and the pidgin of the gold and copper mines called Fanakalo. Thus intellectual isolation is disappearing along with the physical isolation. The numerous 'bush schools' which existed in the Nyakyusa valley in 1938, and at which many of those who attended never even learnt to read and write, have been largely replaced by mission primary schools, state-aided and inspected, and in these and the Native Authority primary and middle schools there are now 9,437 pupils, as against about 500 in similar schools in 1938. Less than 40 per cent of the children between eight and eleven years old[1] are as yet in school in Rungwe District and the demand for places is enormous. Among the most insistent are girls wanting education. During the 1930's the Education Department was trying, with little success, to coax girls to stay in school long enough to learn to read and write, but today nearly a third of the primary school pupils are girls. A handful of boys and girls go out of the district to attend middle or secondary schools, and a few candidates for training as teachers and district nurses come in. Thus an educated person, or one who goes out to work, mixes with people whose backgrounds and languages are quite different from his own.

Then people are richer than they used to be, partly because of the wages earned abroad, and partly because of the coffee and rice grown and exported. There is also some employment within the district on tea estates (especially important to women and girls), and coal and vermiculite mines. The value of peasant crops exported has risen from about £24,000 in 1936[2] to nearly £578,000 from coffee and rice alone in 1955,[3] and some men have made as much as £150 from their coffee in a year. A coffee cheque of £30 to £60 is common. In addition to the peasant crops there is tea from estates—well over a million pounds of made tea in 1955 as well as a quantity of seed. This increase in wealth has involved a change in the division of labour. Because men are not at home to clear and hoe, their wives, perforce, must clear fields and hoe for themselves, assisted by their young sons, boys who twenty years ago would not yet have stopped herding.

There has been a rapid increase in population, more especially in the hills, due partly to the development of health services and

---

[1] Number of children in Mission and Native Authority schools in Rungwe District, 1955:

Boys	Girls	Total	No. of children 8-11 years of age (estimated at 10% of total population)
6,592	2,054	8,646	23,639
Middle Schools			
718	73	791	(This total does not include those who are in middle schools *outside* the District, nor does it include those following a professional course *in* the District)

(Figures provided by the courtesy of the Provincial Education Officer, Mbeya.)
Change in Ngonde is not discussed for it was not possible to visit that area in 1955.

[2] *Good Company*, p. 16.

[3] Calculated from figures kindly supplied by the District Commissioner, Mr. Peter Johnston.

partly to the closer spacing of children. Whereas four years between births was conventional formerly, two or less is now usual. One of the characteristics of the present population is a disproportion between the sexes, the females outnumbering the males by 100 to 87·9 even when due allowance has been made for men away at work.[1] This disproportion is characteristic also of African populations in the south[2] and it appears likely that it is due to a wide difference in the survival rate of men and women, but the vital statistics necessary to test this hypothesis are lacking.

The increase in population, and the demand for coffee gardens and rice fields by men who prefer to earn cash by agriculture rather than as migrant labourers, has led to a shortage of land, already acute in the fertile lake-shore plain, and imminent in the coffee-growing villages of the hills.[3] Much land that was previously pasture land has been taken into cultivation, and signs of overstocking are everywhere apparent. Hillsides that in 1938 were covered with grass, waist high, now have a thin stubble. To aggravate matters, the care of stock is less efficient than it used to be because it is left to very small boys, their seniors being occupied with school and hoeing. Often the cattle are both ill nourished and covered with ticks—something that was never seen when they were herded by adolescents and carefully hand-dressed. The villagers themselves are as much concerned as the agricultural officers over the shortage of pasture and the decrease in the milk supply, but they are not prepared to accept the remedies recommended: namely, reduction of stock and stall-feeding. The advice of Europeans on the growing of rice and coffee crops, which they introduced to the district, is acceptable, but the Nyakyusa argue

[1] The Census figures cannot be taken as exact, but they give some indication of the increase in population, and the disproportion between men and women. In 1931 the population of Rungwe District was given as 195,062. In 1948 it was 236,386. In 1931 the proportion of males to females (Kukwe and Nyakyusa in Rungwe district) was 73·6 : 100 (Tanganyika Territory, *Census of the Native Population 1931*). In 1941 the figure for Tukuyu district as a whole was 80 : 100 (Tanganyika Territory, *East African Population Census, 1948*). Allowing for 8,820 men away without wives (estimate for 1954 less 10 per cent), the proportion is 87·9 : 100 (cf. P. H. Gulliver, Report on the Migration of African Workers to the South from the Southern Highland Province, with special Reference to the Nyakyusa of Rungwe District, February 1955, p. 16). The discrepancy in the figures given for *adults* was 62·2 : 100 in 1948, but the ages of males and females classed as 'adult' are uncertain.

[2] D. H. Houghton and E. M. Walton, *The Economy of a Native Reserve*, Keiskammahoek Rural Survey, vol. ii, pp. 24-6, 51. The sex ratio for Keiskammahoek District is 73·8 males : 100 females.

[3] cf. P. H. Gulliver, *Nyakyusa Land and Population*, 1956.

that they have always been cattle men and they need no instruction on cattle. The tension over stock limitation and soil conservation, so acute in many parts of Africa, is only just appearing in Rungwe district, but potentially it is serious.

Pressure on land, and the planting of a valuable long-term crop such as coffee, have undermined the traditional organization of age-villages. The old men are no longer prepared to move to make way for their sons and, without a new deal in land each generation, the territorial separation of the generations is blurred. Boys villages are no longer visible in the hills near Rungwe mission, partly because so many young men are away, either at school or in employment, but largely because most of the land is taken up with coffee gardens. Homesteads are being built farther apart as men lay out coffee round their houses, and sons often build on a corner of their father's estate instead of in a separate village. On the plain, also, the pressure of population blurs the boundaries between generations. Only in the least heavily populated middle belt are numerous boys' villages still clearly visible, and here too a 'coming out' has recently been celebrated, with some redistribution of land. The scarcest land, that in old volcanic craters, was always inherited, like cattle, not reallocated each generation, and almost all cultivated land is now treated in this way. In many chiefdoms, therefore, a young man looks to his father or senior brother for land, rather than to the village headman, and inheritance is supremely important. But the form of inheritance is changing: property now goes directly from father to son, not as formerly to each of a group of full brothers before reverting to the senior son of the eldest of them. The claims of more distant kinsmen on inherited stock are less than they used to be; such stock becomes the exclusive property of father and sons, rather than property in which members of a lineage of three or four generations have reciprocal rights. The main economic bond which held the lineage together, the exchange of cattle, is thus broken.

Formerly a marriage was a contract between lineages rather than between individuals. A girl was betrothed before puberty to a man of her father's choice and should he die she was still regarded as married to his heir. Should she die a sister replaced her. Ideally a marriage bond between lineages lasted for generations, each man who died being replaced by a brother or son, each woman by a sister or brother's daughter. The choice of a partner in marriage was not an individual one. True, a girl gave her formal consent in the marriage ritual, but the pressure on her to accept the husband selected for her by her kinsmen was almost irresistible. In the thirties Christian women who refused their husband's heir and lived alone, or married an unrelated man of their choice, were regarded by their pagan sisters as very daring, and little girls in pagan families took it as a matter of course that they should replace their dead sisters; today the right of a widow to choose whom she will marry is generally accepted, and the custom of replacing a dead woman by her sister has lapsed. 'Every girl wants her own husband nowadays', the old women say. Thus lineage obligations give way to individual freedom of choice in marriage. At the same time the rituals which emphasized the lineage are dropped or modified. The fearful fecundity of a double birth no longer appals men and the twin ritual which used to bring together all the living members of a lineage of three generations is not celebrated at all. At a puberty ritual a pagan girl may be given the *ikipiki* medicine, the symbol of 'the blood of the lineage' by her mother, but there is no seclusion and elaborate feasting, no sacrifice of the bull of puberty that her father's shades may 'move aside a little' to make way for the shades of her husband's lineage. Only at a funeral do kinsmen still gather and celebrate, for many still fear the shades, and at a funeral the heir is installed and the importance of property and the inheritance of it has not diminished one whit. As we have seen, the traditional religion was formulated in terms of kinship; the gods were senior kinsmen; but today God, *Kyala*, is no ancestor; to pagans as well as to Christians he is separate and supreme. Men are still classified by their lineages, and one of the topics of village questions is how Prince Charles can be heir to the British throne when his father is not of the house of Windsor; but already in the economic field, and increasingly in the religious, it is the family of parents and children which is now dominant, not the lineage.

Divorce is far more frequent than formerly, partly because women claim a greater freedom of behaviour than before, as well as the right of choosing their own husbands, and are supported by the courts. As one village headman put it, 'Formerly a father beat his daughter with a stick if she ran home and sent her back to her husband who also beat her.' The women reject the old pattern of subservience which was expressed in crouching to greet a man, and addressing him in a very deferential fashion; the men observe, and some copy, the manners of Europeans towards their wives, but neither husband nor wife is quite sure what the change in manners implies, and both are often inconsistent in their behaviour. As an educated Nyakyusa put it: 'They do not know what to expect from each other.'

Marriage relationships are complicated by the disproportion in the numbers of men and women; a disproportion which continues while the rule of monogamy is preached and accepted by many. The first effect of the increase in wealth in Rungwe district was for the marriage age of women to go down; in Mr. Punch's phrase 'too many cattle were chasing too few wives'; but the combined pressure of missions and Administration, and some acquaintance with the customs of the outside world, has reversed that tendency, and the marriage of girls below puberty, which was general among pagans in 1938, now appears to be exceptional. Many girls are still betrothed before puberty, but they do not go to their husbands until after that time, and to be still single at puberty with no betrothed to play his part in the ritual is no longer embarrassing to a girl, for the puberty ritual is not celebrated in full. The ruling of the District Council that a man may not recover more than *one* cow given for a girl who has not reached puberty, if the marriage is dissolved, discourages men from giving cattle for girls who have not grown up. At the same time the marriage age of men is going down. Marriage in the early twenties or even the late teens is common now, for young men who have been to work on the mines can buy marriage cattle for themselves, and Christians who are well-to-do provide for the marriages of young sons instead of taking additional wives. Therefore the gap in the marriage age of men and women is very considerably diminished, but it still exists, and combined with the disproportion in the total number of males and females it means that a considerable proportion of the women (perhaps 30 per cent)[1] must become the junior wives of polygynists or remain unmarried altogether, or live alone as widows.

Among pagans polygyny is approved, but young men are irked by their responsibility for elderly widows, a responsibility that was formerly accepted as a matter of course. Able-bodied wives are still economically an asset even now that trade goods are in general use. For Nyakyusa men—pagans—have insisted that as

[1] The masculinity rate is calculated at 87·9 : 100 (*vide supra*) and the *average* difference in the marriage age may well be six years.

their wives took to wearing cloth they should earn it for themselves by growing and selling millet and brewing beer, and many women do the clearing and hoeing in their fields, work that used to fall to men; but it is difficult for a chief to refuse to provide a man to hoe the ridges in his wife's field, or to refuse an elderly woman a cloth or some salt, and young heirs grumble much about their encumbrances.

In the political field there has been a sustained attempt to make local government more democratic and to include in it the educated men. Between 1891, when the German Government first assumed control of the area, and 1938, the tendency was for the power of the chiefs to be increased at the expense of that of the commoners. This was admitted by the chiefs themselves, as we have seen. In 1949 there was established a system of Rural Councils, on which chiefs, village headmen (*amafumu*), and ordinary commoners are represented. Four[1] of each category are chosen as representatives on the Council in their area by an electoral college itself elected by all taxpayers. Rungwe District is divided into five areas. The policy of treating some chiefs as senior to others has been abandoned and each of the seventy-eight recognized rulers (*abatwa*) is eligible for election as a chief's representative on his local Rural Council. Village headmen (two from each chiefdom) and the ordinary commoners are similarly chosen. The five Rural Councils in turn elect one man of each sort to the District Council.[2] The system allows for, and seems to have achieved, a combination of men with traditionally high status and those who are conspicuous by reason of their education or success as coffee or rice farmers. The old feeling that education was not necessary to a chief's son, though it might be useful to a poor man, has vanished, and a considerable number of the educated leaders of the district are sons or grandsons of chiefs. The elected president of the District Council, Mr. Gordon Mwansasu (186) is of the Nyakyusa chiefs' lineage, though not of the most senior line. In the Rural Councils the presidents elected have all, with one exception, been ruling chiefs, but it is not necessarily the genealogically senior who is chosen. There is scope for selection on the grounds of character and ability.

[1] Five in the populous plain, Ntebela (MuNgonde).

[2] cf. Z. E. Kingdon, 'The Initiation of a System of Local Government by African Rural Councils in Rungwe District of Tanganyika', *Journal of African Administration*, vol. iii, 4 (1951).

The office of chieftainship still carries high prestige and the District Council has actually resolved to select a paramount chief. Competition for this position is fierce and it remains to be seen whether the Council will ever agree on a nomination. The persistent suggestion that the Administration should undertake the invidious task and select a paramount is scarcely likely to be acted upon, since the Administration sees no necessity for establishing such an office.

Chiefs, assisted by their village headmen, are the executive officers of the Rural Councils, but they have lost their judicial functions. There are twenty-four recognized courts with a bench of 'courtholders' appointed annually by the Rural Councils, and one superior court, but the annual appointment ceased in 1956 and more permanent appointments were made. The aim is to develop a specialized judiciary independent of the executive. There is also a very important class of full-time civil servants, secretaries of the District and Rural Councils, and clerks of the courts.

The position of village headman is in a fluid state. Where the 'coming out' ritual has been dropped, the traditional occasion for the formal appointment of village headmen no longer arises, and old men continue in office much longer than before. When a headman dies his heir sometimes takes his position or, if neither the heir nor a junior son will accept it, some other man is appointed by the chief. There is evidence that in many chiefdoms men are reluctant to undertake the position, which carries no salary but involves a considerable amount of work and makes it difficult or impossible for a man to engage in paid employment either within or outside the District. As one woman put it, 'Money has killed the office of village headman' (*Indalama sigogile ubufumu*). There is some evidence from the lake-shore plain, however, of men competing for the office, and indeed of a son claiming in the courts the headmanship his father held. Possibly the competition for land on the plain, and the fact that the allocation of land lies with the village headman, account for this. When all the arable land is taken up, it is probable that acquisition will be through inheritance or sale only, and the present headman's power to allocate land is likely to vanish; but one of the most important assets of a village is its pasture-land, and in controlling and developing this the headman may well play a decisive part in the future. Since village headmen are essential executive officers in local administration, and are integrated into the new system of

Councils, the importance of establishing machinery for their appointment in chiefdoms where the 'coming out' is no longer held is obvious.

The traditional communal rituals have not been dropped altogether, but their celebration is sporadic and not everyone supports them. Careful enquiries suggest that in less than half of the chiefdoms has the 'coming out' been celebrated when it was due. In the most conservative portion of the district, Selya, there were celebrations in 1952 and 1954, but even in that area a number of the ruling chiefs have never 'come out'. The omission is due partly to the desire of the old men to retain office, partly to the increase in population and the planting of coffee which makes any new deal in land unacceptable, and partly to the feeling of many that the old ritual is an anachronism, if not directly incompatible with their new faith in Christianity. Some chiefs who have not 'come out' would welcome a celebration; one such told us that 'if the "coming out" died chieftainship would die'; but a young chief's personal wishes are not decisive in this matter. Sacrifices at the groves of chiefs and heroes are not as frequent as before, but they still occur at some groves in time of drought or other emergency. The Kinga came to Lubaga in 1954, and they were expected to come and instal Kasitile's heir in 1955. In 1954 also there were sacrifices to Mwaijonga (82) and Mwakisambwe (30) for it was a season of scarcity. Rituals for cleansing the country and sprinkling the homesteads occur sporadically 'when occasion demands', but not annually in any chiefdom and never in some. And when celebrations do occur they do not unite the people of a chiefdom as they used to do. Christians oppose them and many non-Christians are also sceptical.

In 1935 the traditional rituals celebrated by lineages and chiefdoms formed a coherent system. They were directed towards the shades and the heroes, as was manifest in the sacrifices and in the dramas of death and rebirth when those secluded 'dwelt with the shades' or were 'caught hold of' by Kyala.[1] The older participants were then conscious, in greater or lesser degree, of the symbolism implicit in the actions they performed. By 1955 the ritual cycle was nowhere celebrated in full: what remained were 'bits and pieces' of ritual, none of them fully intelligible without reference to the complete cycle. The link between the rites and the shades and the heroes was less clear, and the symbolism less

[1] *Vide supra*, pp. 27-48, 70-85; *Rituals of Kinship*, pp. 51, 98, 101, 111-13, 205.

conscious. This disintegration of a former coherence, and a decreasing awareness of the meaning of symbols used, are perhaps characteristic of changing societies in Africa.

Despite the growth of the Christian Church, the great demand for schools, and the dropping of the old rituals directed to family shades and the heroes, belief in the power of medicines flourishes. Probably most deaths and misfortunes are still attributed to an enemy using either witchcraft or sorcery. The traditional belief in witchcraft is rejected by educated people, but belief in the power of medicines is general. Autopsies still take place and occasionally the poison ordeal is administered in secrecy; one case was mentioned which occurred in 1942. As we have seen, medicines have always been regarded as a potential instrument of individual competition. They are used in the rituals of kinship to ensure health, fertility, and good manners and morals; in the ritual of chieftainship to buttress authority, and in 'sprinkling the homesteads' to fertilize the fields; but also by individuals to steal the fertility of their neighbours' fields and to grow rich at the expense of their neighbours, and it is their use as an instrument of individual aggrandisement that is most talked of today. There were many reports of their use by rivals to office as chiefs, and the floods of 1955, which washed away the Mbaka bridge and caused a serious landslide on that river, were interpreted as incidents in a prolonged fight between chiefs who were rivals for the position of paramount. The deaths of the heir of one of them in 1953, and of the other chief himself in 1956, were also attributed to their duel with medicines.

Along with the political changes there has been a development of the Churches, more particularly of the Moravian Church, which is now largely self-supporting, with growing congregations served by African ministers.[1] Until 1938 the two main Protestant missions in Nyakyusa valley, the Moravian and Lutheran, were staffed by Germans and their funds came mainly from Germany. The war meant the withdrawal of the missionaries and the cutting off of funds. After a lapse of three years one Moravian missionary, and later one Lutheran, came to take charge of the missions and they were reinforced by other missionaries after the end of the war, but the whole policy in both missions is to build up self-supporting churches staffed by African pastors.

The work of the White Fathers mission was not interrupted by

---

[1] Change in Ngonde is not discussed.

the war and the form of its activities has not altered appreciably.
Three other missions based elsewhere now have small congregations in the District and a Lutheran pastor under discipline broke
away and formed his own 'independent' Church, which differs
from the other 'independent' Churches in that the rule of monogamy is enforced.

The total number of converts has increased very considerably,
much more than keeping pace with the increase in population;
taking the three main missions together, their converts form over
14 per cent of the total population.[1] Figures for the five mission
Churches with small congregations in the District—Pentecostal
Holiness, Assemblies of God, Seventh Day Adventists, Anglican,
and Watch Tower—are not available. Nor do we know the
membership of one of the 'independent' African Churches, but
supposing the membership of the missions with small congregations in the District to be 2,000 (a conservative estimate) the
percentage claiming to be Christian is 24 per cent as against 16
per cent in 1938. Dissimilarities in the response to Christian
teaching in different areas are very marked. Around Rungwe, the
main Moravian mission-station, the bulk of the population is
Christian, and the whole atmosphere is that of a Christian community, whereas in Selya, where mission work began in 1891 as it
did in Rungwe, Christians still form a small minority in domin-
antly pagan chiefdoms. The reasons for this difference are
complex. One factor is that Selya is geographically isolated
whereas Rungwe is near a main road and within easy reach of the
Government and trading centre Tukuyu; but much more important have been differences in mission policy regarding education, and differences in the personalities of missionaries, chiefs,
and early converts.

The change from a society based on kinship to one based on
voluntary association is apparent in the economic field as well as in
the religious. Co-operative societies formed by producers of coffee
and rice, which collect and market the crops, and give opportunity

---

1 Figures supplied by the courtesy of the missionaries directing each mission and
the leaders of two 'independent' Churches were as follows for 1954:

Moravians		29,390
Lutheran		10,000 (approximately)
Roman Catholic		4,700
Last Church (Ngemela)	('independent')	10,721
(Also called 'Native Mission')		
'African Lutheran Church'	('independent')	200

for the local investment of savings are the most important economic undertaking in the District. The seven coffee co-operatives handled a crop of 950 tons in 1955, worth about £427,500, and are organized so efficiently as to be able to return over 90 per cent of the price of the coffee on Moshi market to the producer, after the heavy transport costs (14 per cent) have been paid. One Government-paid officer assists these societies.

In the educational and recreational field also, associations are emerging: football clubs; companies of Scouts and Guides; 'Welfare Centres' with classes in reading for adult illiterates, indoor games, and Saturday-night dances; Women's Clubs for handwork and recreation; and in Tukuyu itself an inter-racial club with its own premises, whose members meet to play games, and get to know one another and discuss common problems. These associations make a visible mark on the face of the country in the shape of new brick Churches, co-operative stores, football fields, and, more rarely, a village club-house.

The change from a subsistence to a money economy, and from a system of government through chiefs and village headmen who were dependent primarily on inherited wealth, which secured to them the labour of many able-bodied wives and sons, to a system of government through European officials, chiefs, and clerks paid out of taxes, and assisted by unpaid village headmen, implies the collection and administration of taxes. The District Council has the responsibility for the budgeting and expenditure of over £60,000 per annum. The greater part of it is spent on the salaries of chiefs, secretaries, and clerks engaged in administration, on courts, on schools, dispensaries, and roads. The development of associations with paid officers also implies the collection of dues and budgeting. As in so many countries the difficulty of building up a tradition of honesty in administration is great. Tax clerks, court clerks, council secretaries, and co-operative society secretaries, and even church elders handle sums of money relatively large in proportion to their earnings and one of the tasks of European officials and missionaries is to secure a sound system of accounting and check corruption. In the traditional society stock theft was a capital offence, but money has not the sanctity of cattle, and often the clerk who has appropriated public funds is treated by others as 'unfortunate' rather than immoral. At the same time villagers show great anxiety lest a man entrusted with some common fund should spend it for himself. The risk of theft of public funds is greater than in England, but it should be added that a European may camp in a Nyakyusa village with nothing locked, and never lose so much as a box of matches.

An attempt has been made to describe the sort of changes which are proceeding in BuNyakyusa. They are not peculiar to that area, but will be familiar to most people who have lived in Africa. Now we turn to the sociological analysis.

CHAPTER XIV

RELIGION AND SOCIAL STRUCTURE

IN this chapter we shall seek to show how the traditional communal rituals both reflect and maintain the traditional political structure, and to consider in what measure the change from paganism to Christianity compels a change in other aspects of the society, or, alternatively, how far the economic and political changes taking place among the Nyakyusa compel a change in religion.

The heroic myths are the charter for chieftainship. The heroes from whom the chiefs are descended are pictured as creators and benefactors, the authors of fertility and civilized living. But myth and ritual also entrench the rights of commoners and unify people of different stocks by asserting their complementary diversity. No ritual can be celebrated without the participation of commoner priests. They 'speak out' at rituals and bring public opinion directly to bear on the chief, whose own health is held to depend upon their goodwill; at the same time the whole country looks to the chief as the source of fertility in man and beast and field.

Ritual was the integrating force with the widest range in the traditional society. Independent chiefs, even those whose people were culturally as different as the Nyakyusa and Kinga, joined in sacrifice to Lwembe and Kyala and were mystically dependent upon one another. As Kasitile put it 'the Kinga come (to Lubaga) both when there is trouble in our land and in theirs'. In Ngonde the 'divine king', the Kyungu, who controlled a flourishing trade in ivory, developed secular as well as ritual functions and emerged as a paramount chief, but in the Nyakyusa valley the ritual bond had no secular backing save the exchange of iron and salt for food, which linked Kinga and Nyakyusa in a tenuous partnership. The sacrifices to the Lwembe did not exclude war between chiefs who acknowledged him, nor did sacrifice to their common ancestor exclude war between Mwaipopo (116) and Mwaihojo (147), but the necessity of co-operation in sacrifice compelled later reconciliation. Perhaps the insistence on the sacredness of the heroes and their living representatives, the elaborate ritual of chieftainship, and the dependence upon medicines as a means of enforcing law were connected with the ineffectiveness of secular authority. Certainly the Kyungu's emergence from seclusion, and the dropping of the taboos which surrounded him were connected with his acquisition of economic power; but we know too little of the conditions that make for elaboration of ritual to postulate any general connexion between the absence of ritual in public life and the effectiveness of secular authority.

The cycle of sacrifices to the heroes and dead chiefs among the Nyakyusa is more than an ancestor cult, for it includes non-relatives among its priests and beneficiaries; but it has many of the features of an ancestor cult, among them the identification of piety with conservatism. A good man follows exactly in the footsteps of his father who becomes his god. This is reconciled with a myth of a new beginning, ten generations ago, when civilized life came to the Nyakyusa valley, and the new beginning is celebrated each generation with the 'coming out' of the young chief and his contemporaries.

All Nyakyusa rituals are cathartic in the sense that they make explicit and seek to dissipate, by their very expression and rejection, certain anti-social tendencies. In the Nyakyusa view the root of evil is 'anger in the heart' unadmitted and corrosive, and only by an open confession can it be overcome.[1] Hence in every situation of misfortune, public or private, men are pressed to 'speak out' (*ukusosya*) and admit their anger. At the 'coming out' the conflict of generations is expressed in the prolonged debate over the date of the celebration and the detailed arrangements, and in the dancing and slaughter of cattle, and is finally resolved when authority and land are handed over to the young men by their fathers. The fissiparous tendencies of a chiefdom are made explicit and canalized in constitutional form by the division of the old chief's country into two, under his senior sons; and criticism of the young chiefs is made explicit in the formal admonition by the father's village headmen. The rejection of conflict is clearest at the annual purification when men throw out the ashes contaminated by family bickering and the cannibalism of witches, and *fight* one another 'that the homesteads may be peaceful'. This fighting is 'to bring out war from within (*ukusosya*)';

---

[1] cf. *Good Company*, pp. 99-112. The belief that a witch or sorcerer must *confess* if the patient was to recover was the reason for the torture of witches in many African societies.

and is therefore to be interpreted as 'confession of anger', rather than as 'rebellion'.

Sometimes there is an expression of *opposite* tendencies, both implicitly approved. The sacrifices to the heroes and at the groves of the chiefs emphasize seniority and precedence, and express the dependence of junior on senior kinsmen, but the myth, recalled in every celebration, tells of the surpassing power of the son or younger brother in the beginning of time, and the junior brother of a chief often holds office as a priest. Then there is the drama of driving away the shade and bringing him back transformed, which is so characteristic of the rituals of kinship and appears again at the cleansing of the country. Such contradictions are doubtless expressions of ambivalent attitudes among the participants themselves, and of the attempt in ritual to reconcile conflicting social principles—in these instances authority with the rights and duties of juniors, and change with continuity.

In a society without written records legal certainty depends very largely on publicity. This is apparent in the law relating to marriage contracts and family inheritance,[1] and still more so in the law of the chiefdom. The ritual of 'coming out' celebrates radical changes in social status, and the public recognition of the leaders, members, and territorial boundaries of villages, as well as of the heirs to chieftainship. Thus certainty in these matters is assured. There is no positive value of the co-regency of father and son (as in ancient Egypt),[2] but the installation of the young chiefs before the death of their father serves to mitigate conflicts over the succession. Confusion over village boundaries and village leadership often appears when the ritual has not been celebrated, for there is no public definition to refer to.

How close is the link between religious belief and practice and social structure? There is no doubt that the sacrifices to the dead chiefs and heroes and the traditional rituals of kinship supported the former political and kinship structure of the Nyakyusa. Their performance compelled co-operation between kinsmen,[3] between neighbouring chiefs, and between chiefs and people. How far then does the change in religion, begun when the first Christian convert professed his new faith, compel a change in the social

[1] Godfrey Wilson, 'An Introduction to Nyakyusa Law', *Africa*, vol. ix, 1937, p. 29.
[2] H. Frankfort, *Kingship and the Gods*, pp. 101-2.
[3] cf. *Rituals of Kinship*, pp. 190-200, 227.

structure? And how far does the new economic and political organization produce a change in religion? These theoretical questions can be answered only by a series of comparative studies. Here there is evidence for one area alone, and the connexions which we postulate can be established only if they hold in a whole range of societies.

Christianity implies an emergence from the nexus of kinship, for the worshipping group is two or three believers, not a body of kinsmen, and conversion is a personal choice. This is more obvious in a missionary church than in one long established, for, as we have seen, the convert in a pagan community must withdraw from his kinsfolk to become a Christian,[1] but it remains true, even in a Christian society. The new doctrine implies a body of believers— a Church. The particular form varies, but the Church has appeared wherever the Christian faith has been established. In short, we argue that the change in religion necessarily disrupts an organization based primarily on kinship and establishes a new type of organization based partly on voluntary association. With the change from the ritual of the lineage to the ritual of the Church the authority and leadership of senior kinsmen is diminished; they are replaced by 'elders' and priests or pastors whose basis of authority is not birth, but selection by the Church. Furthermore, association for worship becomes a pattern for association in other fields, and the Church is the training ground among the Nyakyusa, as it has been among so many other peoples, for organizers of other types of societies.

And not only is kinship subordinated to faith; the forms of kinship are themselves modified. From the time of their first arrival the missionaries have taught that Christianity implies monogamy and they have baptized no polygynist who does not put away his additional wives. This teaching has been questioned by many Africans and by some European missionaries themselves, who doubt the wisdom of persuading a man already married to send away his wives—or even of countenancing such an action. But the rule of monogamy has remained as a condition of membership in all the Churches with European connexions.[2] It has been rejected, as we have seen, by two of the 'independent' African

---

[1] *ibid.*, pp. 197-9.

[2] The rule was suspended for a brief period in one mission working not far from the Nyakyusa area, but was later enforced. cf. Lyndon Harries in *Survey of African Marriage and Family Life* (edited by A. Phillips), pp. 341-2.

Churches in the area. Nevertheless the bulk of professing Christians are monogamists, though it is still customary and, in Rungwe District, economically profitable, for a rich man who is not a Christian to have more than one wife. The difficulties of establishing monogamy are accentuated by the great disproportion in the numbers of men and women. If the figures available are accurate, a general acceptance of monogamy would mean that only about 70 per cent of the women could be married; therefore the Church is necessarily concerned in seeking an adjustment in the disproportion of the population—in keeping the men alive if our assumption that the shortage of men is due to a heavy male death rate is true.

The yeast of the gospel permeates still further. It is taken to imply the freedom of an individual to accept or reject a partner in marriage. This has been maintained from the first in the Nyakyusa Church, and is enforced by the courts, which apply a conception of personal rights springing from the Christian tradition.

Most Nyakyusa men attribute the rapid rise in the divorce rate to this new 'freedom' of women. Christian teaching stresses the family and the sanctity of marriage, but it ignores the lineage. In the traditional rituals of kinship the lineage is represented again and again, while in Christian ritual it is the elementary family and the Church that are pictured. The preoccupation with fertility and the reproductive cycle was linked with the glorification of the lineage itself, and it disappears when the lineage ceases to be the basis of social grouping.

How closely linked are symbols to other aspects of a society? Our hypothesis is that they are relatively free, but it can be shown that many of the symbols used in the traditional rituals of the Nyakyusa reflect the economy, and vary somewhat from one area to another, with the staple crops. The development of trade or of new crops is a prerequisite for using the symbols of bread and wine traditional in the Christian rituals, and even the 'independent' African Churches use new foods, not the beer and bananas of the country; thus change in material symbols and change in economy may be directly connected. The imagery changes also with the changing social structure; Kyala ceases to be pictured as a senior kinsman, when the lineage organization begins to weaken; he is God the father of a family rather than an early member of the royal lineage. But there is no evidence that *particular* symbols are tied to a particular social structure; the poet makes his choice within the whole range of the familiar.

The impetus to change has come both from the religious field and from the secular. For example, the pressure towards monogamy among the Nyakyusa has been religious; given plentiful land and cash crops additional wives are an economic asset, not a liability. In this respect the contrast with the Ciskei in South Africa, where families are dependent for food on wage-earners in towns, and no man can support two families,[1] is marked. On the other hand, the decay of Nyakyusa age-villages is primarily due to economic pressure, though it is facilitated by the insistence of Christians that there is no danger in father-in-law and daughter-in-law meeting one another. The first generation of Christians living on mission land built villages apart for their sons, despite the teaching that avoidance of a father-in-law by his daughter-in-law was foolish, if not sinful. But a radical change in pagan observance of ritual avoidance is brought about by the general practice of going out to work for long periods, and the competition for coffee and rice-lands, which makes the territorial separation of fathers and sons impossible. As we have shown, young men going to work commonly leave their wives in their fathers' homesteads, valuing the support and supervision given them there above the old stringency of avoidance and, where land is scarce and valuable, fathers do not move aside each generation to make way for their sons. Avoidance between father-in-law and daughter-in-law continues only in an attenuated form.

From German times control by a European government has compelled a modification of the traditional sacrifices to the heroes and of the ritual of chieftainship. How the Kinga priests came to Lubaga 'in secret' and how they failed to instal a new Lwembe after the death of Mwakisisya about 1914 has been described. Killing a child to anoint a drum or make medicine for the fields, compelling a man to accept a dangerous office, killing chiefs because they are ailing, or plucking off their nails before they die; all these are actions which are held, and must be held, to be 'contrary to natural justice' by any Western government. Here the change in political organization compels a change in ritual and there is evidence that belief in the traditional forms is much diminished, though not dead. The European government also

---

[1] Keiskammahoek Rural Survey. Vol. ii, *The Economy of a Native Reserve*, by D. H. Houghton and E. M. Walton; vol. iii, *Social Structure*, by M. Wilson *et al*.

found the administration of the poison ordeal, driving out people alleged to be witches, and killing supposed sorcerers 'contrary to natural justice'. Here the change is not in the celebration of a ritual but in the execution of 'justice' based on traditional religious beliefs.

The early missionaries were very important as employers of labour and a market for produce; indeed at one time they were the *sole* source of western trade-goods among the Nyakyusa. For long they provided the only skilled medical attention. They were the source of new learning, teaching, from the start, reading and writing and new manual skills, and the link between learning and religion, so familiar in the history of Europe, is still strong. Therefore acceptance of Christianity *tended* to go along with acceptance of the new economic and political structure, but it was never identified with it. Already in the thirties a popular song contrasted Christians with Europeans, and African nationalism was finding expression in 'independent' Churches.

Secularism fits as well with the new economic and political structure as Christianity, and it has been argued elsewhere that one of the characteristics of the change from a small-scale, isolated, self-sufficient people to a large-scale society is increasing secularism.[1] The evidence from BuNyakyusa does not so far support this, but there is a *separation* of religious and other activities. Religion is not interwoven with the modern political system as it was with the old. Traditionally the fusion between ritual and political activities was almost complete; village headmen became priests as they grew old, and chiefs became gods. Now there is a separation between Church and state, between Government and mission, which co-operate closely only in the organization of schools. It is true that Christian congregations pray regularly for 'those set in authority over us', but for the most part religious ritual does not enter into state functions. The flag is hoisted and saluted at sunrise and sunset at administrative and military centres; certain occasions, such as the Queen's birthday or the visit of the Queen's representative, the Governor, are celebrated with secular ceremonial. Only at the Coronation, to which African representatives from Rungwe district were sent, did the state ceremonial and the Christian ritual merge.[2] Political tension is not now directly

[1] R. Redfield, *The Folk Culture of Yucatan*, Chicago (1941); *A Village that Chose Progress*, Chicago (1950).

[2] 'The entire solemnity of the Coronation, from start to finish, is distinctly a religious rite.' Canon Charles Smyth, 'The Coronation Rite', *The Listener*, 28th May 1953.

expressed or resolved in ritual. The place for *ukusosya*—speaking out—is the council chamber not the sacred grove or the homestead where the shades gather, and the reconciliation of conflicts between chiefs, or between chiefs and District Commissioner or chiefs and commoners, is sought in a committee rather than a Church. Perhaps the greatest difficulty in modern administration in Africa lies in this very separation of activities, in the *thinness* of the bonds across the colour line, in the cleavage between secular and sacred. Some separation of the different aspects of a society is a concomitant of the increase in scale—it is one manifestation of specialization—but it is greater in Tanganyika with its diversity of religious traditions than it is in Britain with its common Christian history.

That there is a connexion between the form of faith and ritual and the form of social structure few would deny. The concern of the anthropologist is to define it; to plot the limits of autonomy between different aspects within societies. This can be done only by the patient analysis and comparison of many societies and this book is offered as a humble contribution towards such a comparative study.

MEMBERSHIP OF VILLAGES

(a) *Lupando* (Senior village of Generation IV)

Members	Village of father	Villages of fathers-in-law	Kinsmen in village
1. Mwanyilu (177)	Igembe	Bujege Itebe Iringa Igembe	Half-brother Half-sister married to headman Father's half-brother
2. Kilasile (headman)	Kituli Father's heir in Kibonde	Igembe Heir in forest village	Married half-sister of chief
3. Ndungundeli Mwaipopo	Igembe	Mwangomo's (C 28) chiefdom	Half-brother of chief
4. Mwasikambo	Bujege. Moved to Kibonde	Another chiefdom	None traced
5. Mwambambale	Bujege	Bujege Moved to Ndola	Married daughter of chief's father's half-brother
6. Mwakalinga	Igembe	Igembe	None traced
7. Mwampora	Kisyero	Igembe	None traced
8. Musika	Ipoma	Ipoma	None traced
9. Mwakipesile	Ipoma	Igembe	None traced
10. Mwakilasa	Kisyero	Igembe	None traced
11. Mwakipokera	Another chiefdom	Mwandosya's chiefdom (C 27)	None traced
12. Mwakipesile	Another chiefdom	Ipoma	None traced
13. Mwakalebela	Mwangomo's chiefdom (C 28)	Mwangomo's chiefdom (C 28) Kabula	None traced
14. Mwambipile	Igembe	Lupondo	None traced
15. Mwakinyolobe	Ipoma	Mwaihojo's chiefdom (C 23)	None traced
16. Mwakasio	Kibonde	Lupondo	None traced
17. Mwajojele	Another chiefdom	Another chiefdom	None traced
18. Mwansale	Itiki	Igembe Kisyero	None traced
19. Kigasya Mwaipopo	Bujege	bachelor	Half-brother of chief's father
20. Mwampise	Kisyero	Igembe	None traced

i.e. out of twenty members, three are close kinsmen, and two are married to kinswomen of these three. The remaining fifteen members are not connected by kinship ties.

(b) *Katumba* (Generation III)

Members	Village of father	Villages of fathers-in-law	Kinsmen in village	Kinsmen elsewhere
1. Gwemelese	Kisyero		Elder brother of 2	Son in Ndola. Elder brother in another chiefdom (C 27)
2. Anganile	Kisyero	Not married	Younger brother of 1	
3. Syapabwingi	Kisyero	Lugombo Kasambala's chiefdom (C 2)		Brother in forest village. Brother in chiefdom (C 2). Brother in plain. (All at first built in Katumba).
4. Kileke	Bujege	(a) Bujinga (b) Kisyero	Half-brother of 5	Elder brother Igembe, moved to C 28. Brother in Christian village Kabembe (at first built in Katumba). Brother in Mbeya at work. Brother in Itiki (but away at work).
5. Nkokwa	Bujege		Half-brother of 4	
6. Mwalumu	Bujege	(a) Kisyero (b) Mwangomo's country (C 28) (c) Kibonde	Half-brother of 7	No full brothers. 2 half-brothers moved to other chiefdoms, another to Zanzibar. Daughter married Kibonde, another married Ndola.
7. Nsana	Bujege	not married	Half-brother of 6	
8. Nathan	Bujege	Kibonde moved to Igembe		He only son of mother, 2 half-brothers in Ndola.
9. Pabulosi	Another chiefdom (C 23)	Ndupaso		Father's younger brother's son headman of Iringa.
10. Mwalibaki				

i.e. out of ten members, there are one pair of brothers and two pairs of half-brothers, but *all* have close kinsmen (brothers, half-brothers, or father's brother's sons) in other villages or chiefdoms. Katumba has diminished from fifty-three members in 1938 to ten in 1955. Many members have died and many have moved, some to the forest colony, some to the plain to plant rice, four to Lupando.

(c) *Katela* (Generation IV and V)

Boys (none married)		Father	Father's village
Andulu	} full brothers	Mwaseba (152)	Mpunga
Alijesi			
Jestina			
Mololo			
Freda	} half-brothers	Mwaseba (152)	Mpunga
Tukafika			
Laseki			
Kimamba			
Abandubandu		Bampolile	Masoko
Andambile		Peteli	Masoko
Lalogwa		Mbukanya	Masoko
Bandadanwile		Imilano	Masoko
Anigwile		Mungile	Masoko
Kofia		Gusike	Masoko
Kaswelile		Mwaiposi	Masoko
Akipwele		Mwankuni	Masoko
Bajeko		Mwangosi	Masoko
Adumile		Gwilliam	Masoko (Inherited in Lupondo)
Kajobene		Mwalusamba	Masoko
Fryin		Anitike	Masoko
Mwitingi		Simeon	Masoko
Ndalwisye		Mwangoje	Masoko
Osijah		Mwaipaja	Mfumbi

i.e. out of twenty-three members, two are full brothers and six others are half-brothers. No other kinship connections were traced.

COMMONER PRIESTS MENTIONED

Kikungubeja, Kyamba Kitali, Nsyanigwa, Silobwike	Hereditary Kinga priests who come to Lubaga and visit Kasitile on the way
Kissoule, Mwamalunguka, Mwambipili	Hereditary priests of Lubaga
Mwamakunda	Kasitile's assistant priest
Mwalukuta, Nyama	Hereditary priests of Mbyanga, the grove of Mwakisambwe (30)
Kissogota, Ngulyo, Njobakosa	Village headmen of Mwaijonga (82) and priests of his grove
Mwambuputa, Kakuju	Village headmen of Mwankuga (150) and priests responsible for 'coming out' of Mwanyilu (177)

INDEX

For Product Safety Concerns and Information please contact our EU
representative GPSR@taylorandfrancis.com
Taylor & Francis Verlag GmbH, Kaufingerstraße 24, 80331 München, Germany

www.ingramcontent.com/pod-product-compliance
Lightning Source LLC
Chambersburg PA
CBHW070856270326
41926CB00050B/2602